the Awkward Yeti™ Presents

Heart and Brain

BODY LANGUAGE

ANOTHER!

Andrews McMeel
PUBLISHING®

Heart and Brain: Body Language

Andrews McMeel Publishing
a division of Andrews McMeel Universal
1130 Walnut Street, Kansas City, Missouri 64106

www.andrewsmcmeel.com

17 18 19 20 21 TEN 10 9 8 7 6 5 4 3 2 1
ISBN: 978-1-4494-8712-6
Library of Congress Control Number: 2017932230

Editor: Allison Adler
Art Director/Designer: Diane Marsh
Production Editor: Kevin Kotur
Production Manager: Chuck Harper

ATTENTION: SCHOOLS AND BUSINESSES

Andrews McMeel books are available at quantity discounts with bulk purchase for educational, business, or sales promotional use. For information, please e-mail the Andrews McMeel Publishing Special Sales Department: specialsales@amuniversal.com.

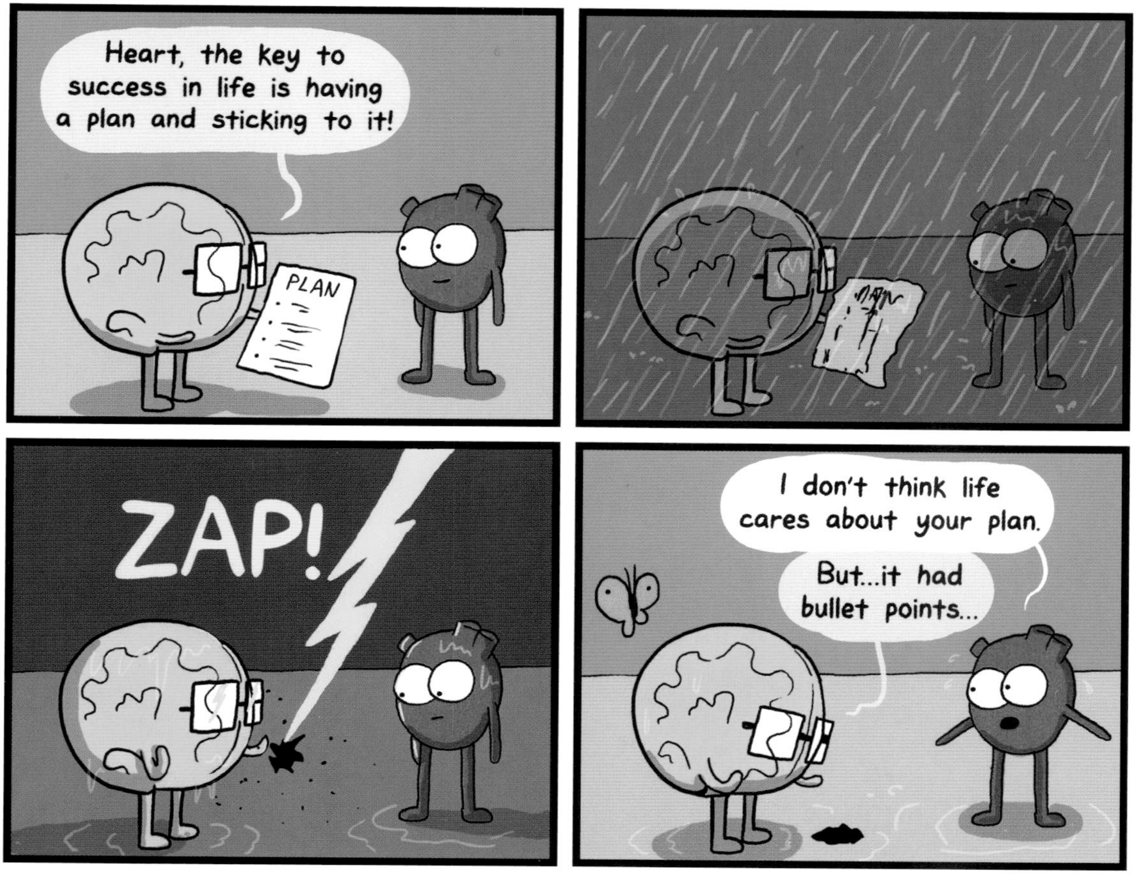
Heart, the key to success in life is having a plan and sticking to it!
PLAN
ZAP!
I don't think life cares about your plan.
But...it had bullet points...

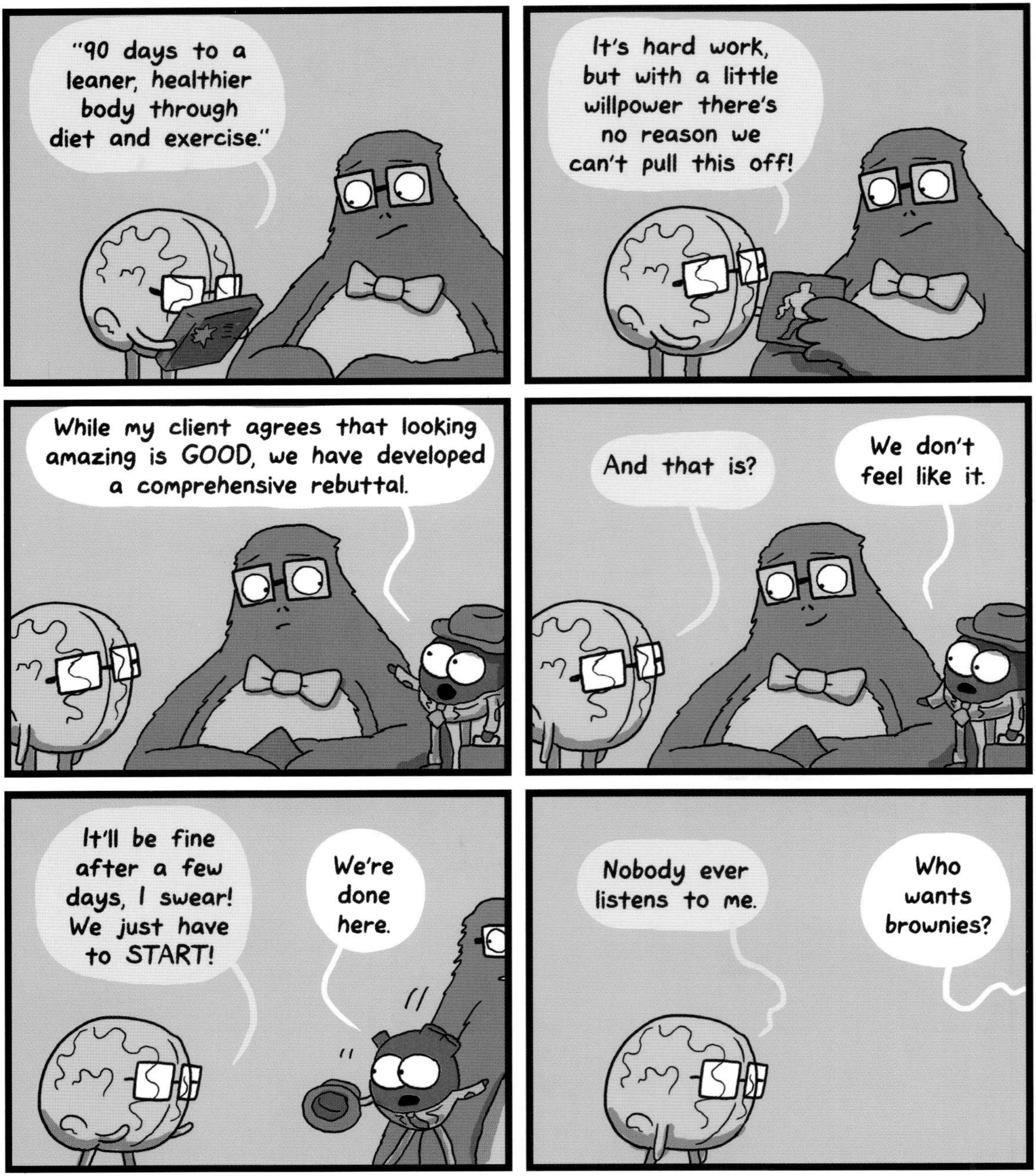
"90 days to a leaner, healthier body through diet and exercise."
It's hard work, but with a little willpower there's no reason we can't pull this off!
While my client agrees that looking amazing is GOOD, we have developed a comprehensive rebuttal.
And that is?
We don't feel like it.
It'll be fine after a few days, I swear! We just have to START!
We're done here.
Nobody ever listens to me.
Who wants brownies?

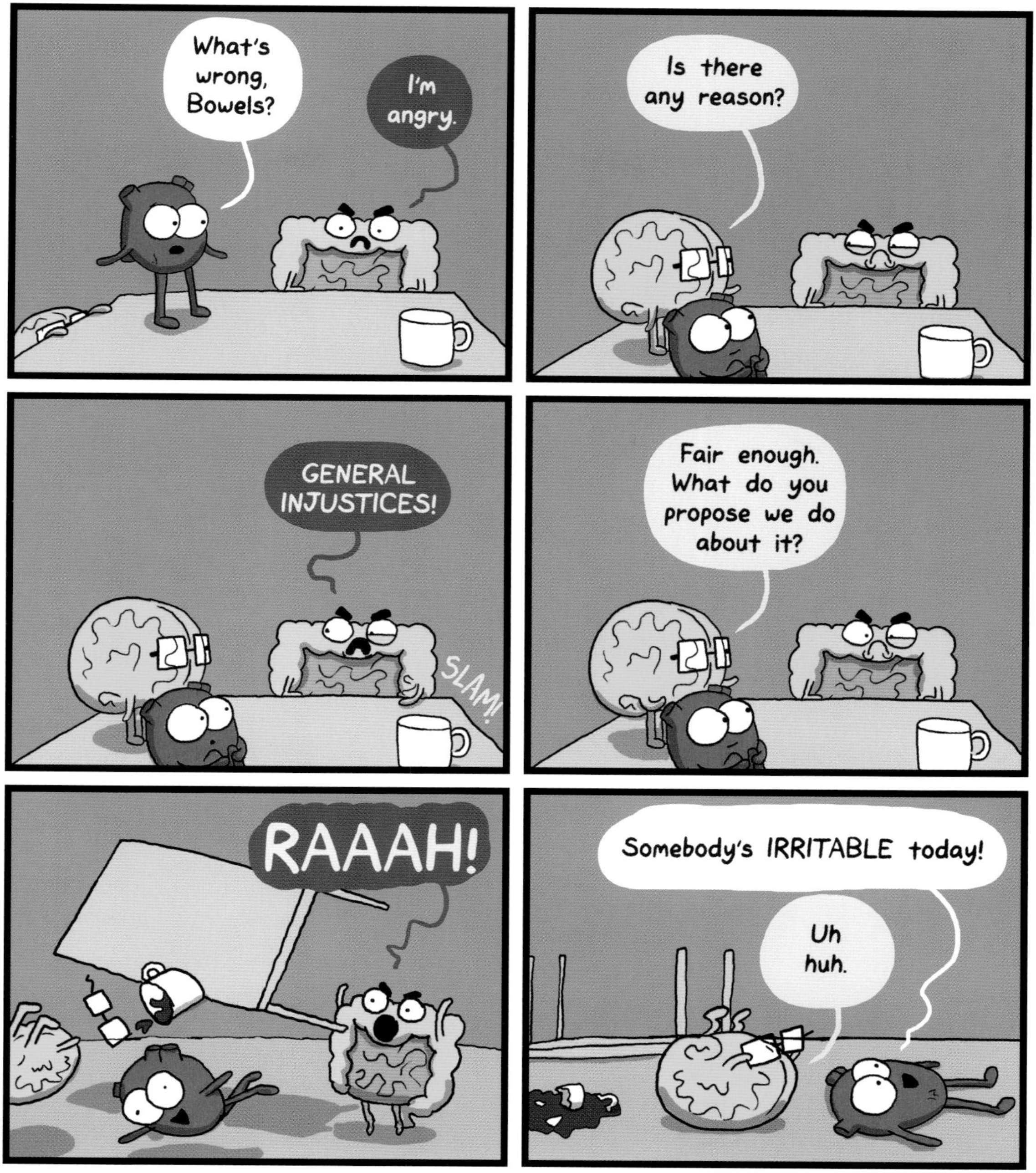
What's wrong, Bowels?
I'm angry.
Is there any reason?
GENERAL INJUSTICES!
SLAM!
Fair enough. What do you propose we do about it?
RAAAH!
Somebody's IRRITABLE today!
Uh huh.

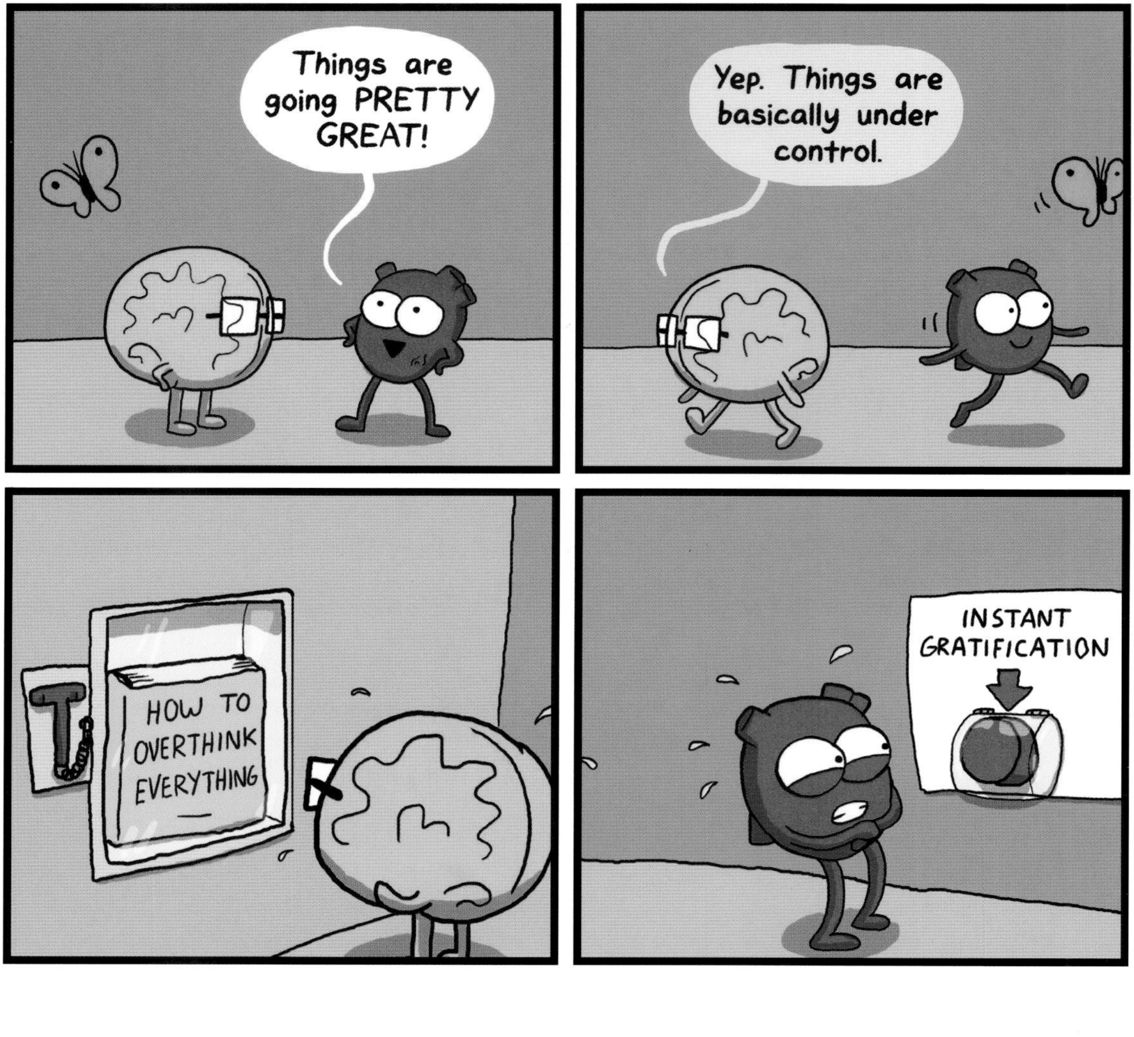
Things are going PRETTY GREAT!
Yep. Things are basically under control.
HOW TO OVERTHINK EVERYTHING
INSTANT GRATIFICATION

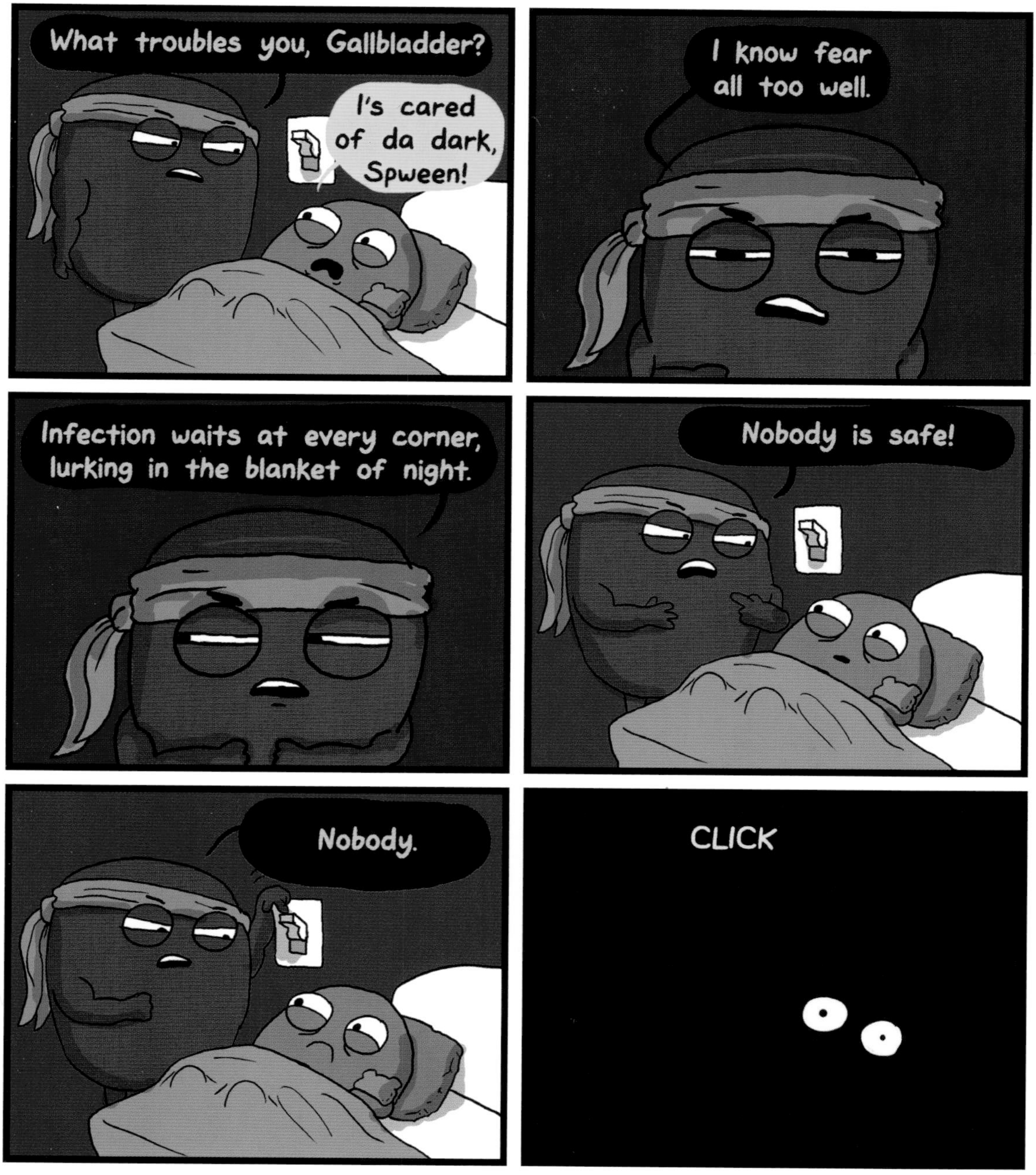
What troubles you, Gallbladder?
I's cared of da dark, Spween!
I know fear all too well.
Infection waits at every corner, lurking in the blanket of night.
Nobody is safe!
Nobody.
CLICK

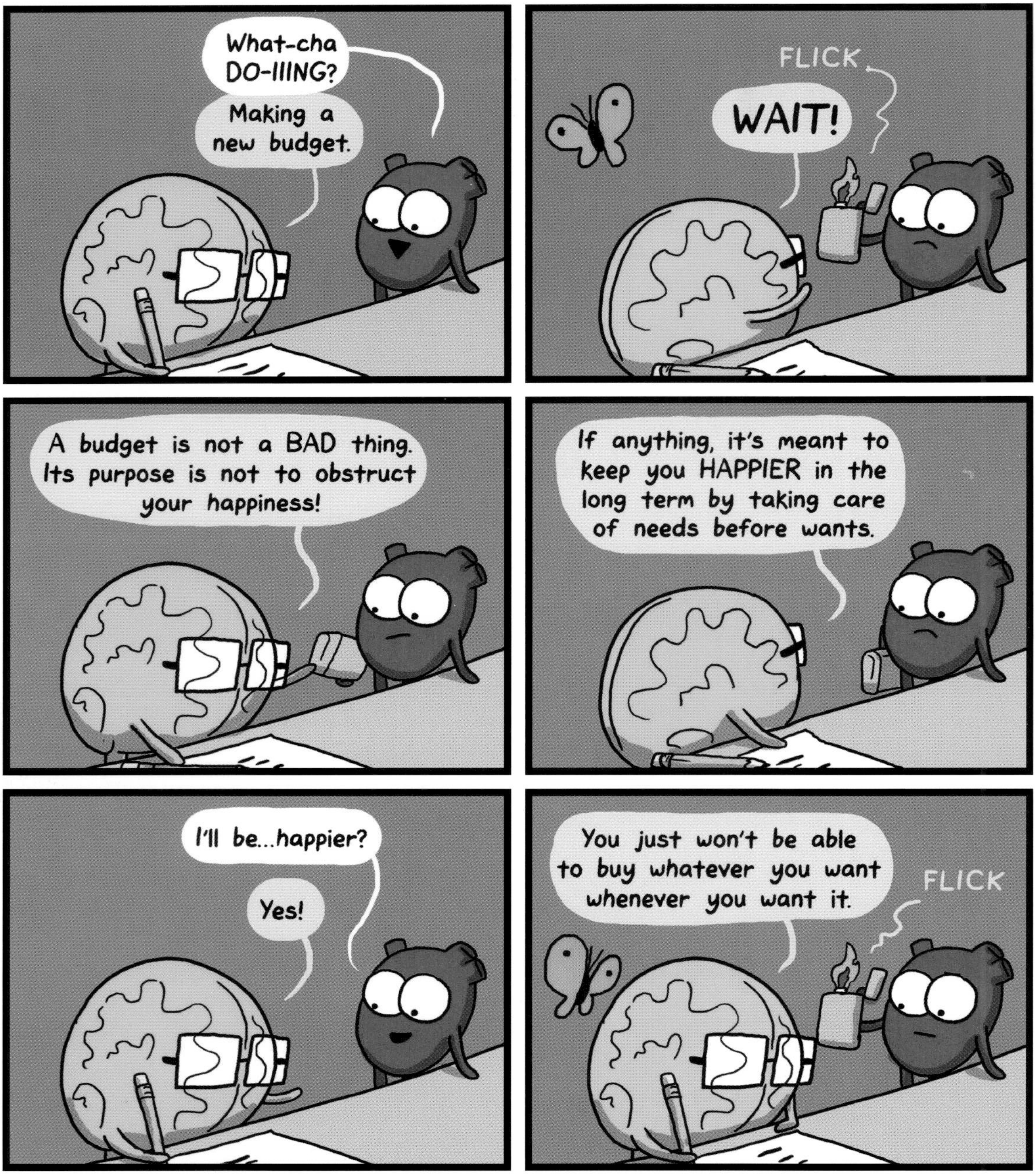
What-cha DO-IIING?
Making a new budget.
FLICK
WAIT!
A budget is not a BAD thing. Its purpose is not to obstruct your happiness!
If anything, it's meant to keep you HAPPIER in the long term by taking care of needs before wants.
I'll be...happier?
Yes!
You just won't be able to buy whatever you want whenever you want it.
FLICK

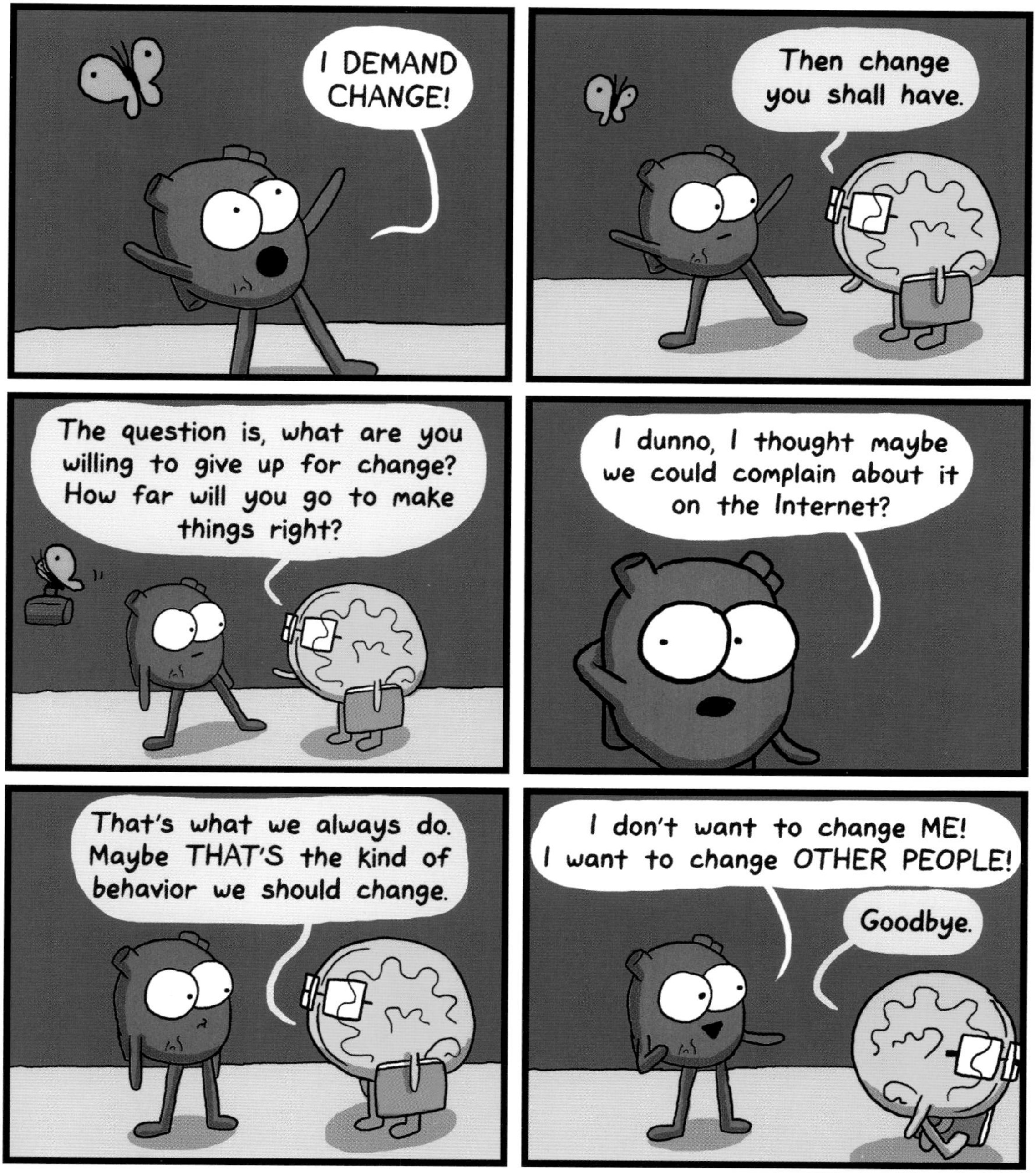
I DEMAND CHANGE!
Then change you shall have.
The question is, what are you willing to give up for change? How far will you go to make things right?
I dunno, I thought maybe we could complain about it on the Internet?
That's what we always do. Maybe THAT'S the kind of behavior we should change.
I don't want to change ME! I want to change OTHER PEOPLE!
Goodbye.

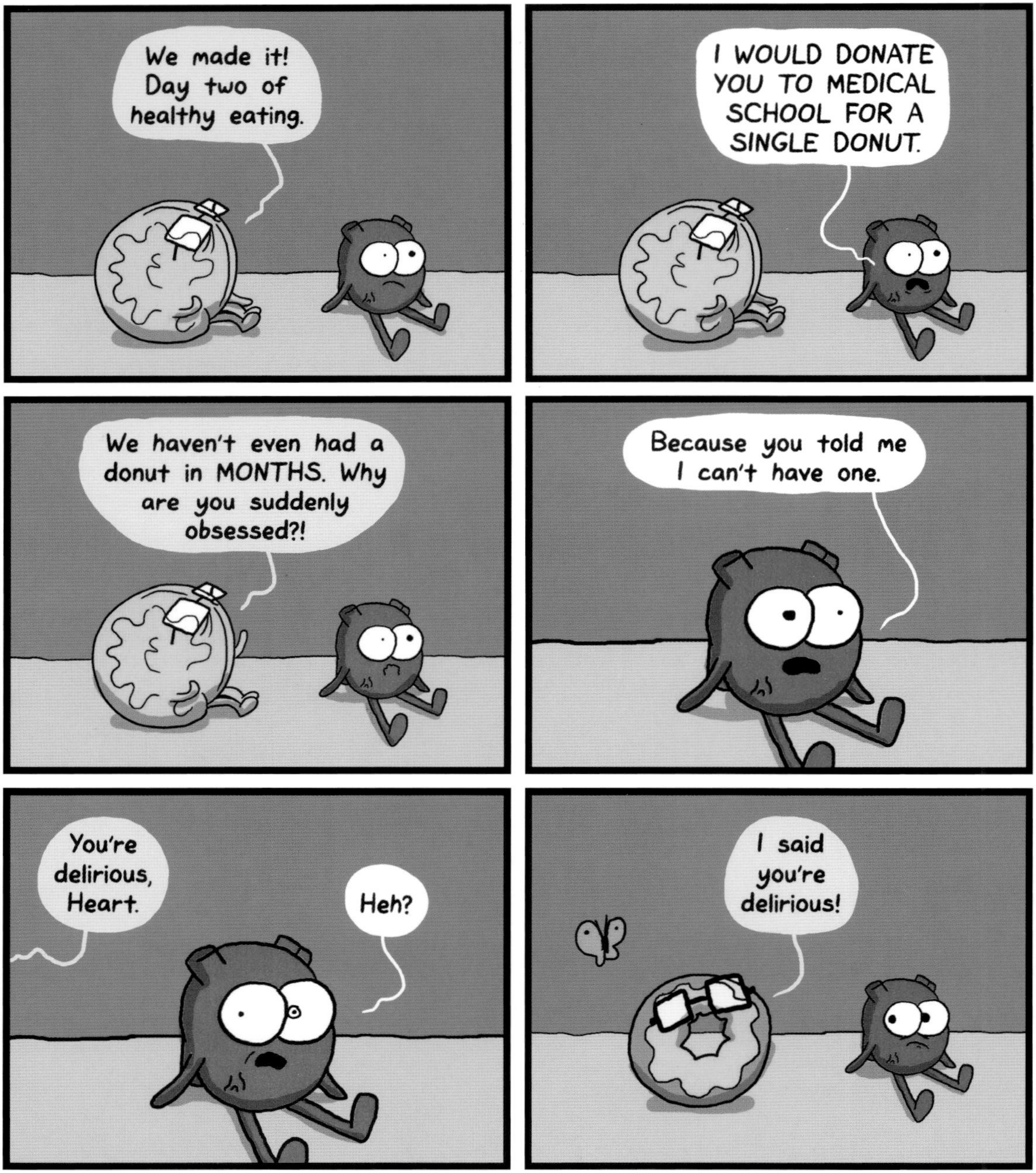
We made it! Day two of healthy eating.
I WOULD DONATE YOU TO MEDICAL SCHOOL FOR A SINGLE DONUT.
We haven't even had a donut in MONTHS. Why are you suddenly obsessed?!
Because you told me I can't have one.
You're delirious, Heart.
Heh?
I said you're delirious!

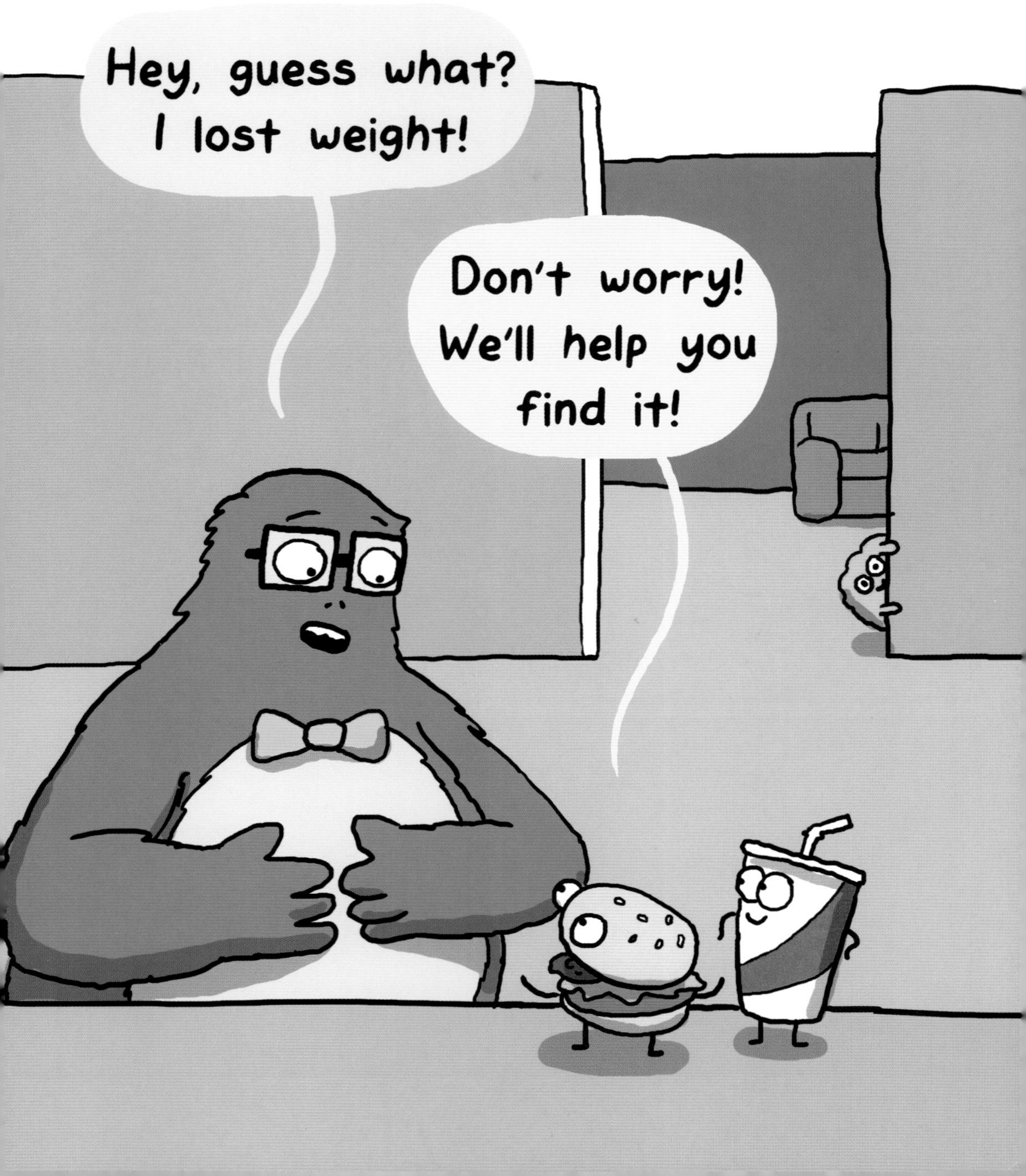
Hey, guess what? I lost weight!
Don't worry! We'll help you find it!

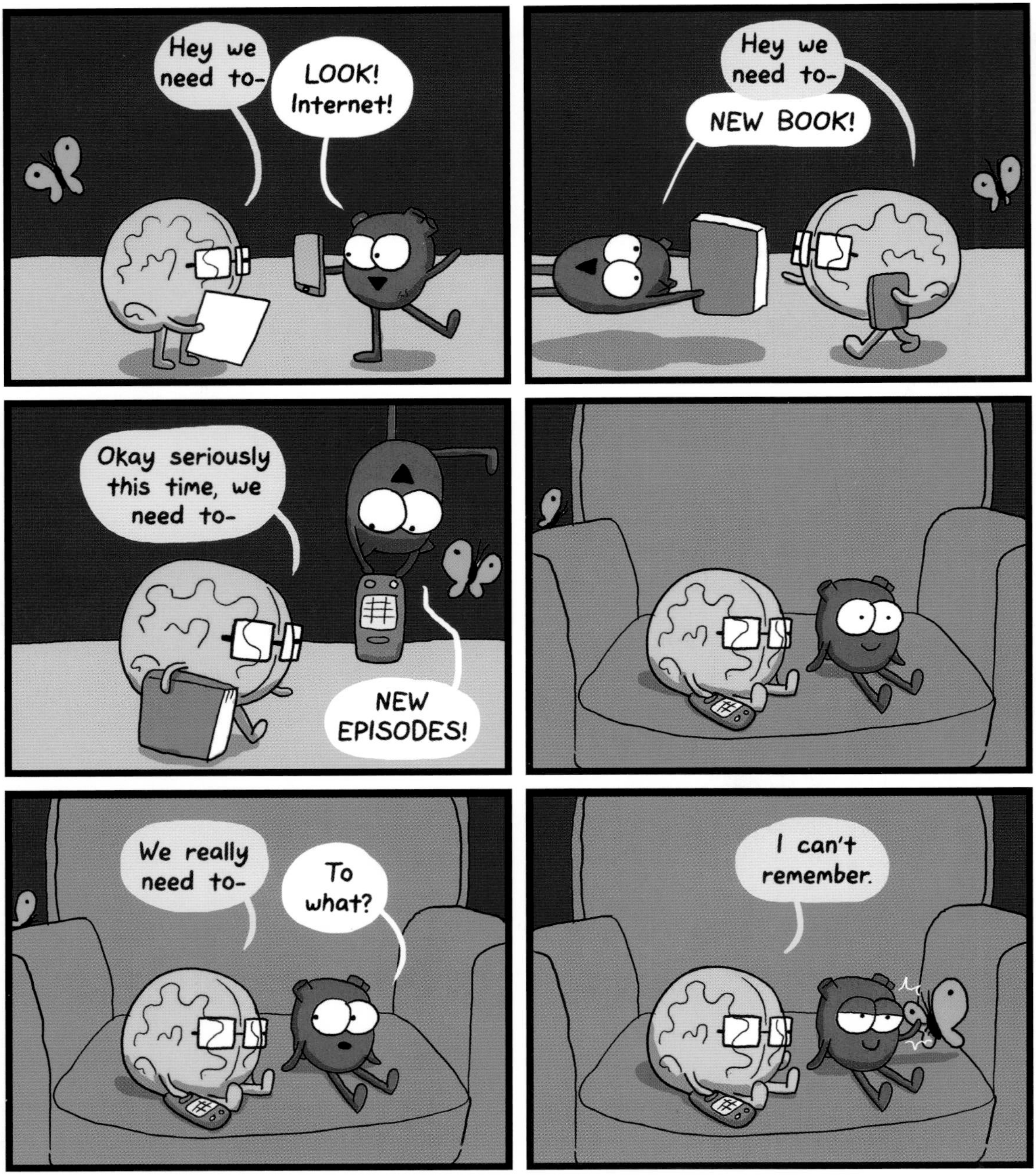
Hey we need to-
LOOK! Internet!
Hey we need to-
NEW BOOK!
Okay seriously this time, we need to-
NEW EPISODES!
We really need to-
To what?
I can't remember.

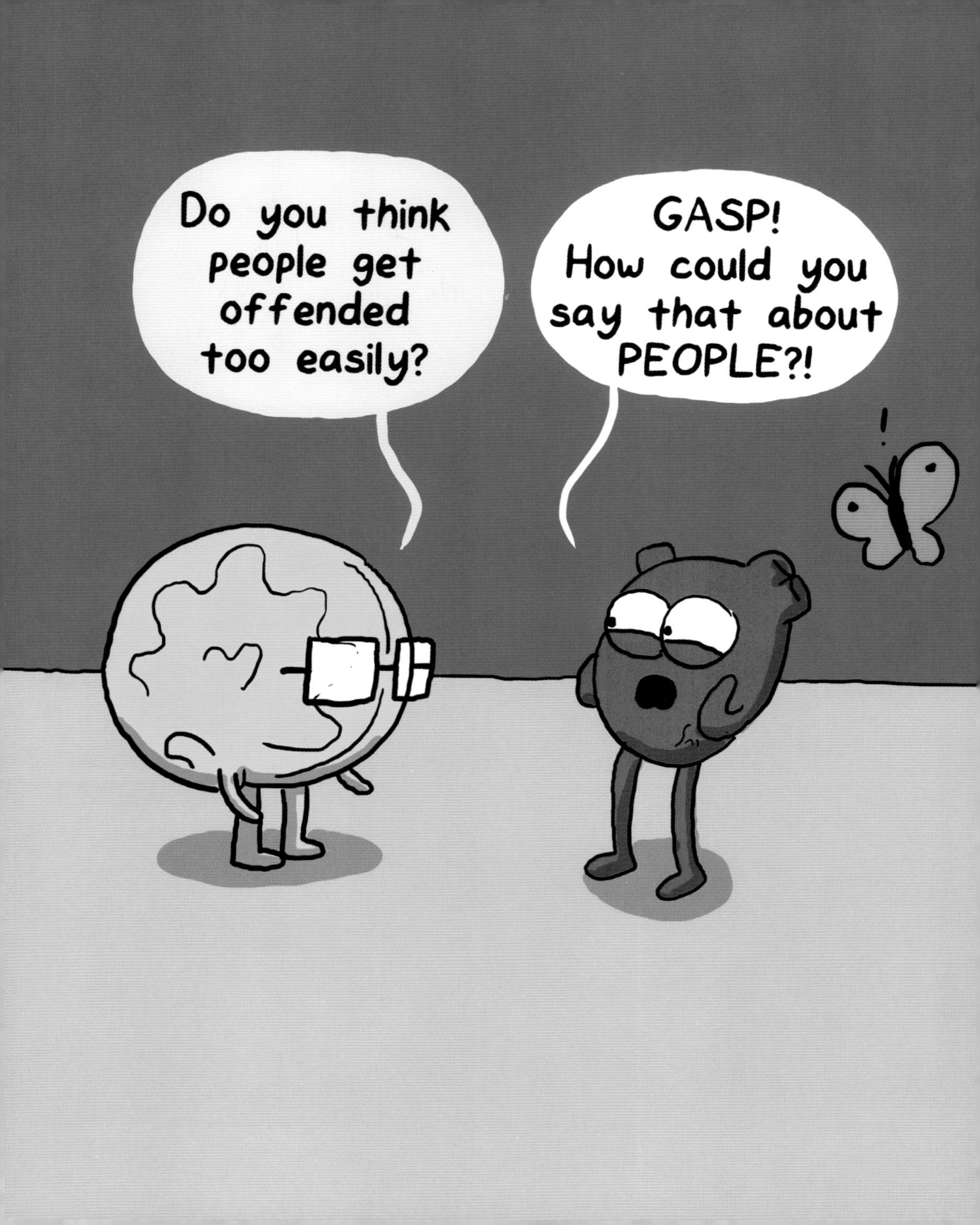
Do you think people get offended too easily?
GASP! How could you say that about PEOPLE?!
!

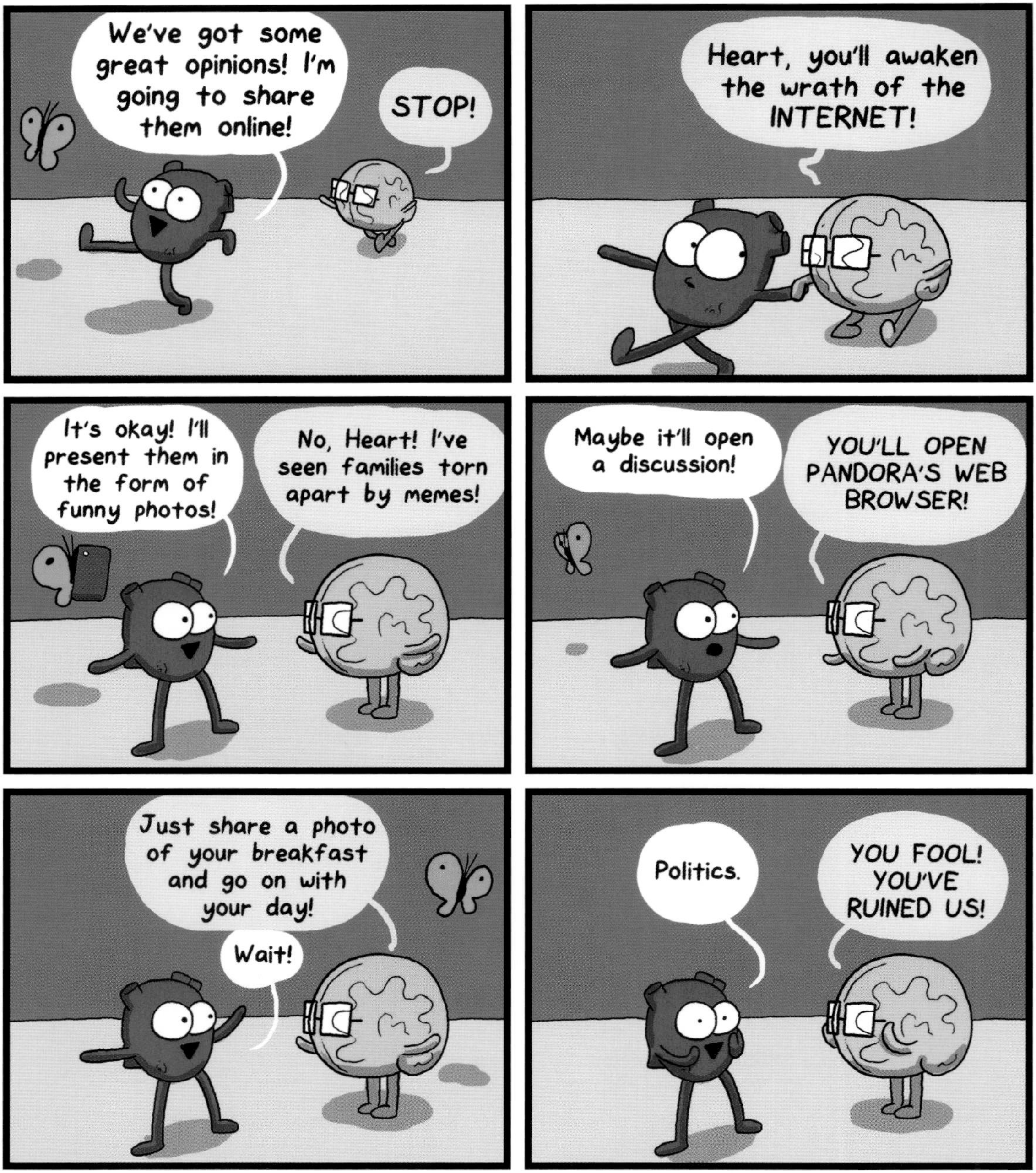
We've got some great opinions! I'm going to share them online!
STOP!
Heart, you'll awaken the wrath of the INTERNET!
It's okay! I'll present them in the form of funny photos!
No, Heart! I've seen families torn apart by memes!
Maybe it'll open a discussion!
YOU'LL OPEN PANDORA'S WEB BROWSER!
Just share a photo of your breakfast and go on with your day!
Wait!
Politics.
YOU FOOL! YOU'VE RUINED US!

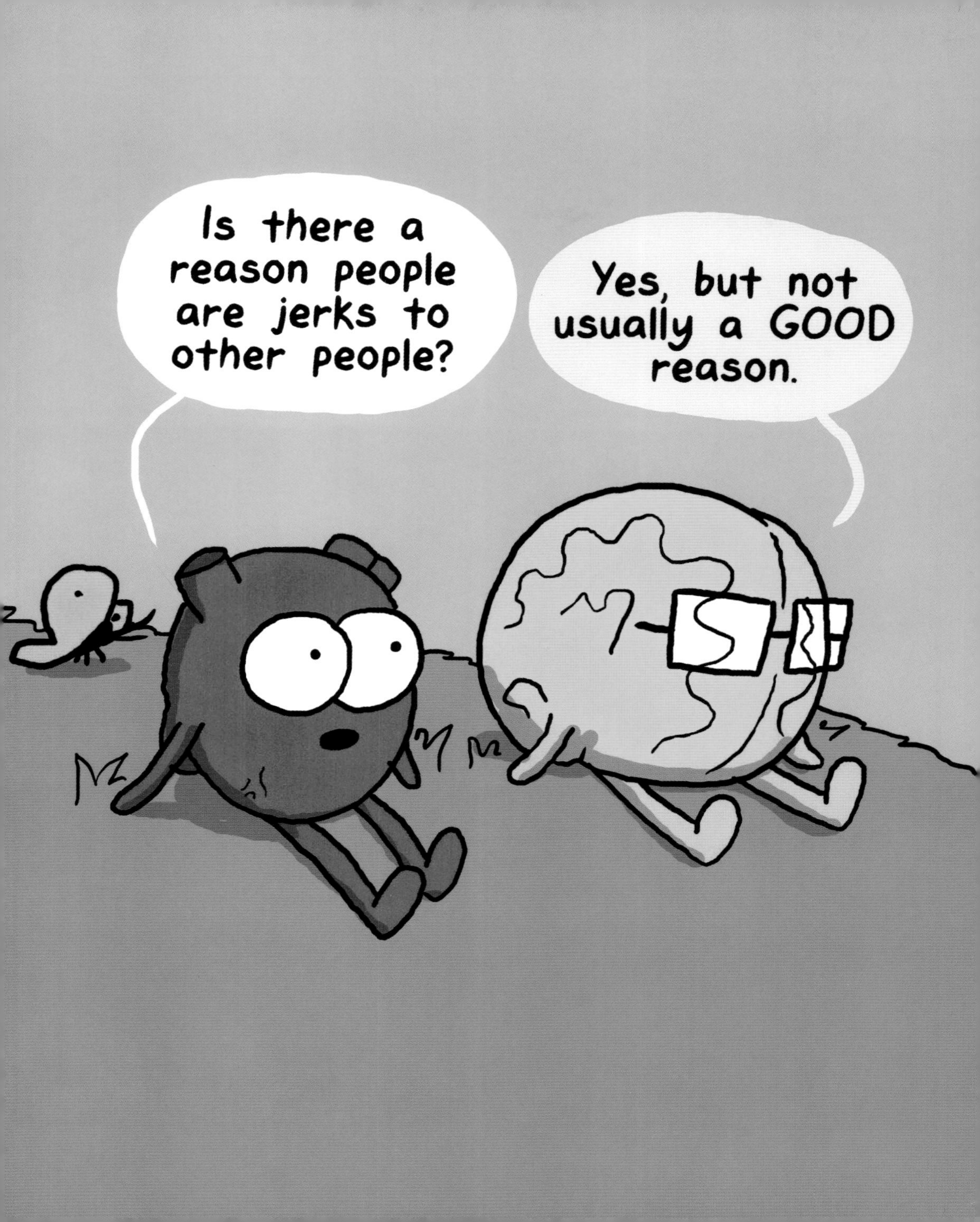
Is there a reason people are jerks to other people?
Yes, but not usually a GOOD reason.

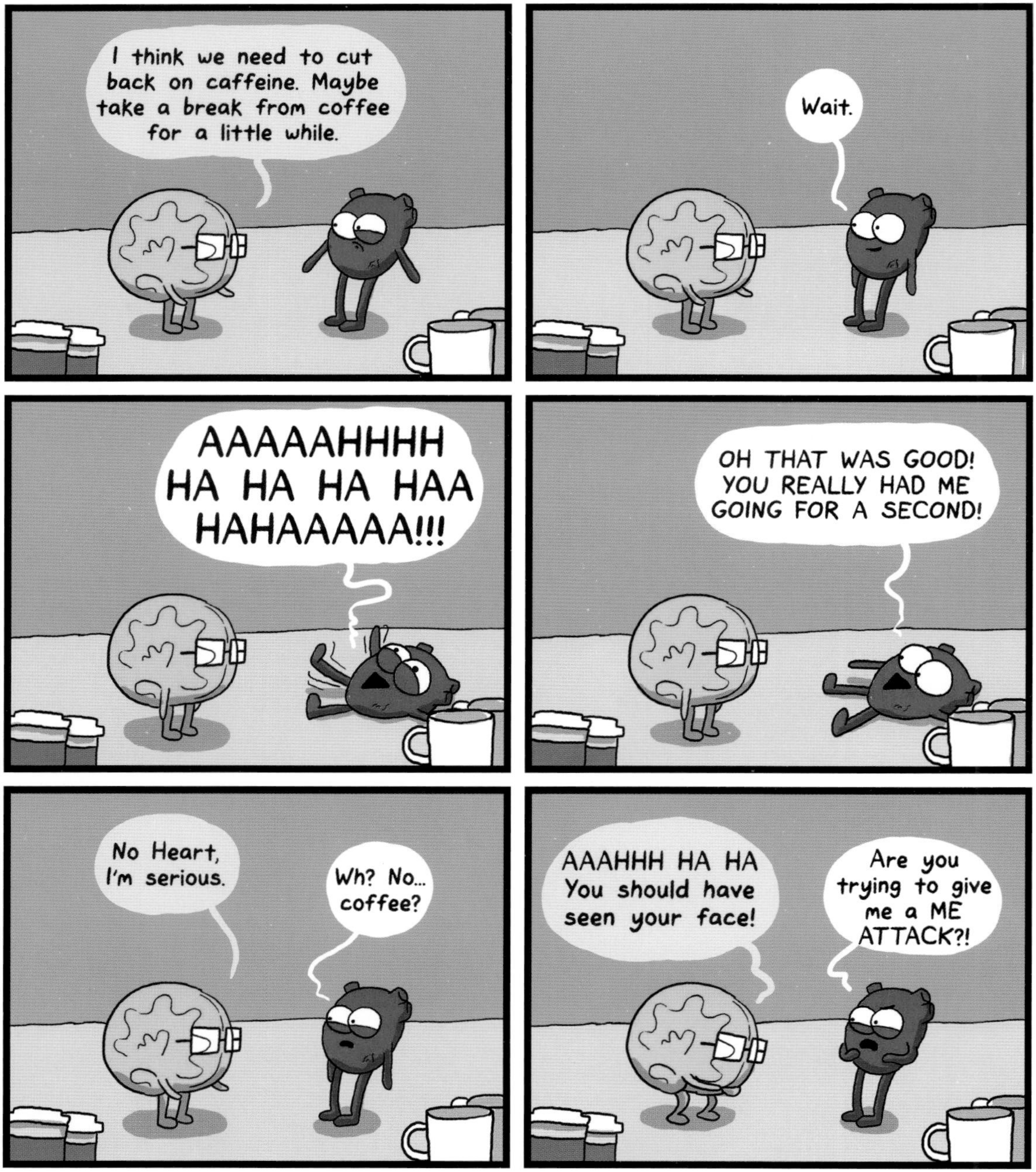
I think we need to cut back on caffeine. Maybe take a break from coffee for a little while.
Wait.
AAAAAHHHH HA HA HA HAA HAHAAAAA!!!
OH THAT WAS GOOD! YOU REALLY HAD ME GOING FOR A SECOND!
No Heart, I'm serious.
Wh? No... coffee?
AAAHHH HA HA You should have seen your face!
Are you trying to give me a ME ATTACK?!

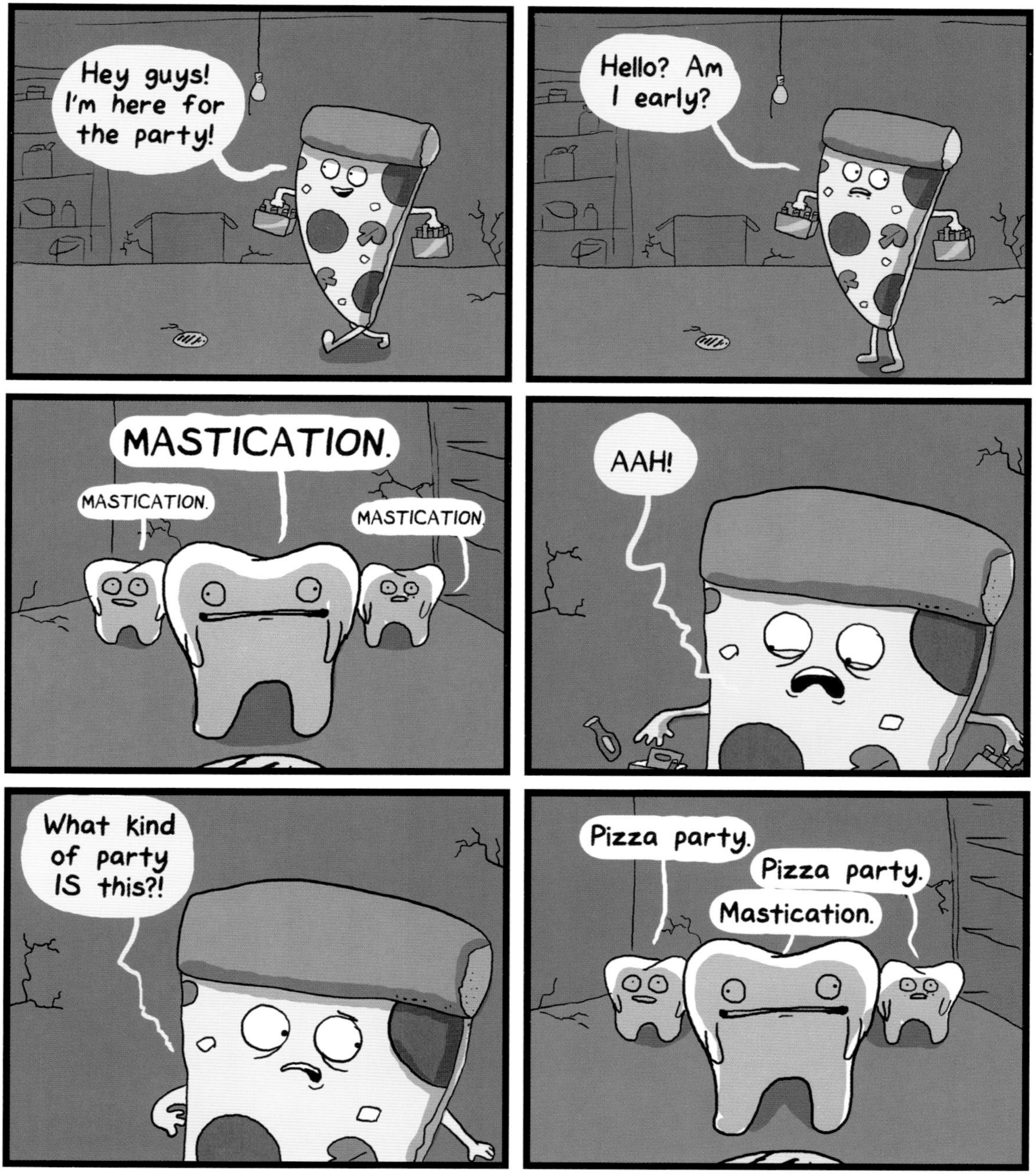
Hey guys! I'm here for the party!
Hello? Am I early?
MASTICATION.
MASTICATION.
MASTICATION.
AAH!
What kind of party IS this?!
Pizza party.
Pizza party.
Mastication.

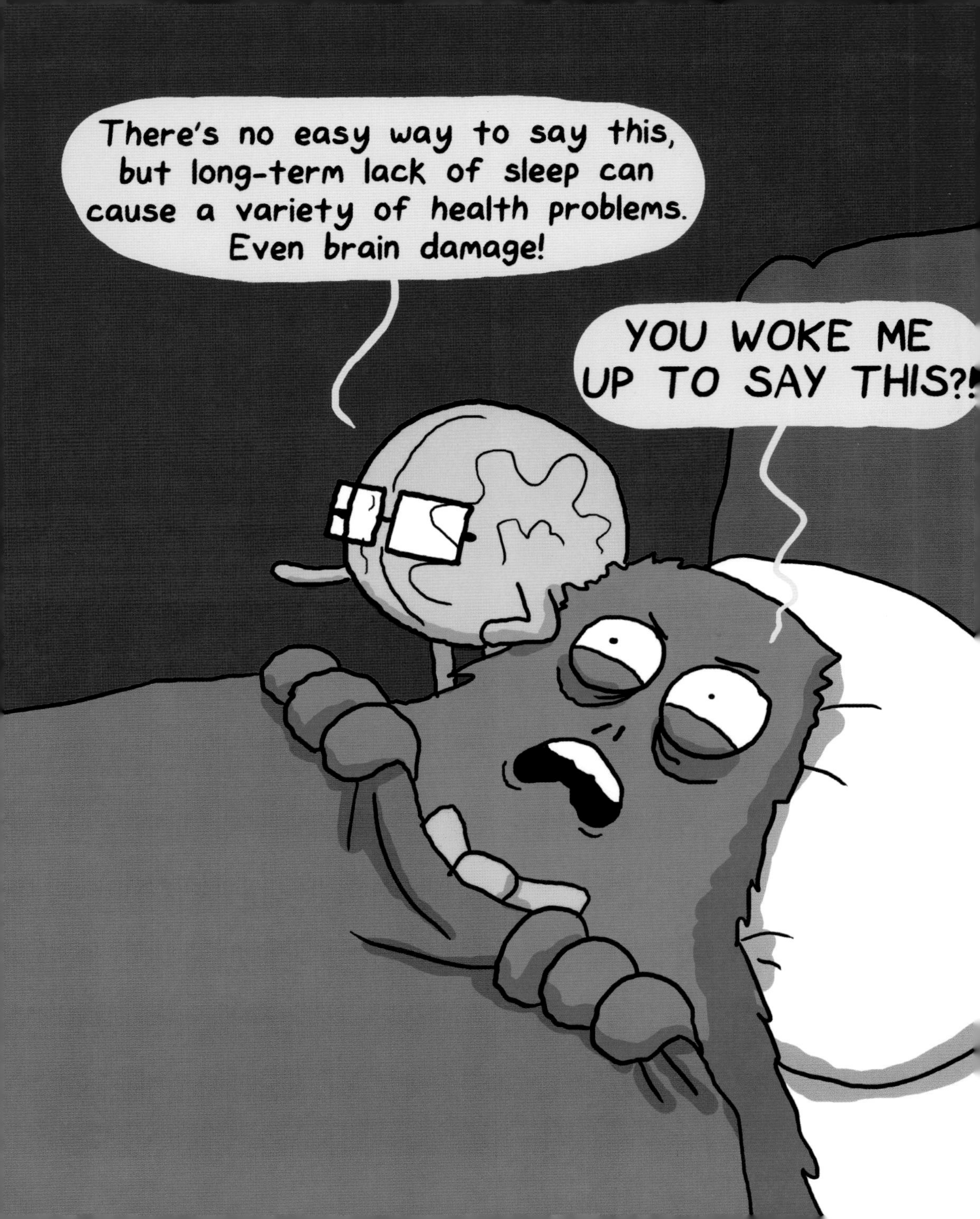
There's no easy way to say this, but long-term lack of sleep can cause a variety of health problems. Even brain damage!
YOU WOKE ME UP TO SAY THIS?!

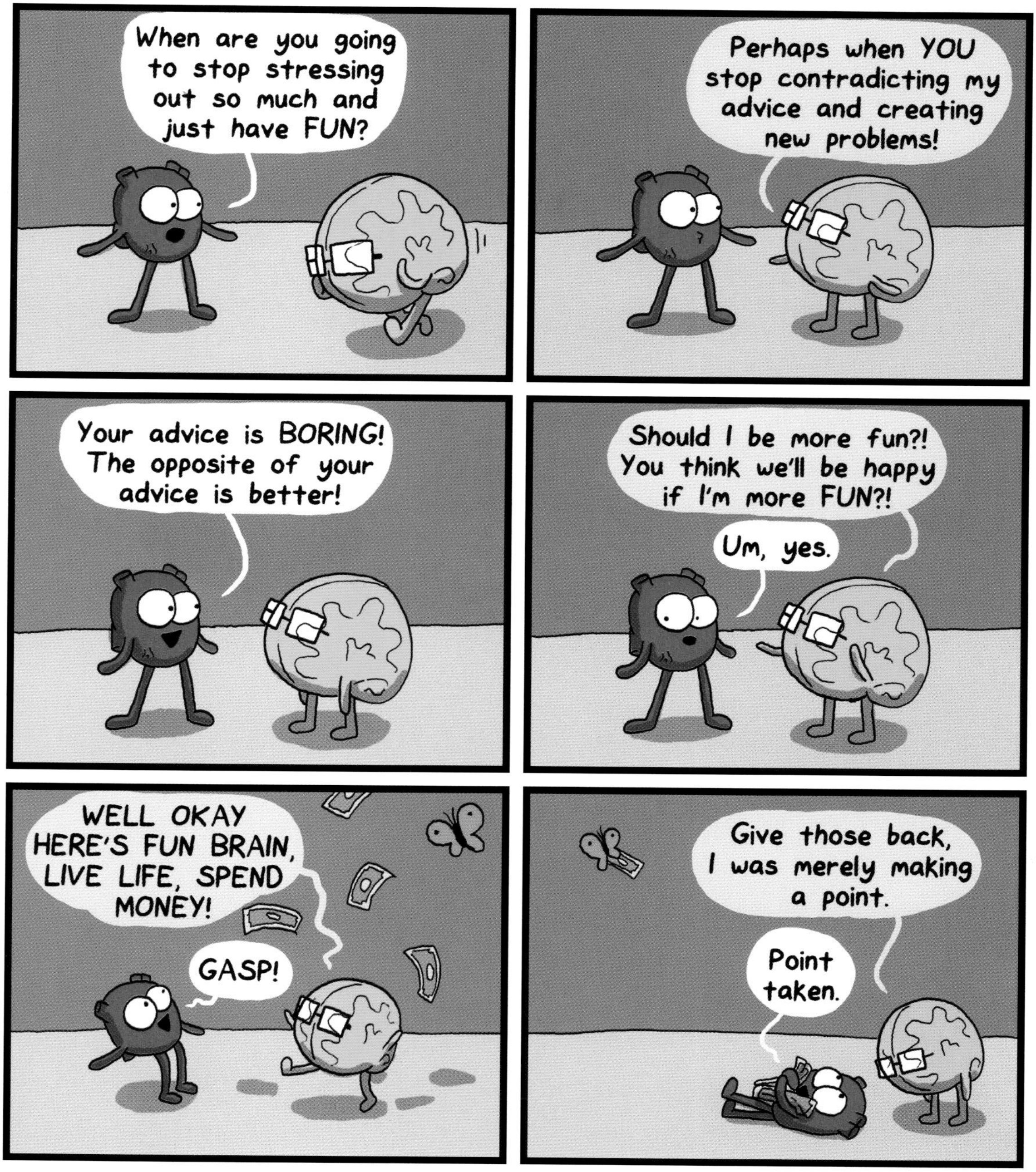
When are you going to stop stressing out so much and just have FUN?
Perhaps when YOU stop contradicting my advice and creating new problems!
Your advice is BORING! The opposite of your advice is better!
Should I be more fun?! You think we'll be happy if I'm more FUN?!
Um, yes.
WELL OKAY HERE'S FUN BRAIN, LIVE LIFE, SPEND MONEY!
GASP!
Give those back, I was merely making a point.
Point taken.

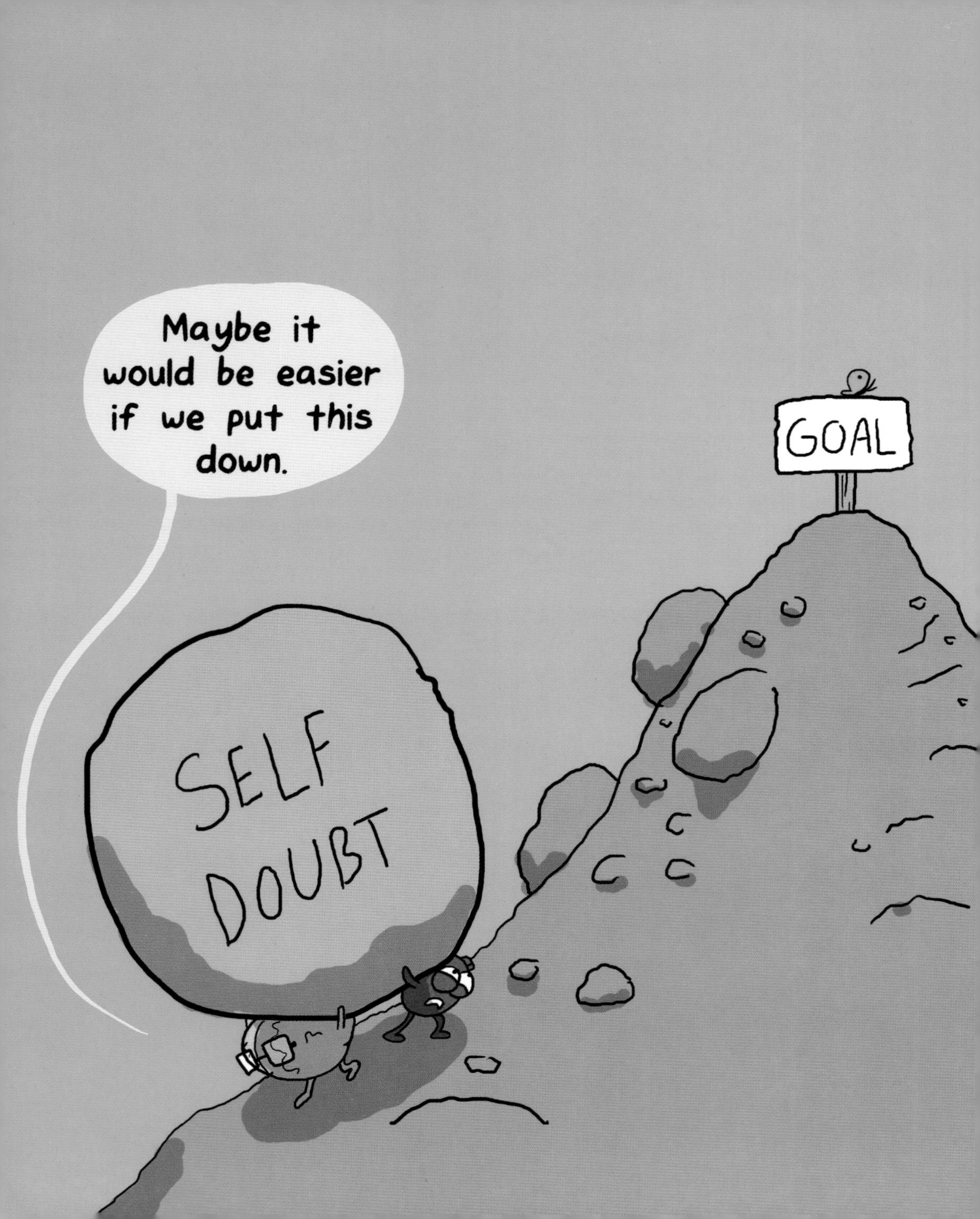
Maybe it would be easier if we put this down.
GOAL
SELF DOUBT

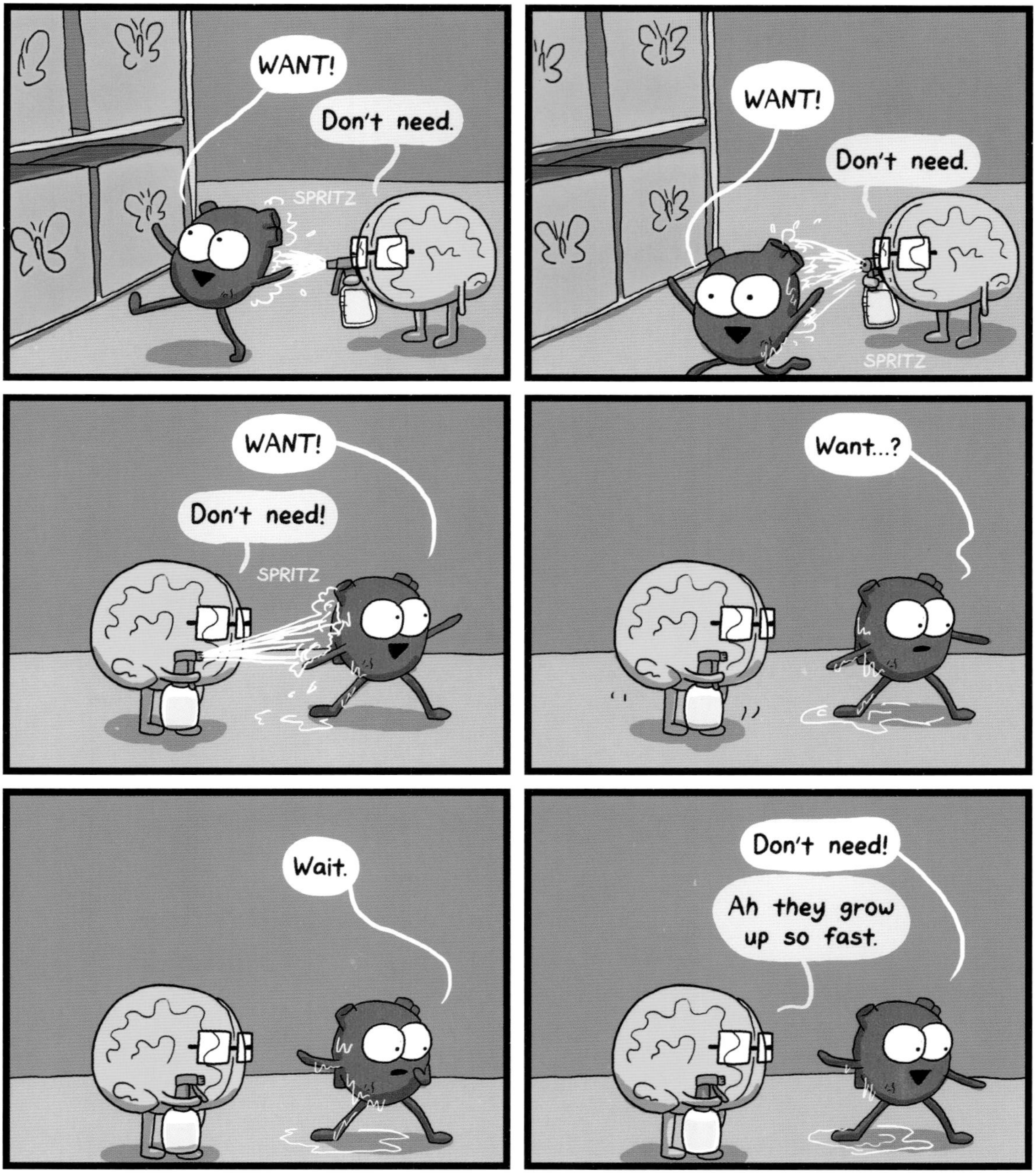
WANT!
Don't need.
SPRITZ
WANT!
Don't need.
SPRITZ
WANT!
Don't need!
SPRITZ
Want...?
Wait.
Don't need!
Ah they grow up so fast.

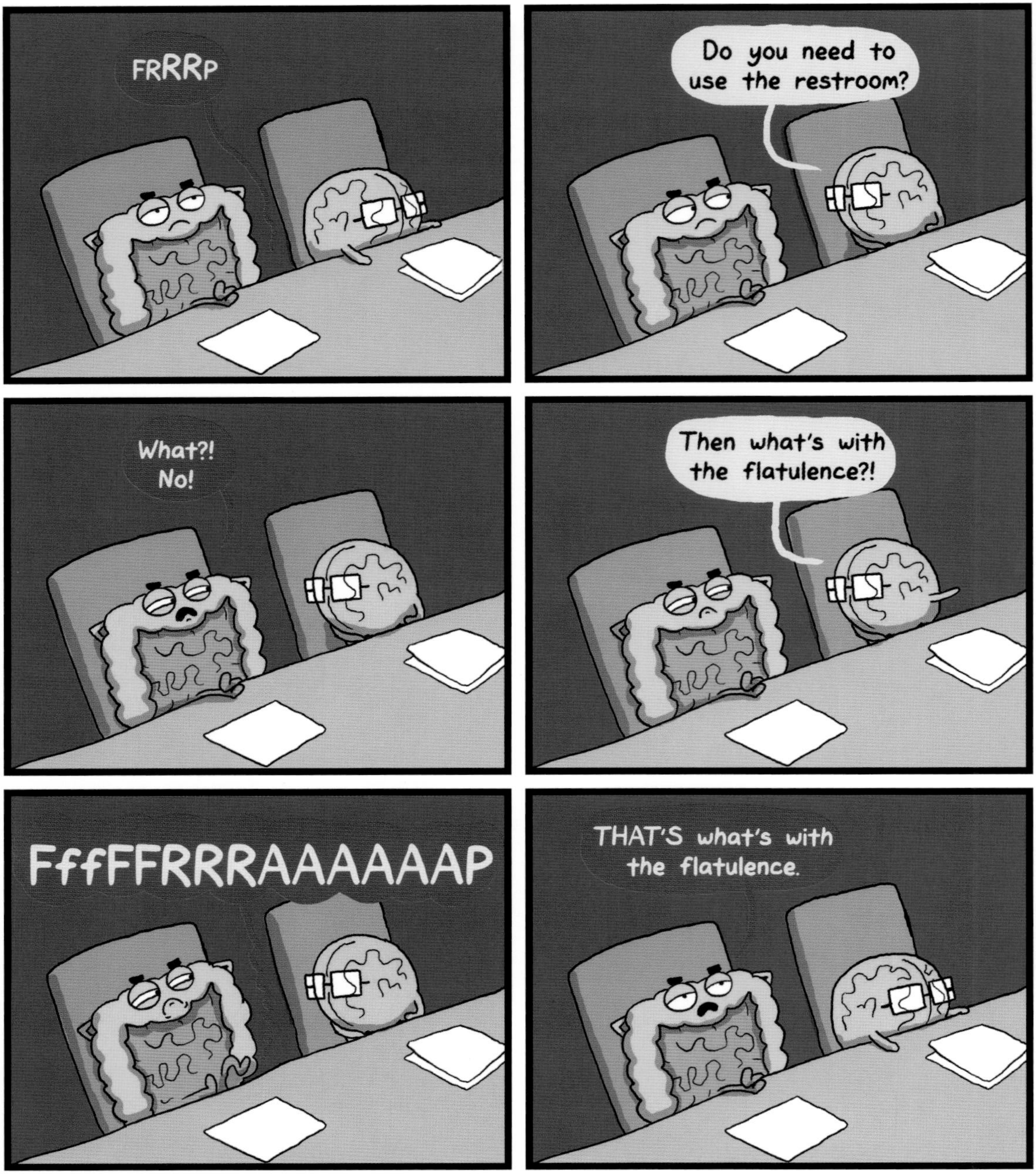
FRRRP
Do you need to use the restroom?
What?! No!
Then what's with the flatulence?!
FfFFFRRRAAAAAAP
THAT'S what's with the flatulence.

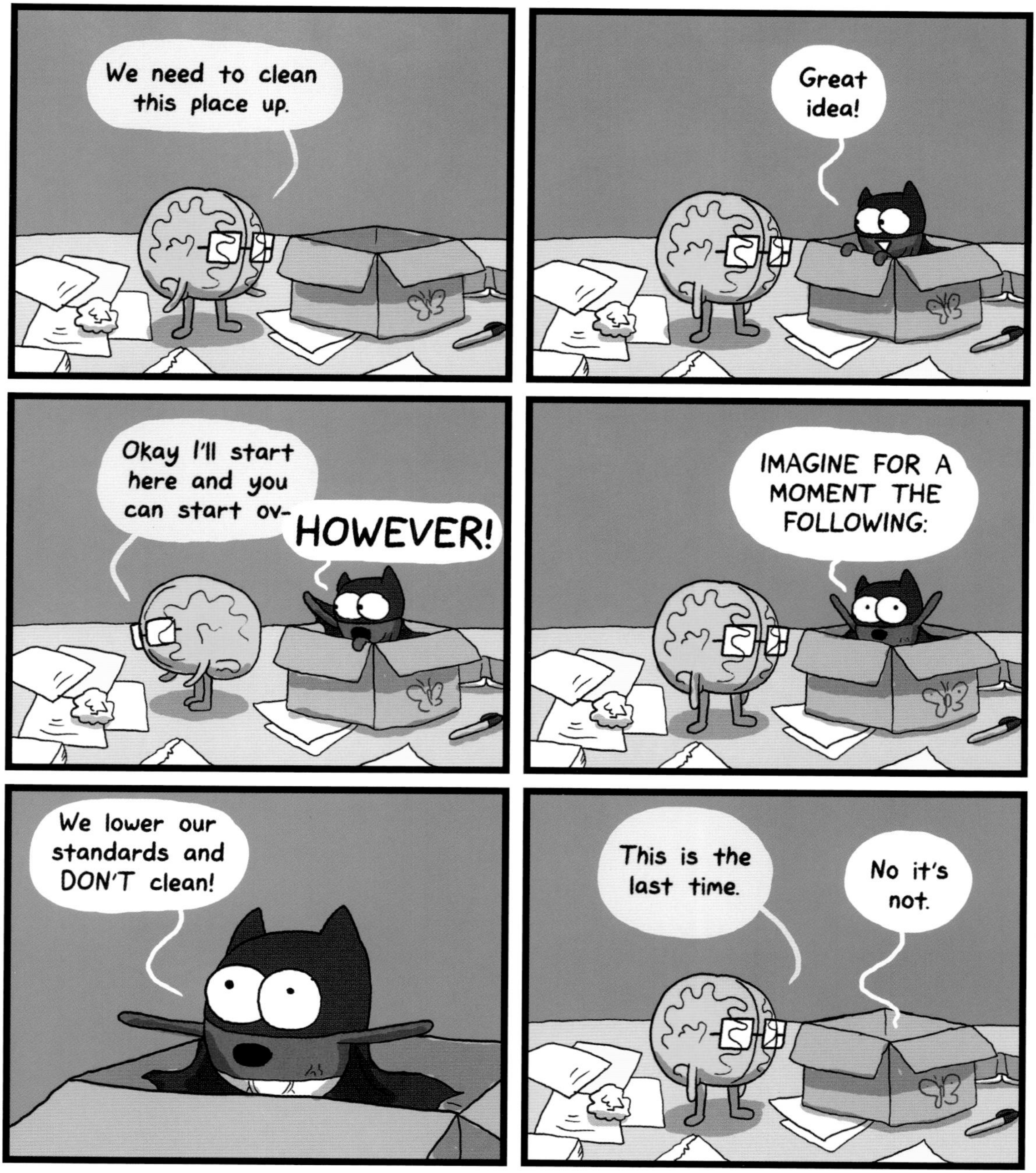
We need to clean this place up.
Great idea!
Okay I'll start here and you can start ov-
HOWEVER!
IMAGINE FOR A MOMENT THE FOLLOWING:
We lower our standards and DON'T clean!
This is the last time.
No it's not.

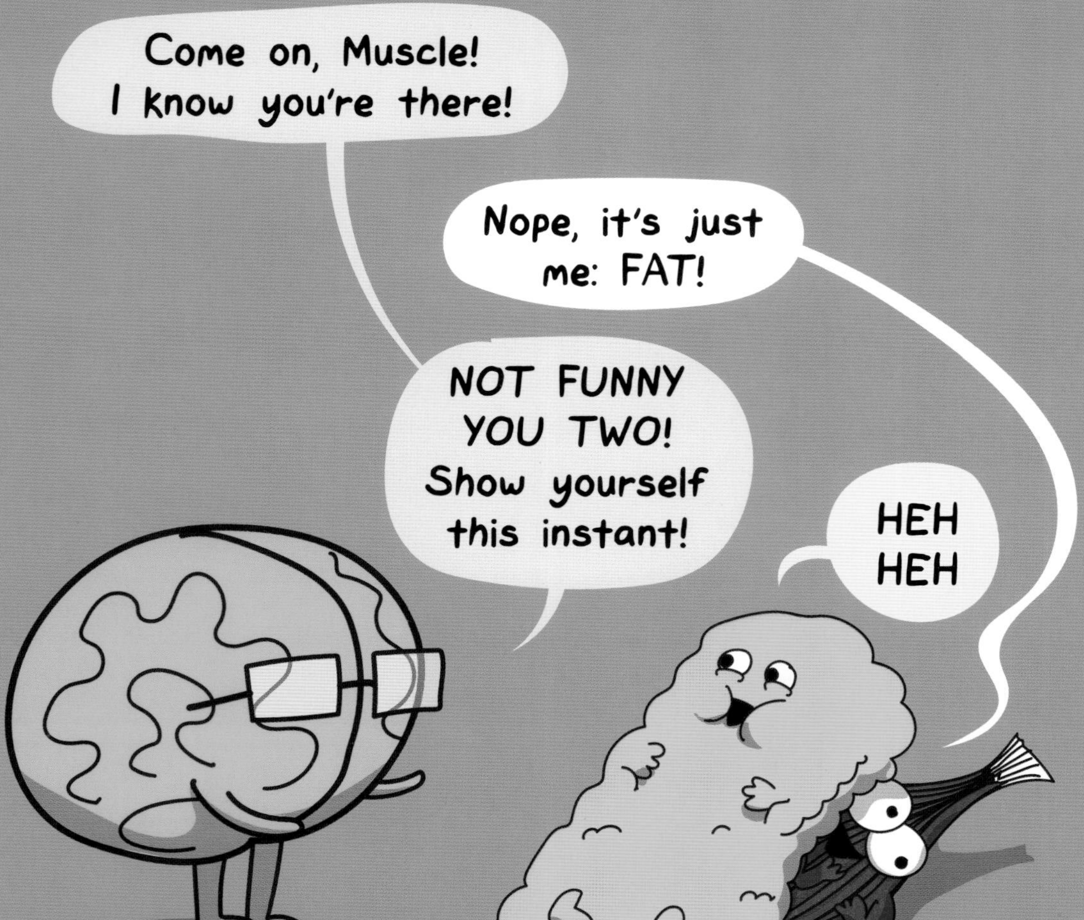
Come on, Muscle! I know you're there!
Nope, it's just me: FAT!
NOT FUNNY YOU TWO! Show yourself this instant!
HEH HEH

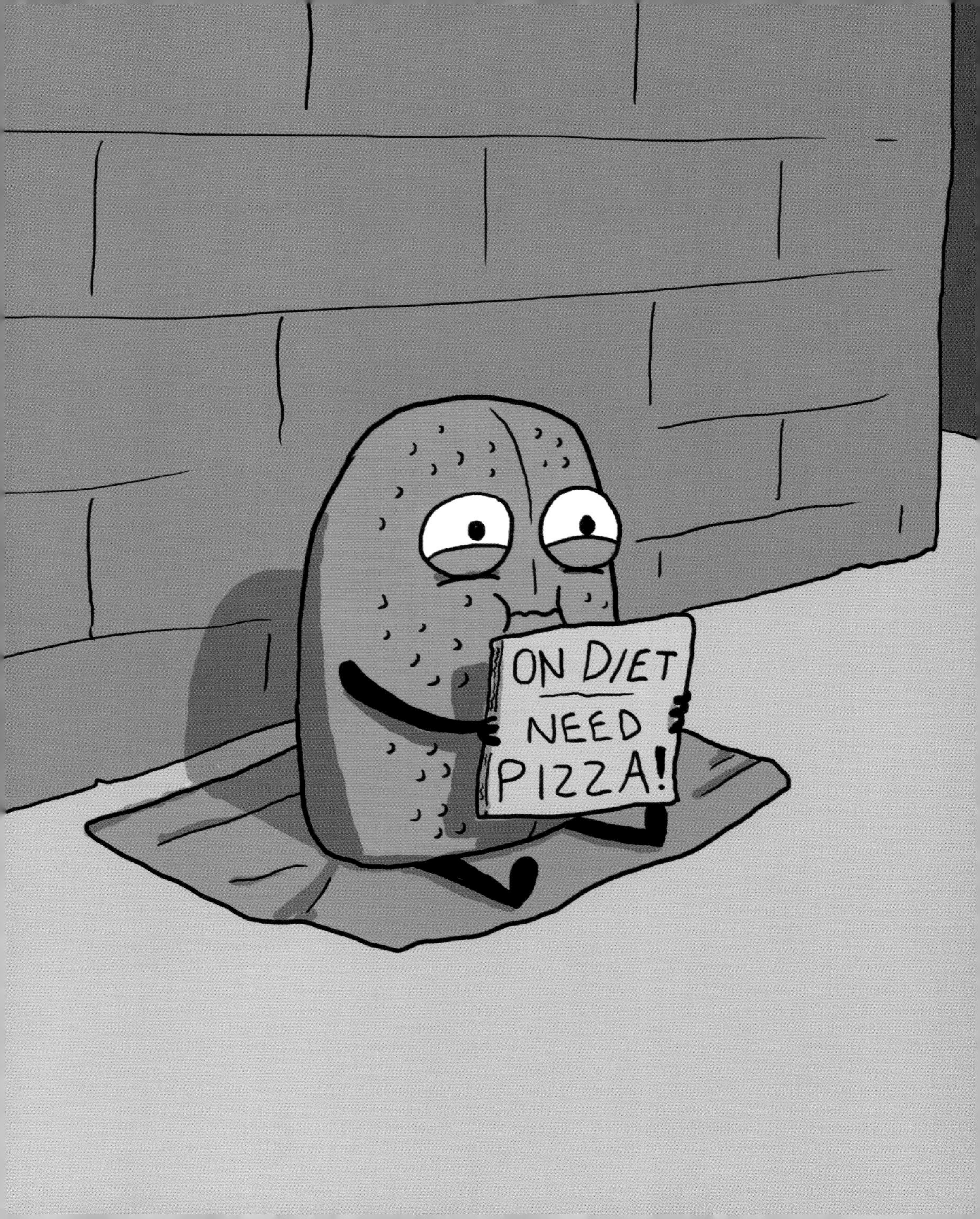
ON DIET
NEED
PIZZA!

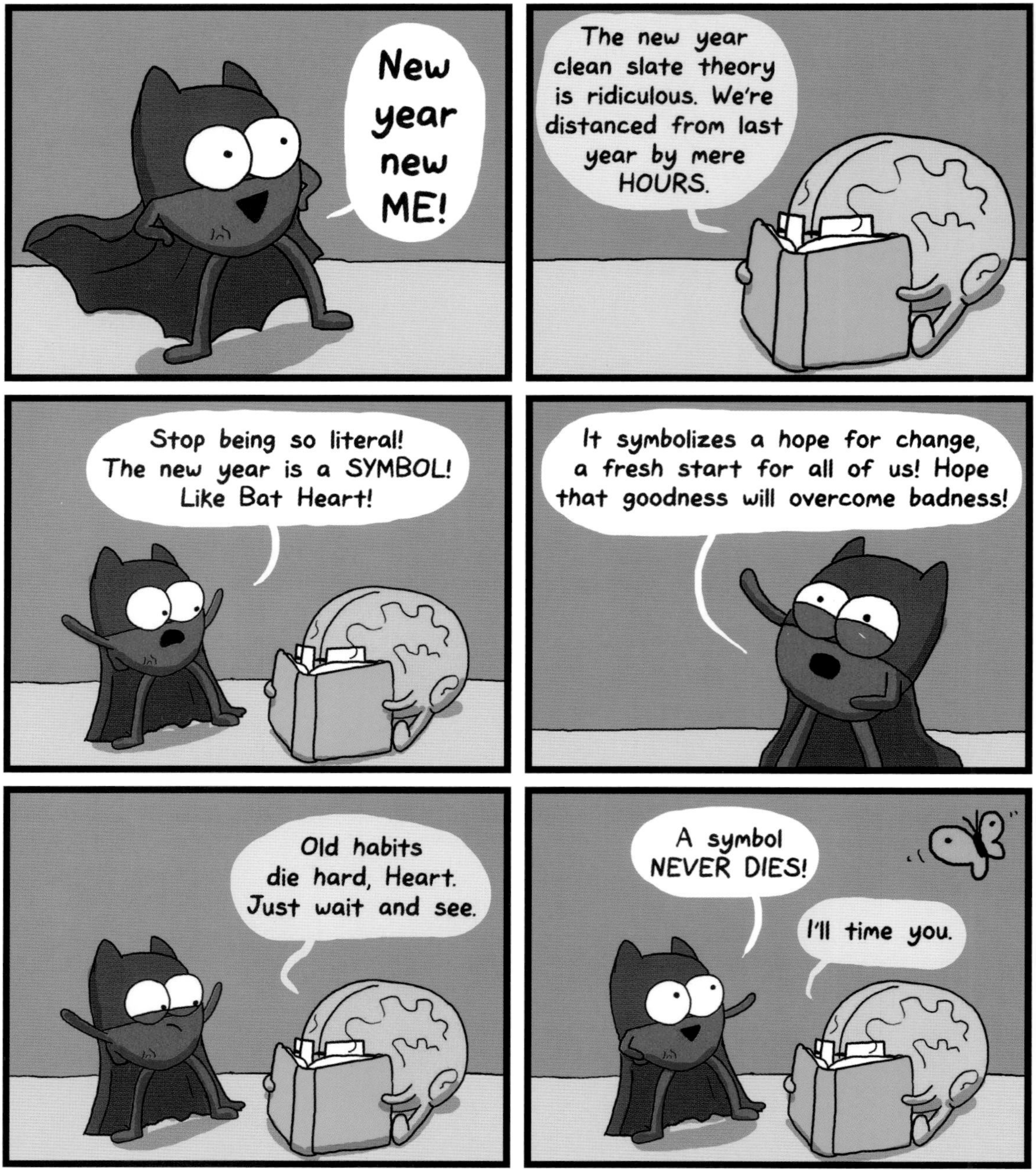
New year new ME!
The new year clean slate theory is ridiculous. We're distanced from last year by mere HOURS.
Stop being so literal! The new year is a SYMBOL! Like Bat Heart!
It symbolizes a hope for change, a fresh start for all of us! Hope that goodness will overcome badness!
Old habits die hard, Heart. Just wait and see.
A symbol NEVER DIES!
I'll time you.

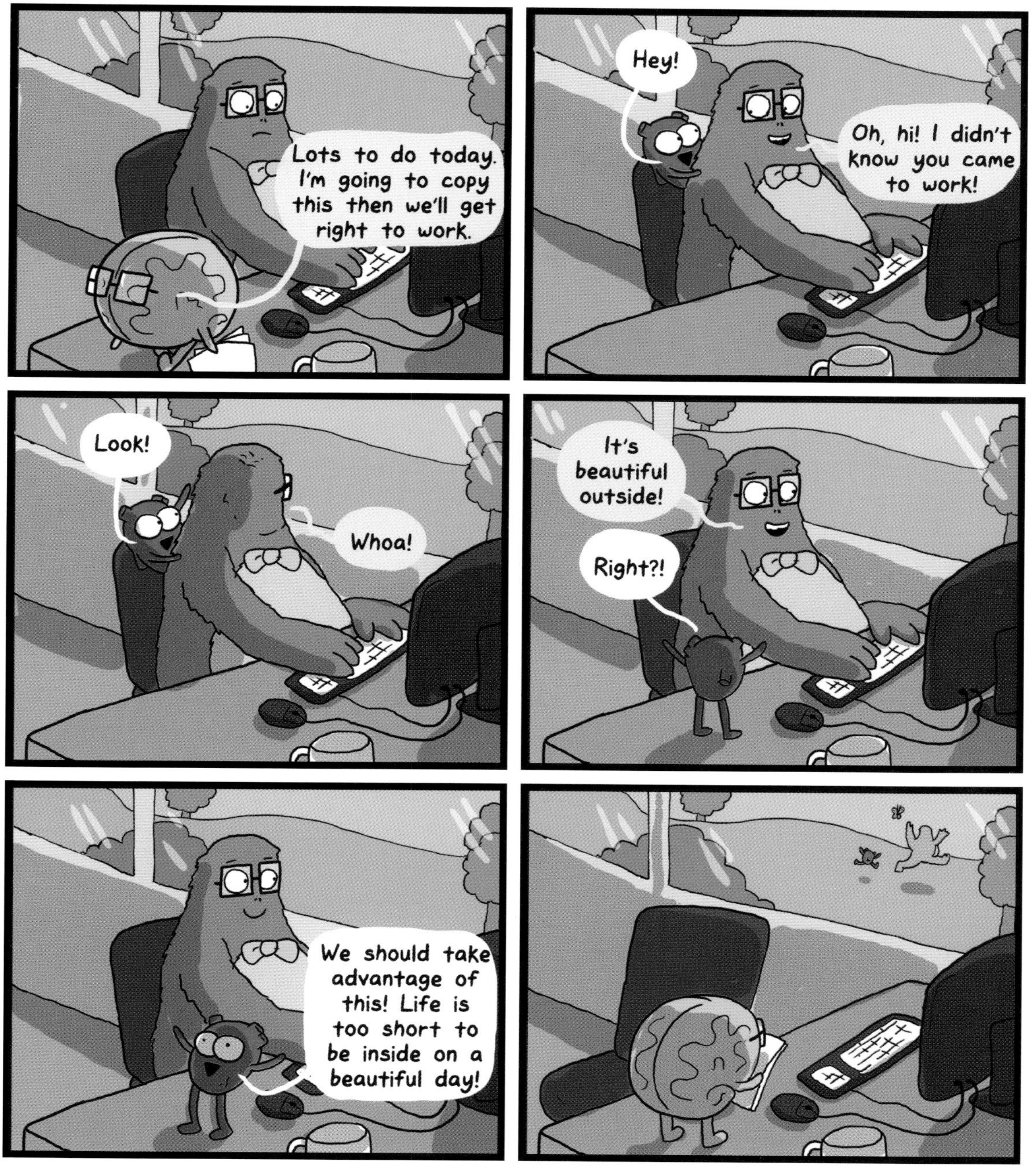

Lots to do today. I'm going to copy this then we'll get right to work.
Hey!
Oh, hi! I didn't know you came to work!
Look!
Whoa!
It's beautiful outside!
Right?!
We should take advantage of this! Life is too short to be inside on a beautiful day!

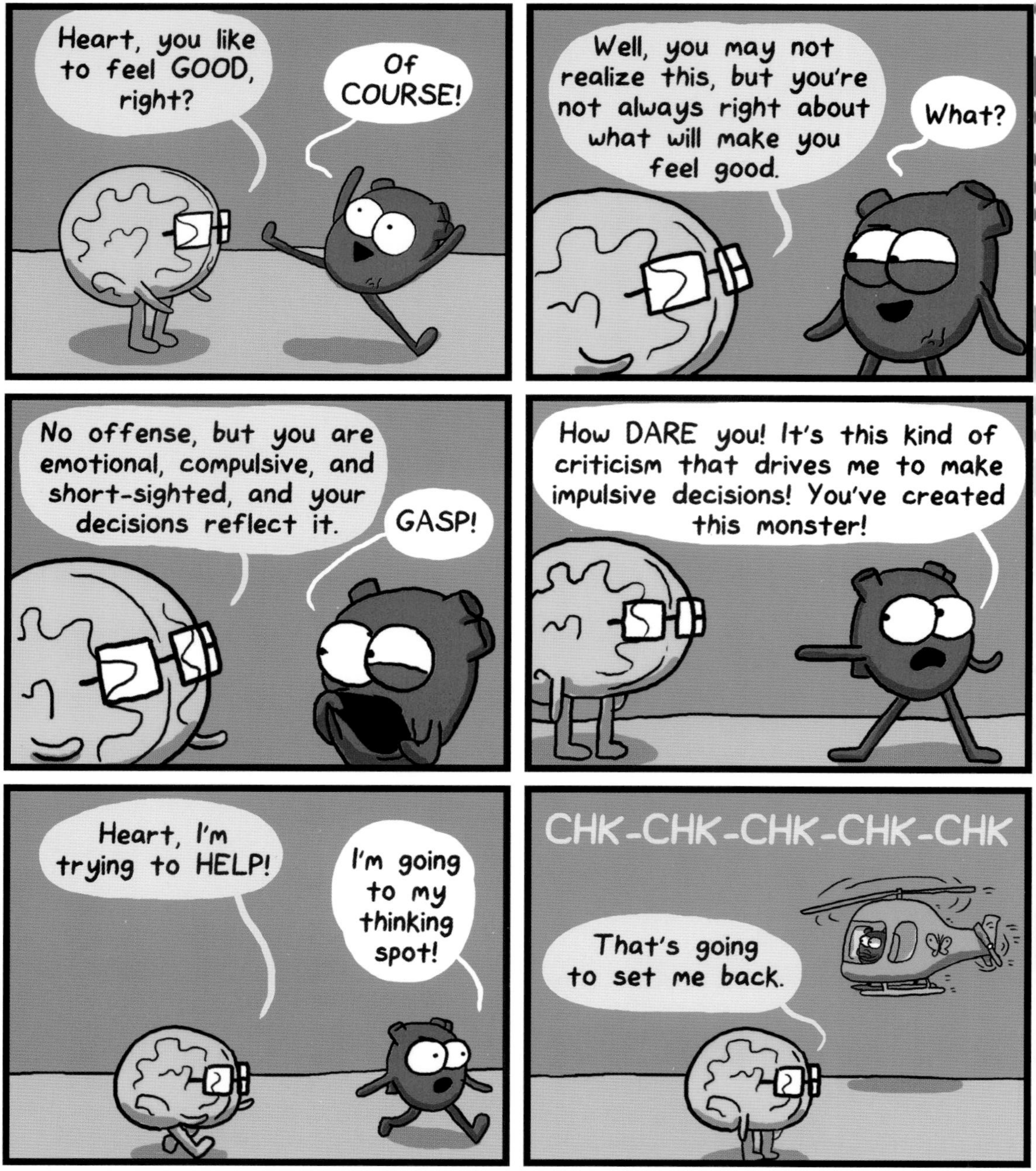
Heart, you like to feel GOOD, right?
Of COURSE!
Well, you may not realize this, but you're not always right about what will make you feel good.
What?
No offense, but you are emotional, compulsive, and short-sighted, and your decisions reflect it.
GASP!
How DARE you! It's this kind of criticism that drives me to make impulsive decisions! You've created this monster!
Heart, I'm trying to HELP!
I'm going to my thinking spot!
CHK-CHK-CHK-CHK-CHK
That's going to set me back.

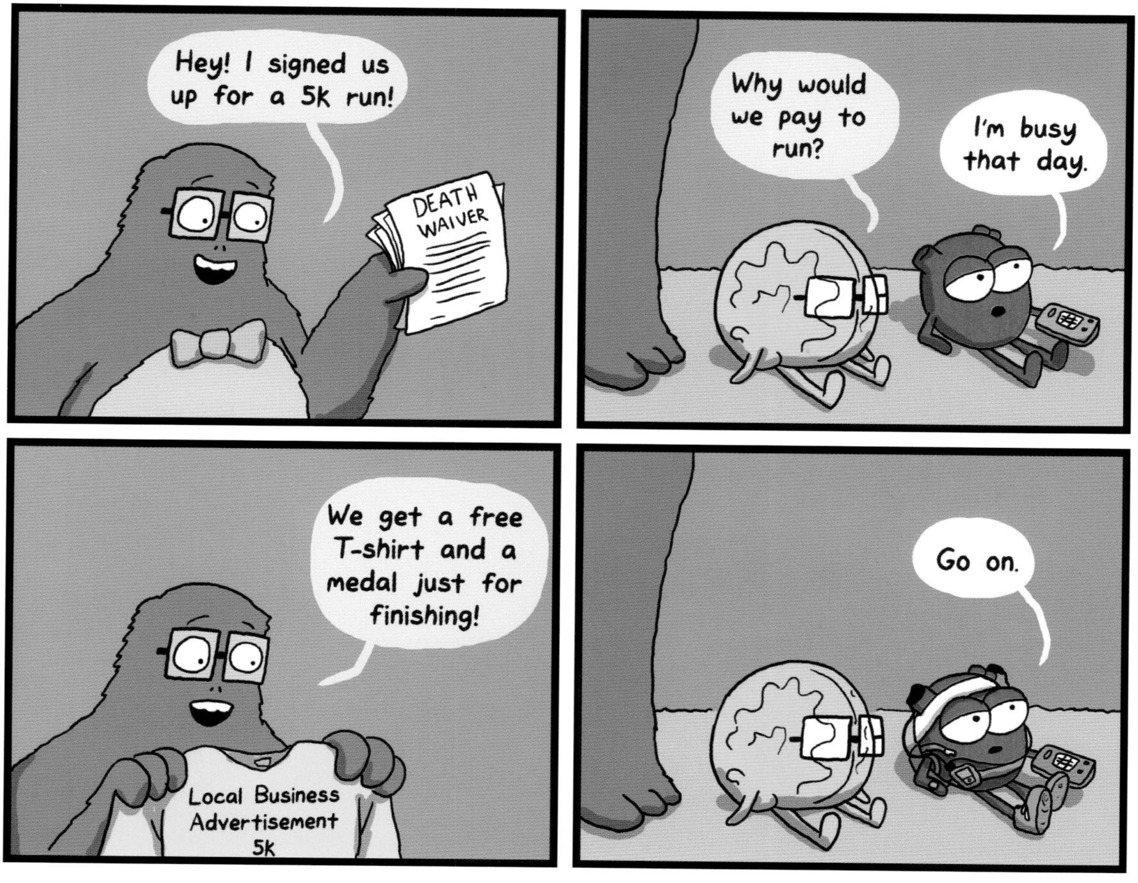
Hey! I signed us up for a 5k run!
DEATH WAIVER
Why would we pay to run?
I'm busy that day.
We get a free T-shirt and a medal just for finishing!
Local Business Advertisement 5k
Go on.

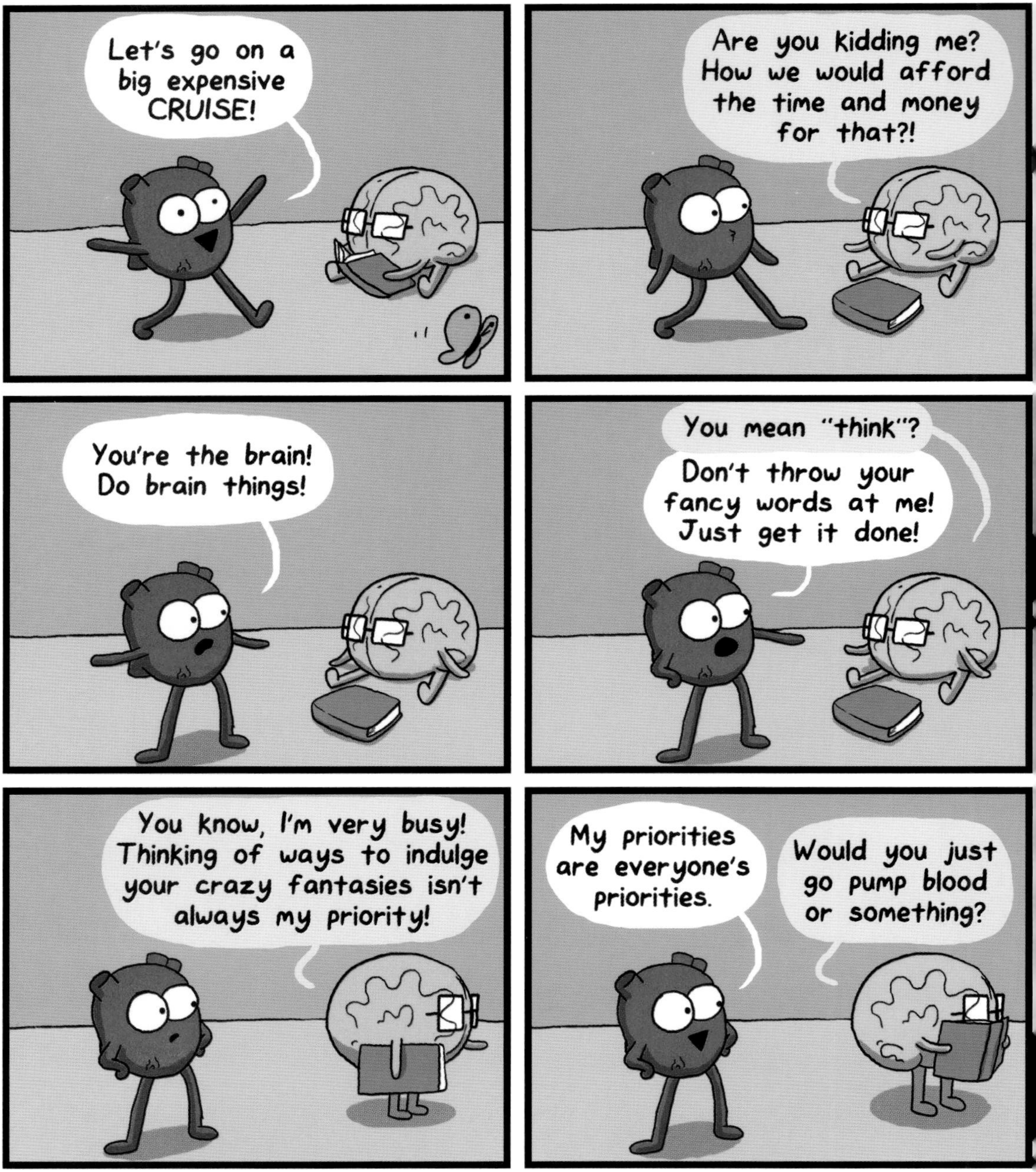
Let's go on a big expensive CRUISE!
Are you kidding me? How we would afford the time and money for that?!
You're the brain! Do brain things!
You mean "think"?
Don't throw your fancy words at me! Just get it done!
You know, I'm very busy! Thinking of ways to indulge your crazy fantasies isn't always my priority!
My priorities are everyone's priorities.
Would you just go pump blood or something?

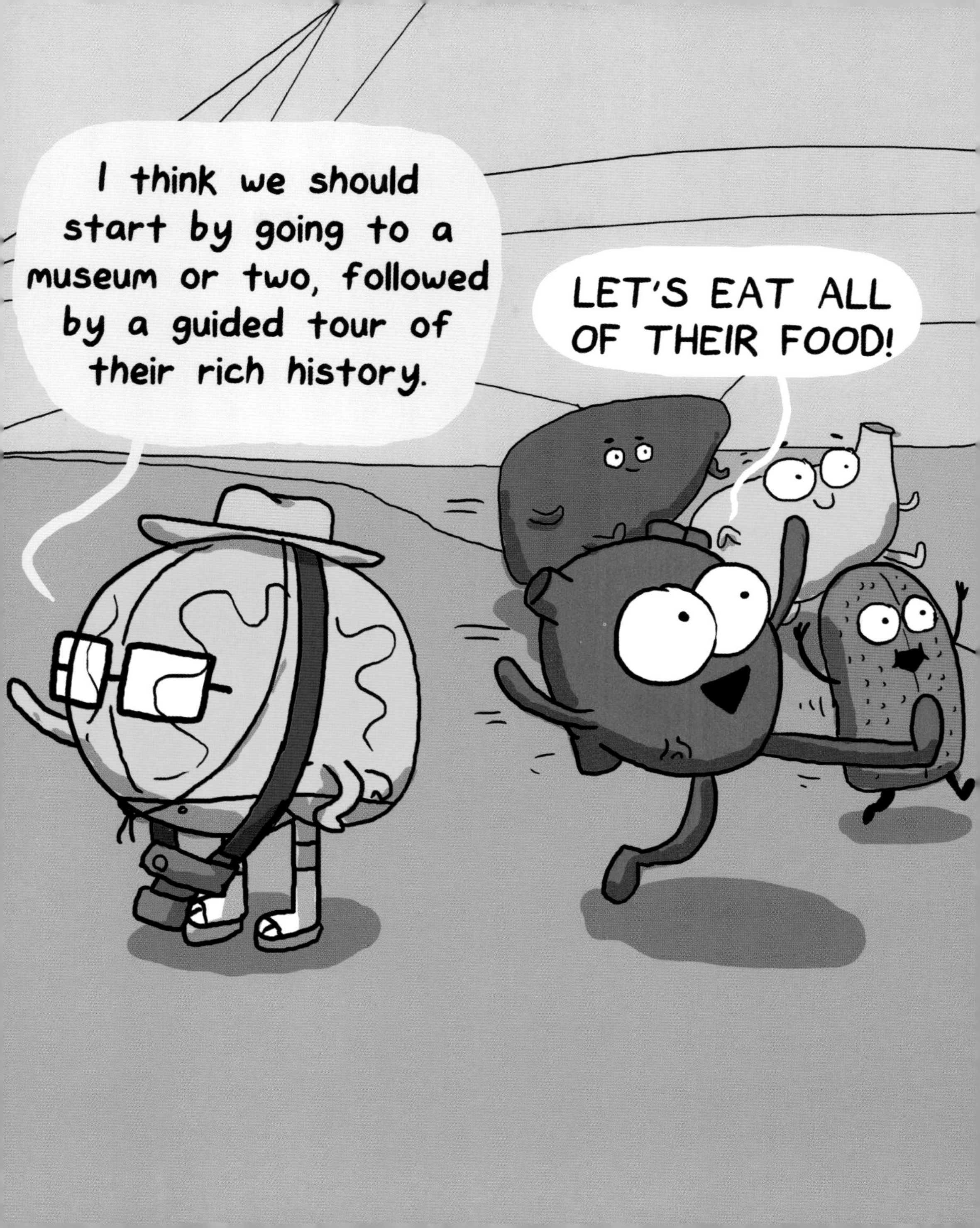
I think we should start by going to a museum or two, followed by a guided tour of their rich history.
LET'S EAT ALL OF THEIR FOOD!

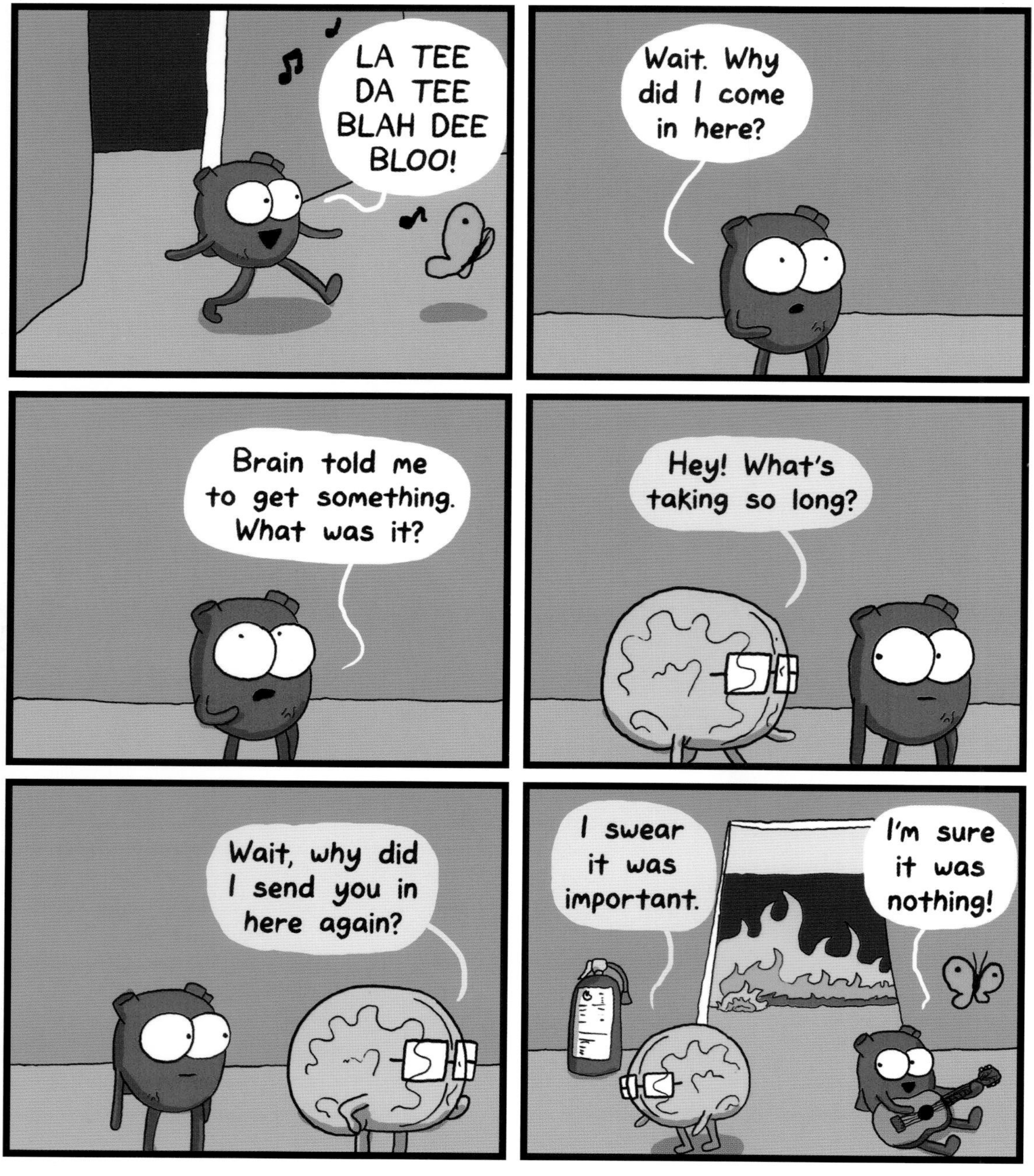
LA TEE DA TEE BLAH DEE BLOO!
Wait. Why did I come in here?
Brain told me to get something. What was it?
Hey! What's taking so long?
Wait, why did I send you in here again?
I swear it was important.
I'm sure it was nothing!

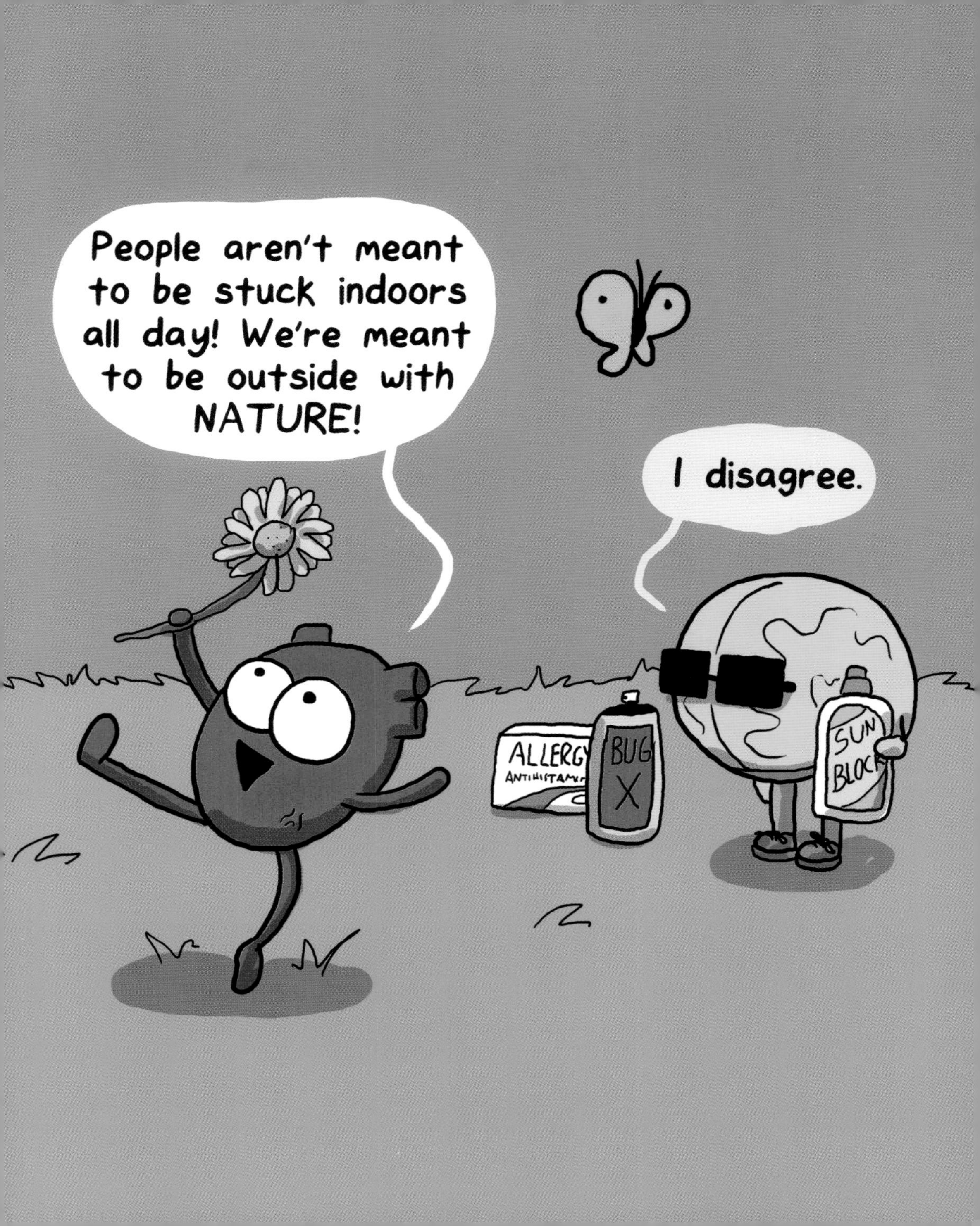
People aren't meant to be stuck indoors all day! We're meant to be outside with NATURE!
I disagree.
ALLERGY
BUG X
SUN BLOCK

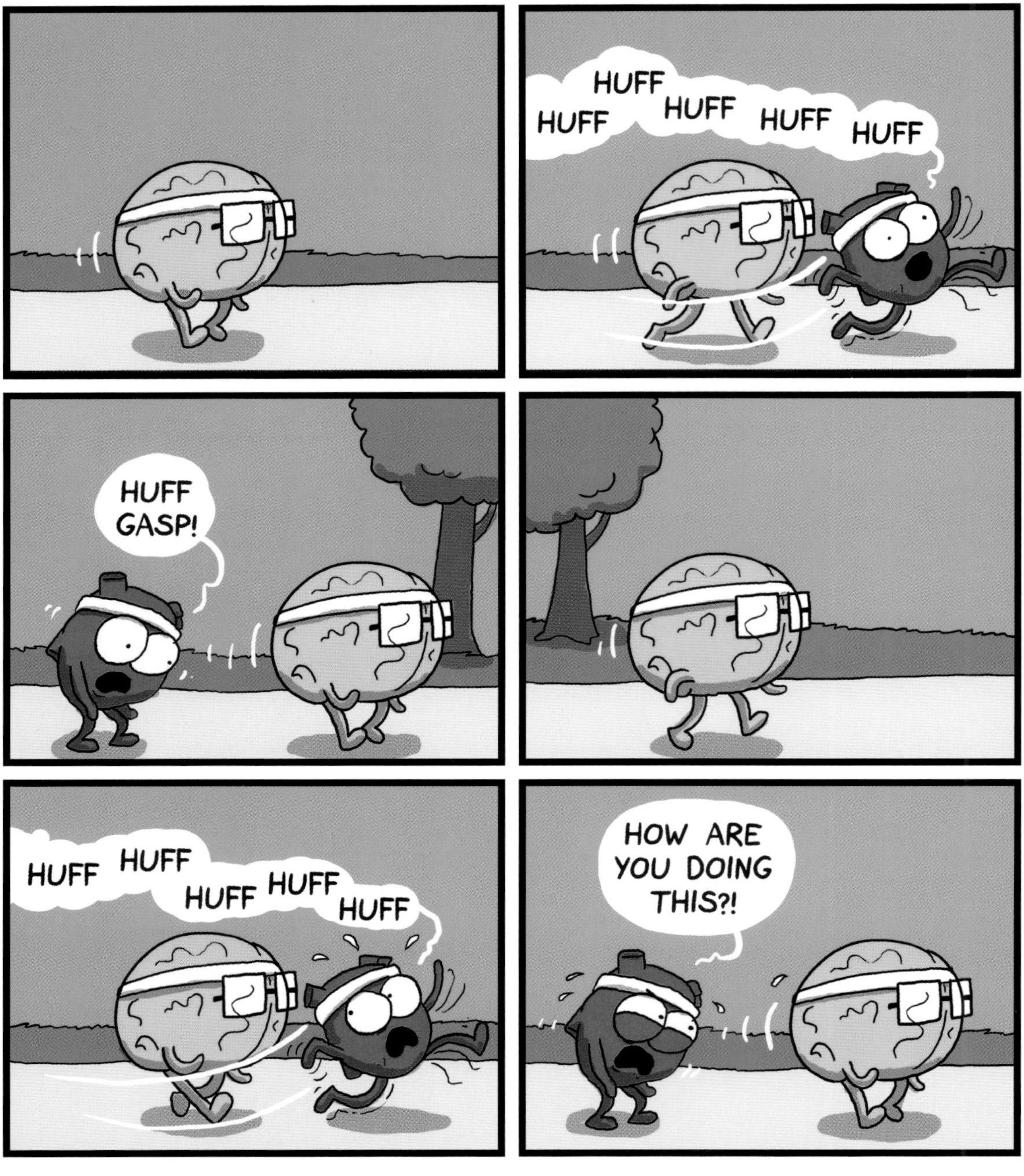
HUFF HUFF HUFF HUFF HUFF
HUFF GASP!
HUFF HUFF HUFF HUFF HUFF
HOW ARE YOU DOING THIS?!

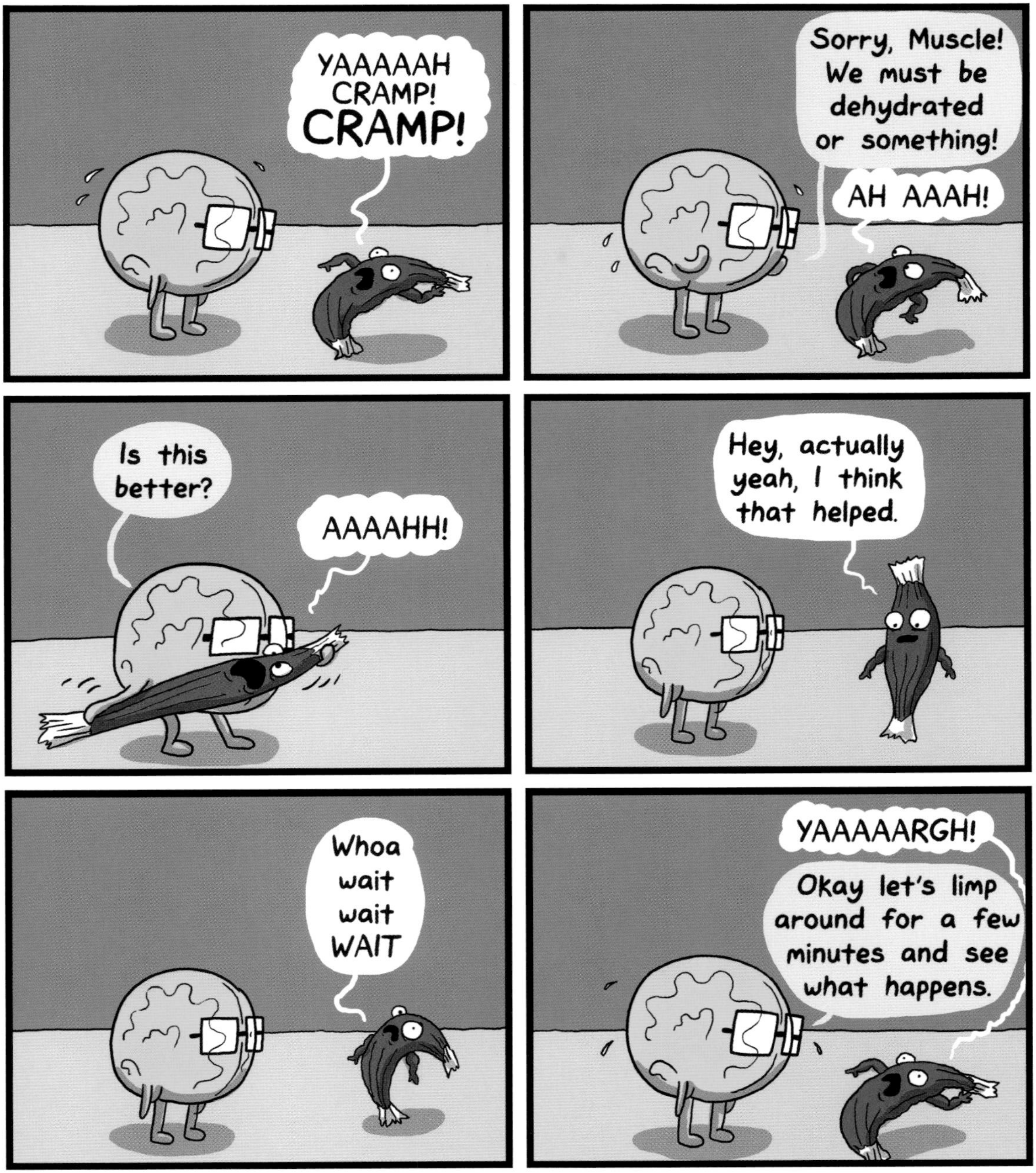
YAAAAAH CRAMP! CRAMP!
Sorry, Muscle! We must be dehydrated or something!
AH AAAH!
Is this better?
AAAAHH!
Hey, actually yeah, I think that helped.
Whoa wait wait WAIT
YAAAAARGH!
Okay let's limp around for a few minutes and see what happens.

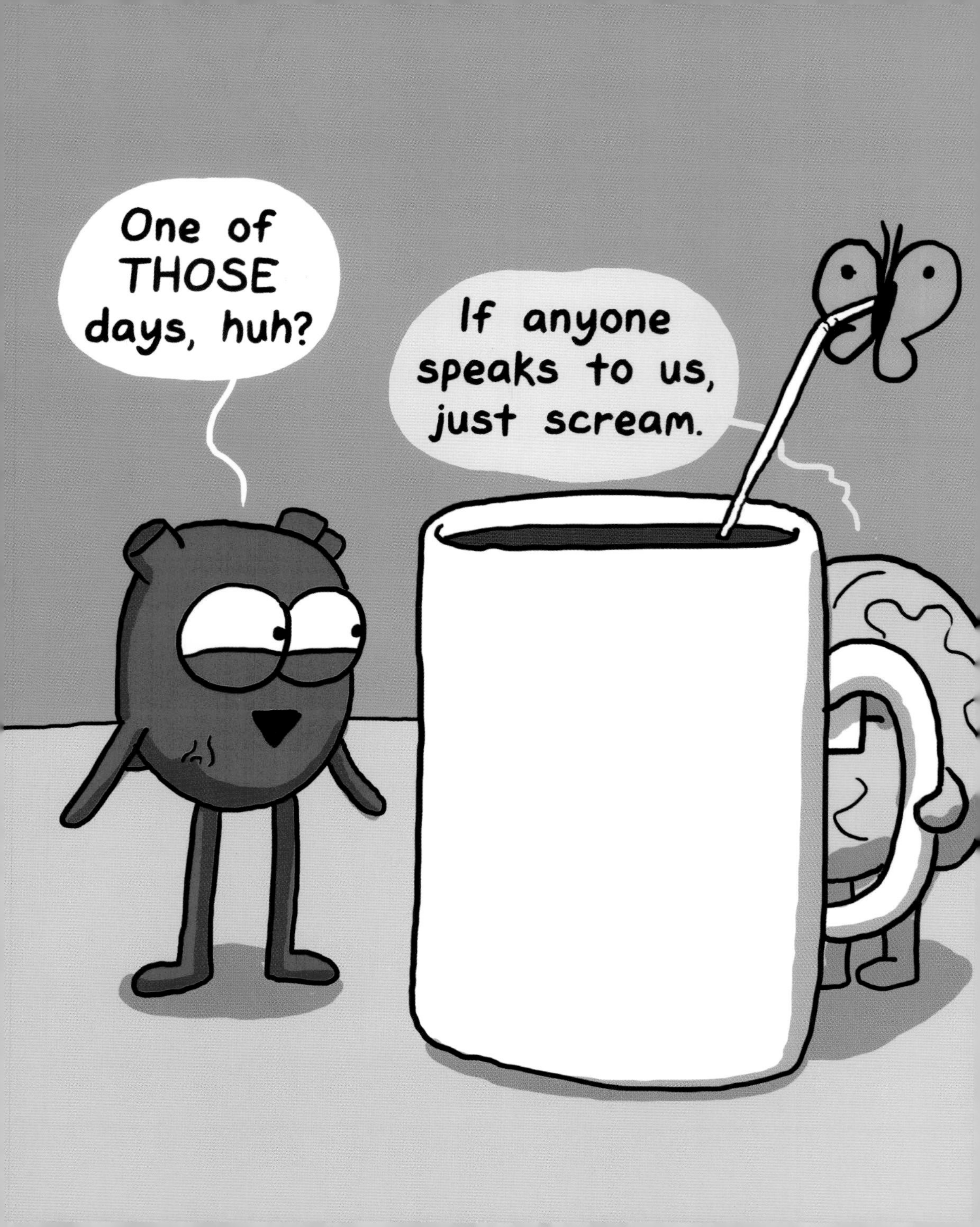
One of THOSE days, huh?
If anyone speaks to us, just scream.

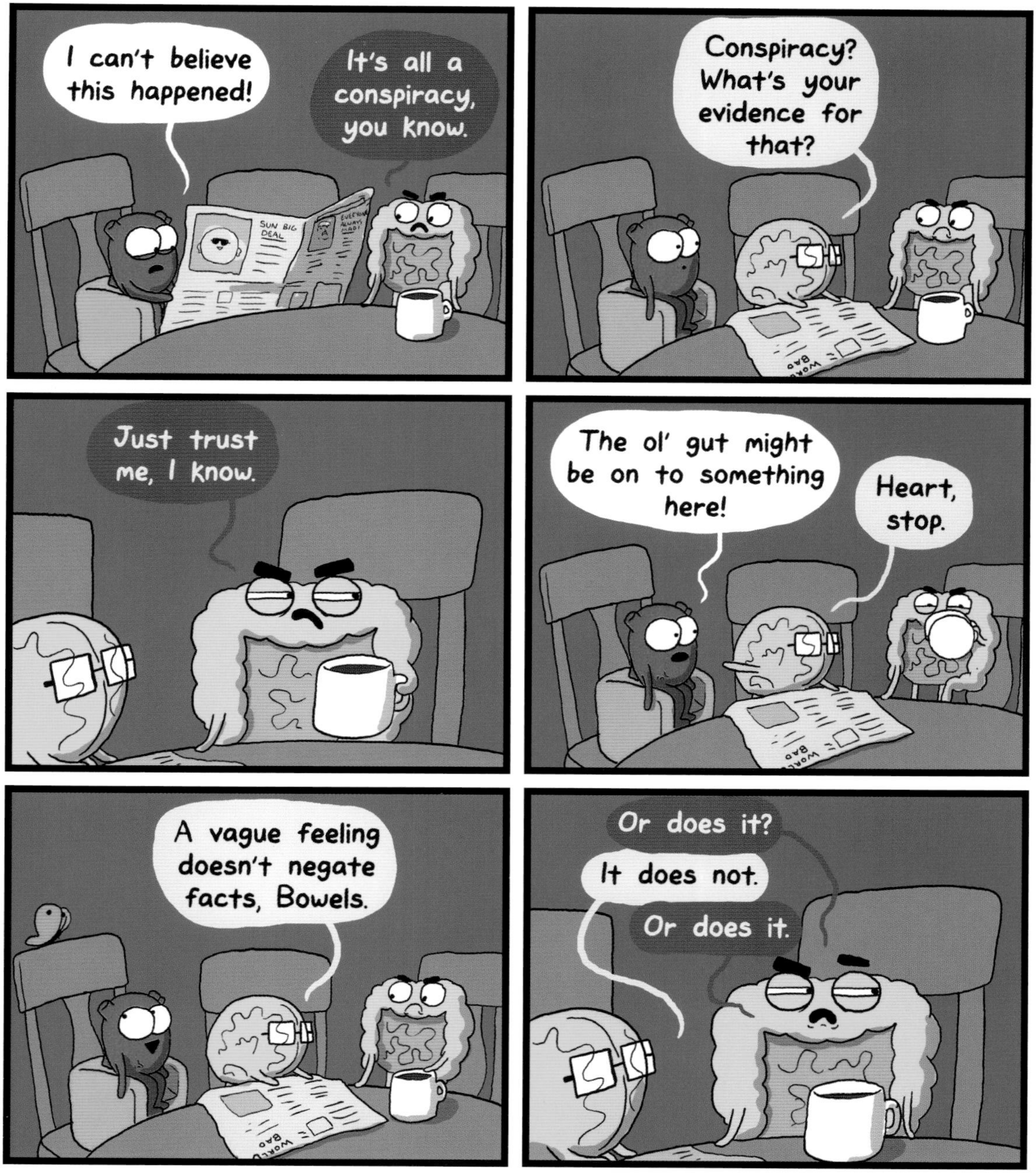
I can't believe this happened!
It's all a conspiracy, you know.
SUN BIG DEAL
Conspiracy? What's your evidence for that?
Just trust me, I know.
The ol' gut might be on to something here!
Heart, stop.
A vague feeling doesn't negate facts, Bowels.
Or does it?
It does not.
Or does it.

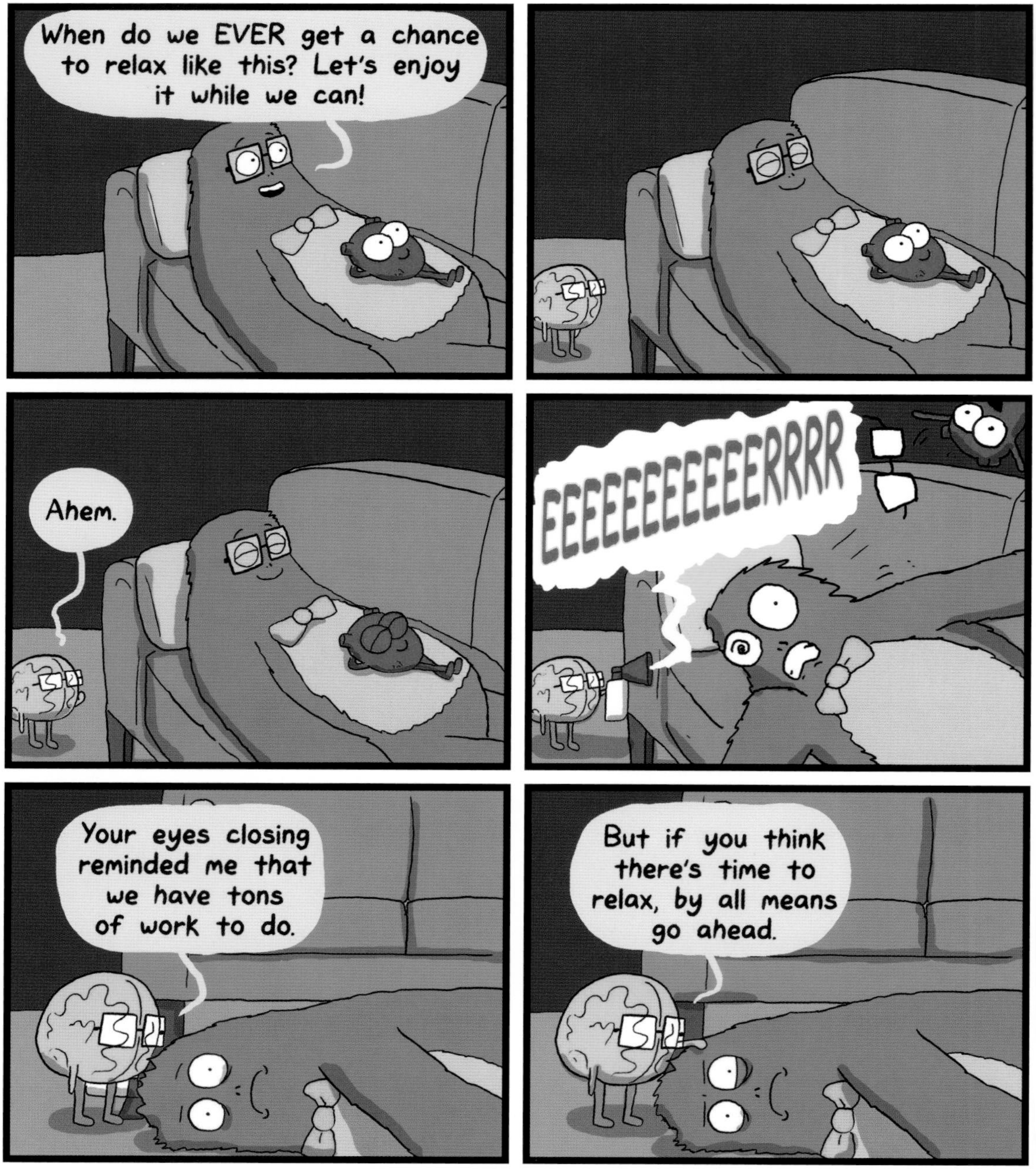
When do we EVER get a chance to relax like this? Let's enjoy it while we can!
Ahem.
EEEEEEEEEEERRRR
Your eyes closing reminded me that we have tons of work to do.
But if you think there's time to relax, by all means go ahead.

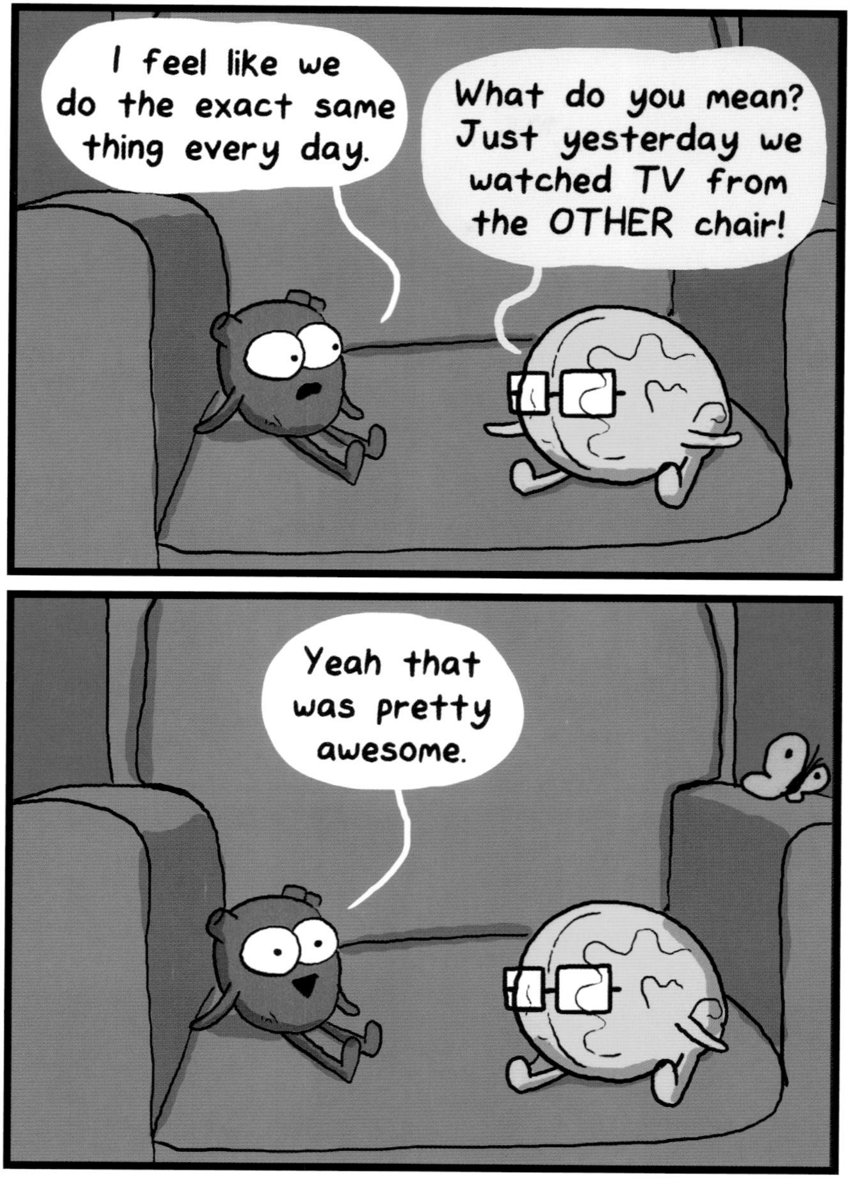
I feel like we do the exact same thing every day.
What do you mean? Just yesterday we watched TV from the OTHER chair!
Yeah that was pretty awesome.

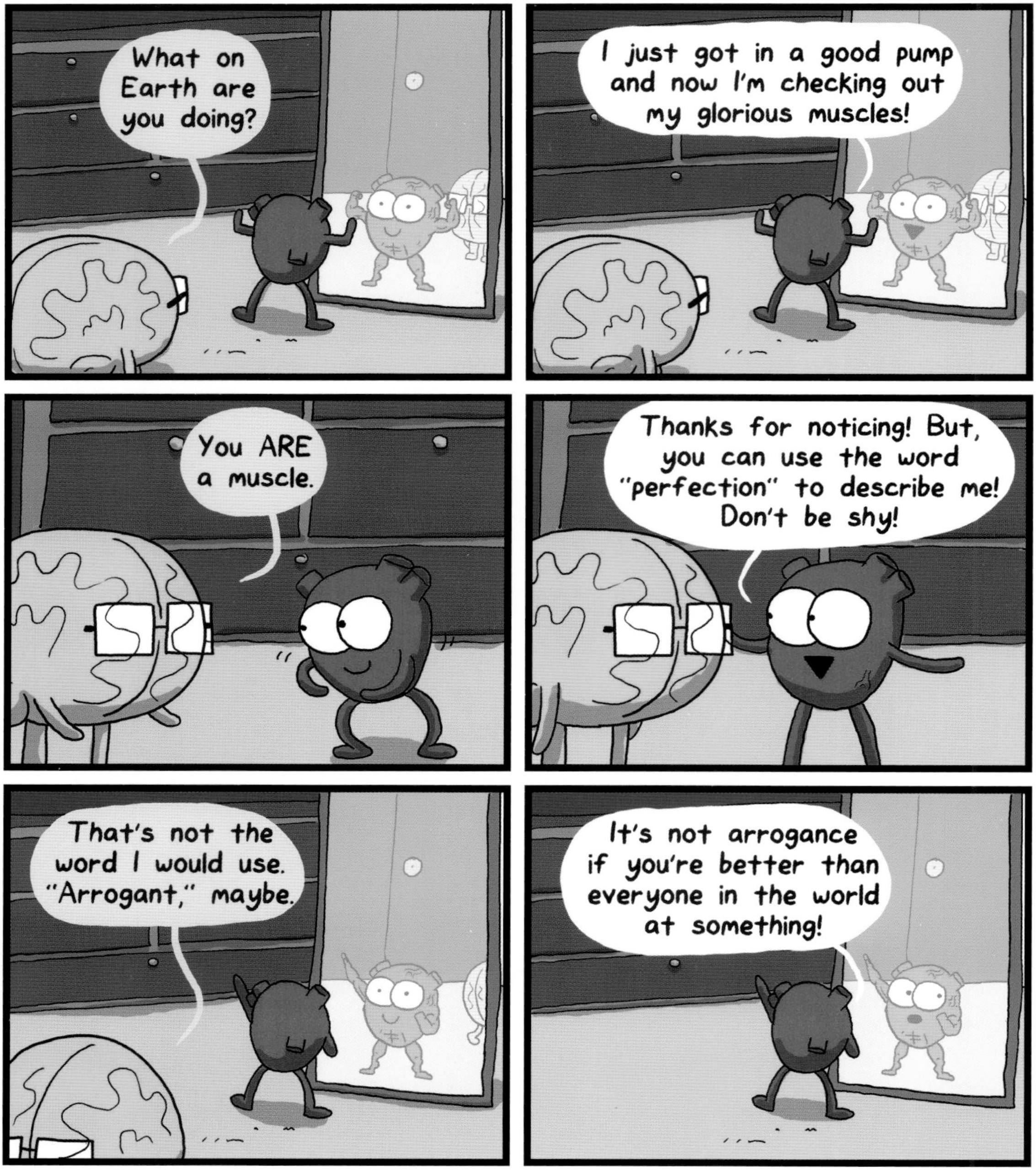
What on Earth are you doing?
I just got in a good pump and now I'm checking out my glorious muscles!
You ARE a muscle.
Thanks for noticing! But, you can use the word "perfection" to describe me! Don't be shy!
That's not the word I would use. "Arrogant," maybe.
It's not arrogance if you're better than everyone in the world at something!

In a hundred years, nobody you know will exist anymore.
Why would you feel the need to say that?!

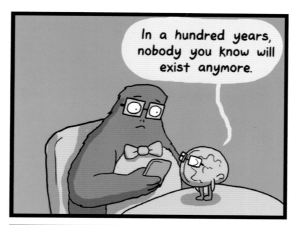

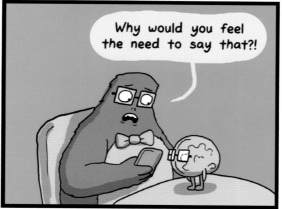

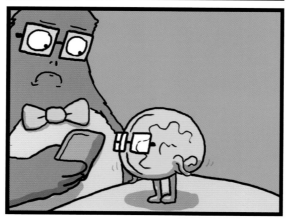

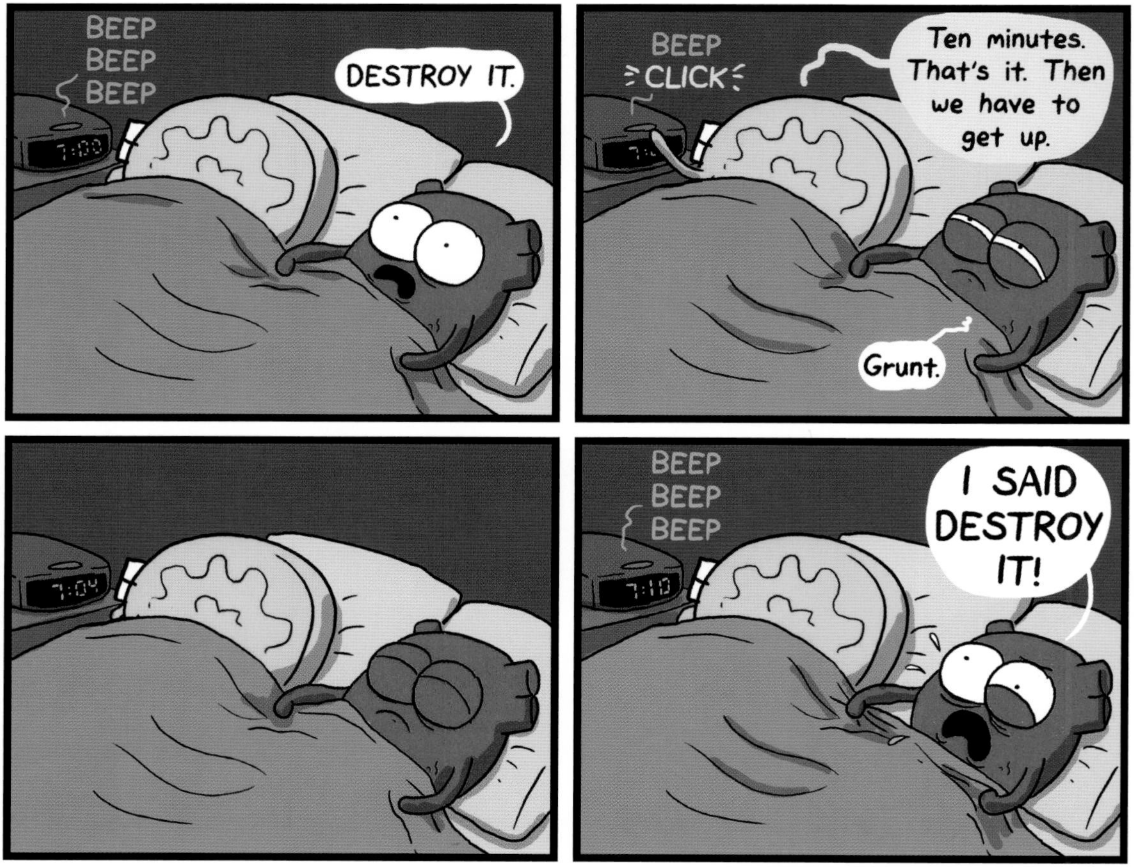
BEEP
BEEP
BEEP
DESTROY IT.
7:00
BEEP
CLICK
Ten minutes. That's it. Then we have to get up.
Grunt.
7:04
BEEP
BEEP
BEEP
7:10
I SAID DESTROY IT!

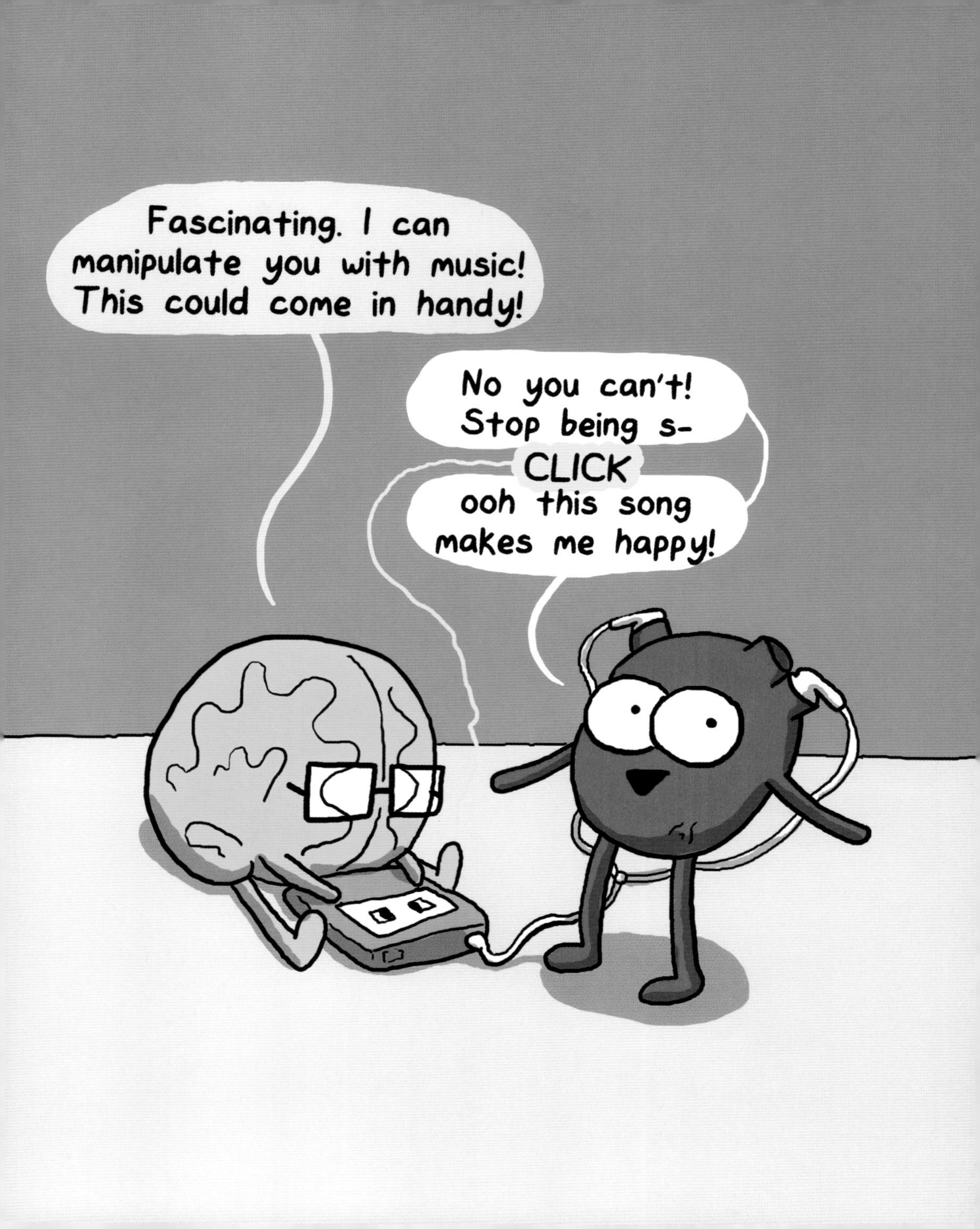
Fascinating. I can manipulate you with music! This could come in handy!
No you can't! Stop being s-
CLICK
ooh this song makes me happy!

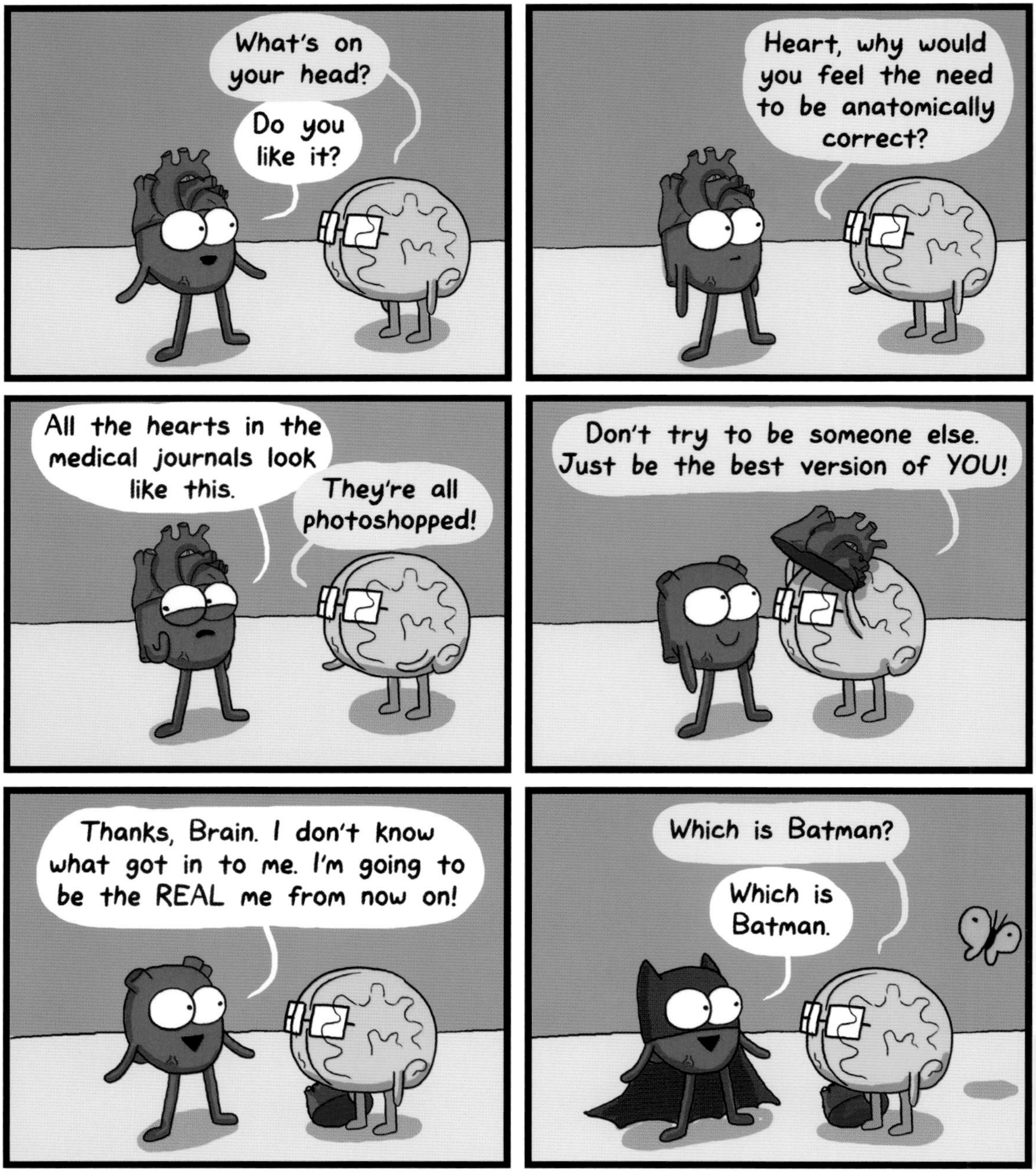
What's on your head?
Do you like it?
Heart, why would you feel the need to be anatomically correct?
All the hearts in the medical journals look like this.
They're all photoshopped!
Don't try to be someone else. Just be the best version of YOU!
Thanks, Brain. I don't know what got in to me. I'm going to be the REAL me from now on!
Which is Batman?
Which is Batman.

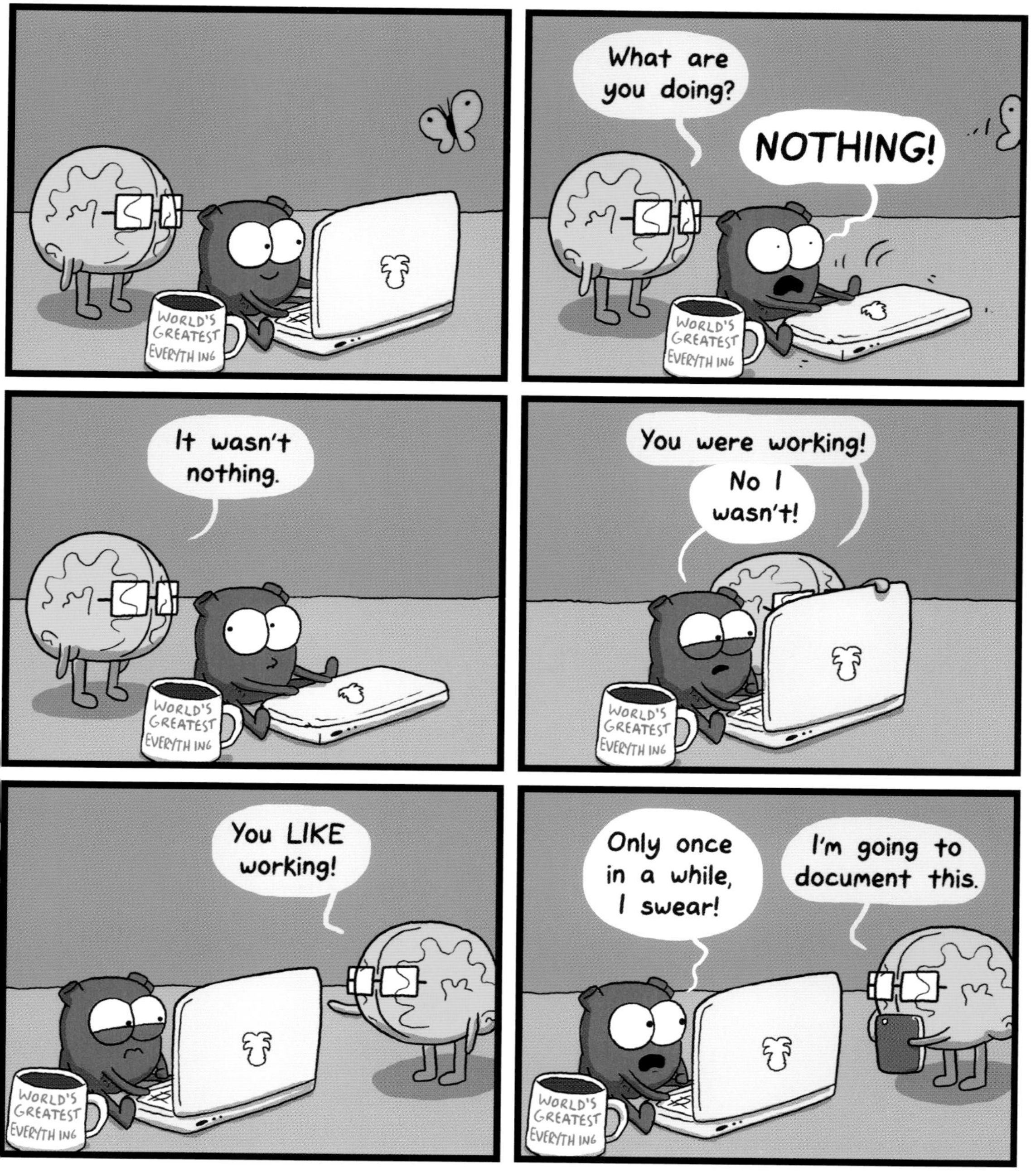
WORLD'S GREATEST EVERYTHING
What are you doing?
NOTHING!
It wasn't nothing.
You were working!
No I wasn't!
You LIKE working!
Only once in a while, I swear!
I'm going to document this.

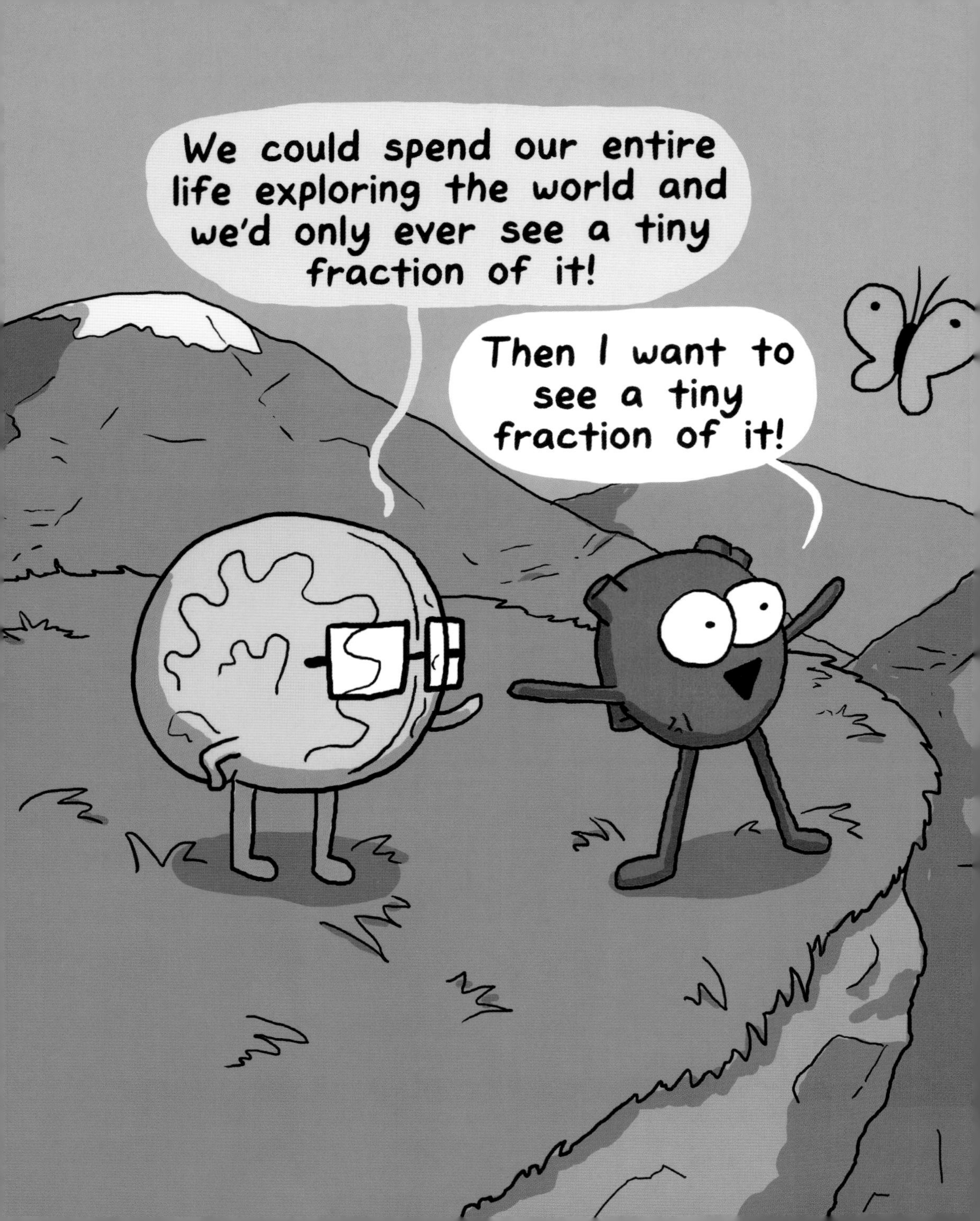
We could spend our entire life exploring the world and we'd only ever see a tiny fraction of it!
Then I want to see a tiny fraction of it!

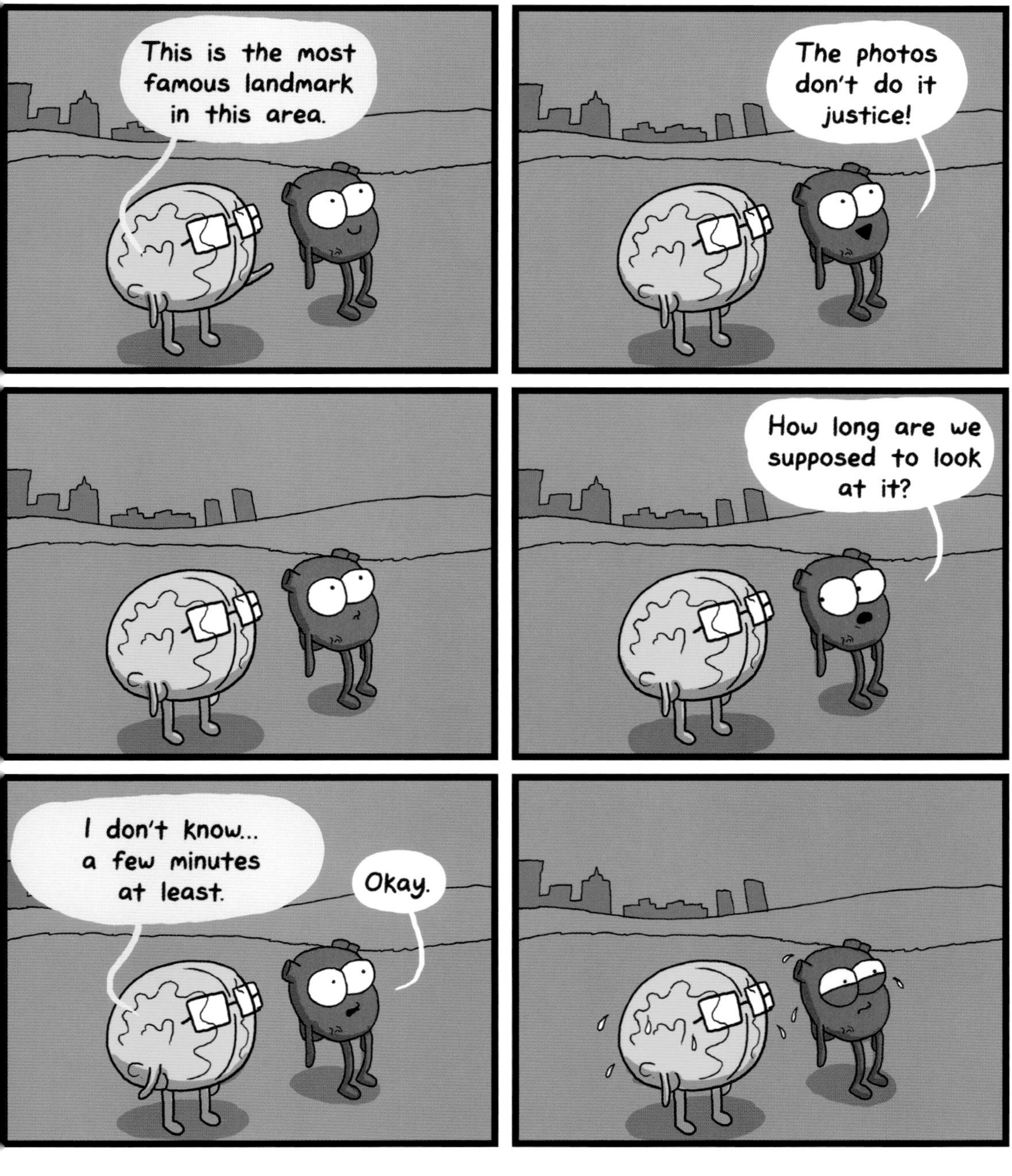
This is the most famous landmark in this area.
The photos don't do it justice!
How long are we supposed to look at it?
I don't know... a few minutes at least.
Okay.

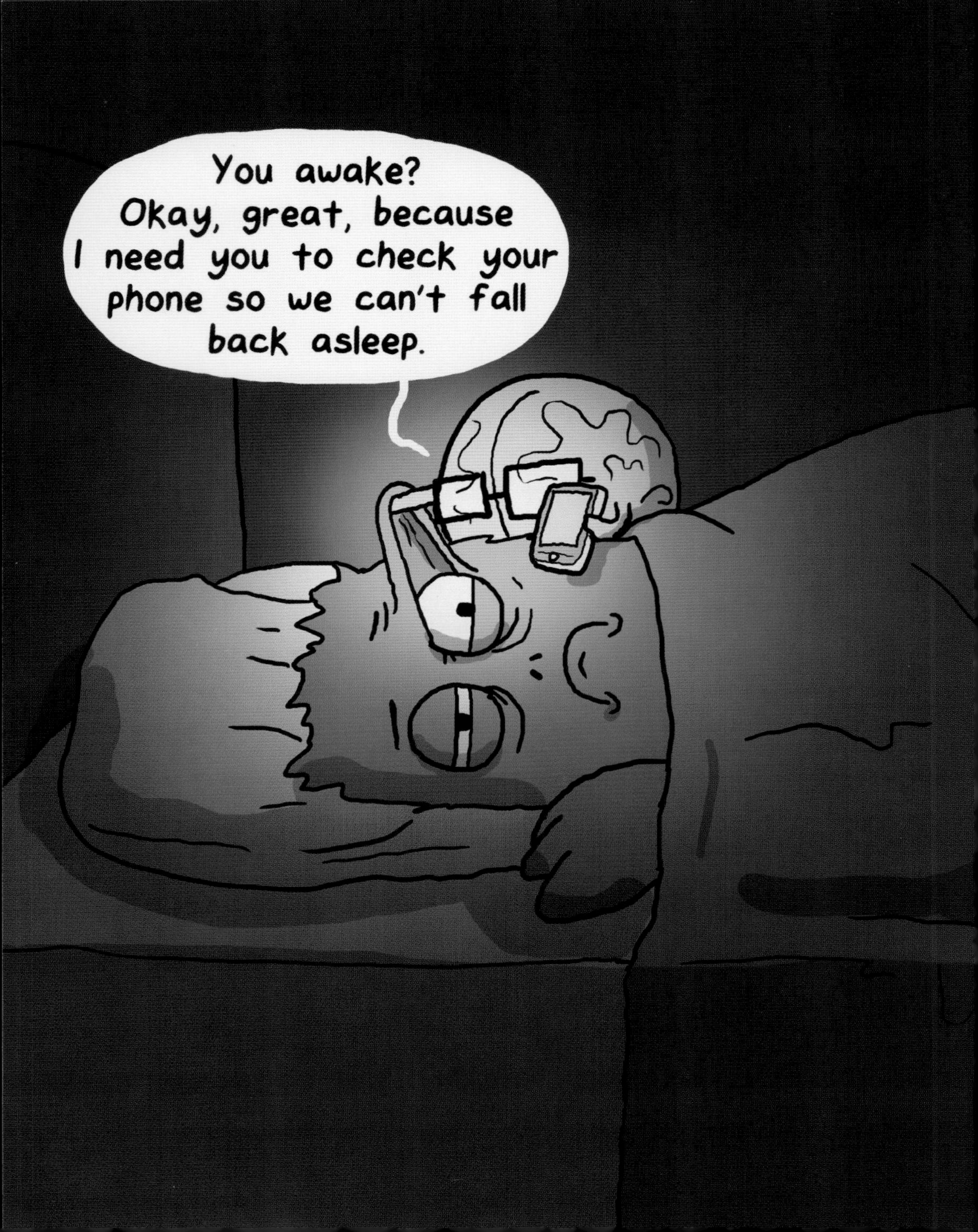
You awake?
Okay, great, because
I need you to check your
phone so we can't fall
back asleep.

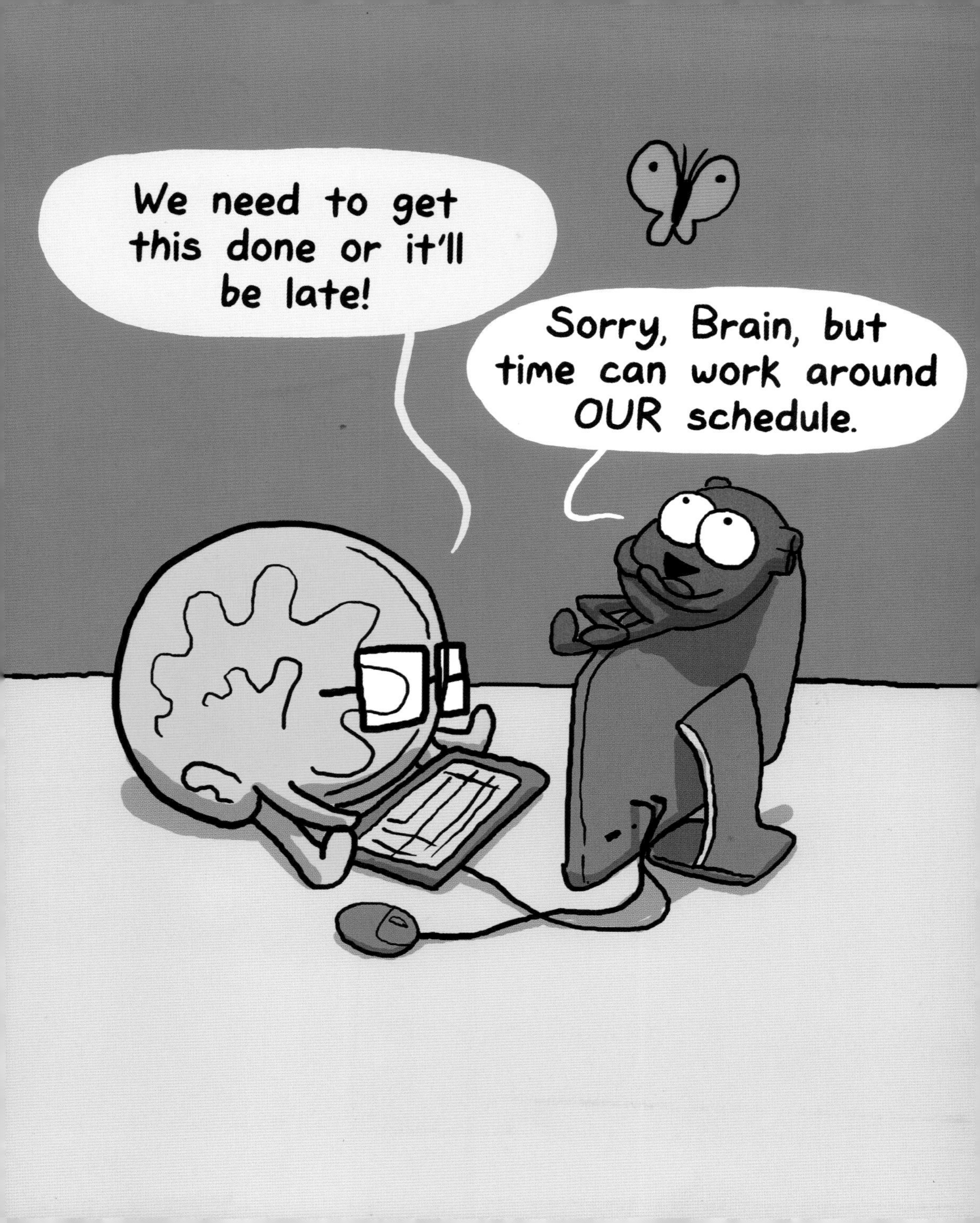
We need to get this done or it'll be late!
Sorry, Brain, but time can work around OUR schedule.

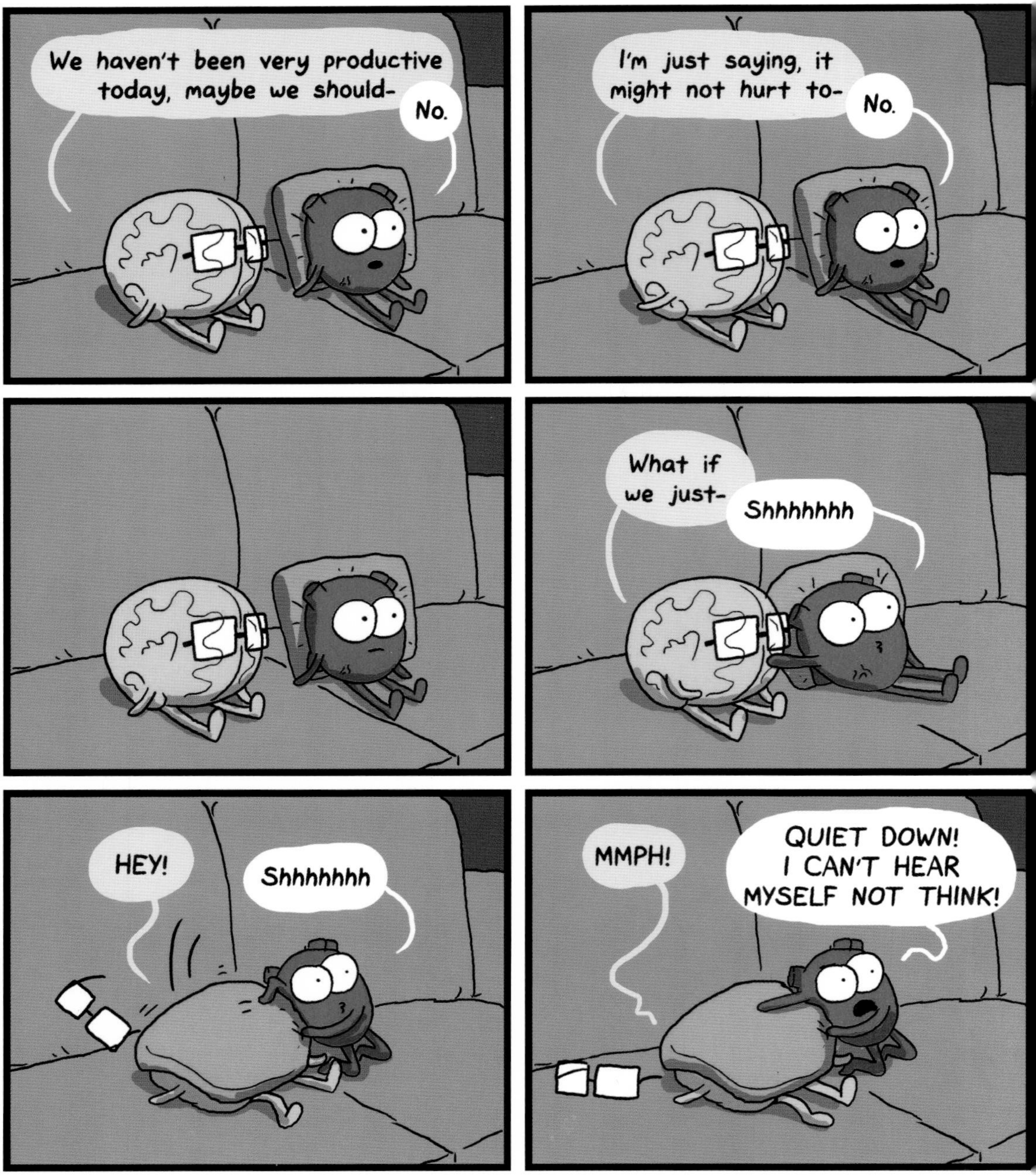
We haven't been very productive today, maybe we should-
No.
I'm just saying, it might not hurt to-
No.
What if we just-
Shhhhhhh
HEY!
Shhhhhhh
MMPH!
QUIET DOWN! I CAN'T HEAR MYSELF NOT THINK!

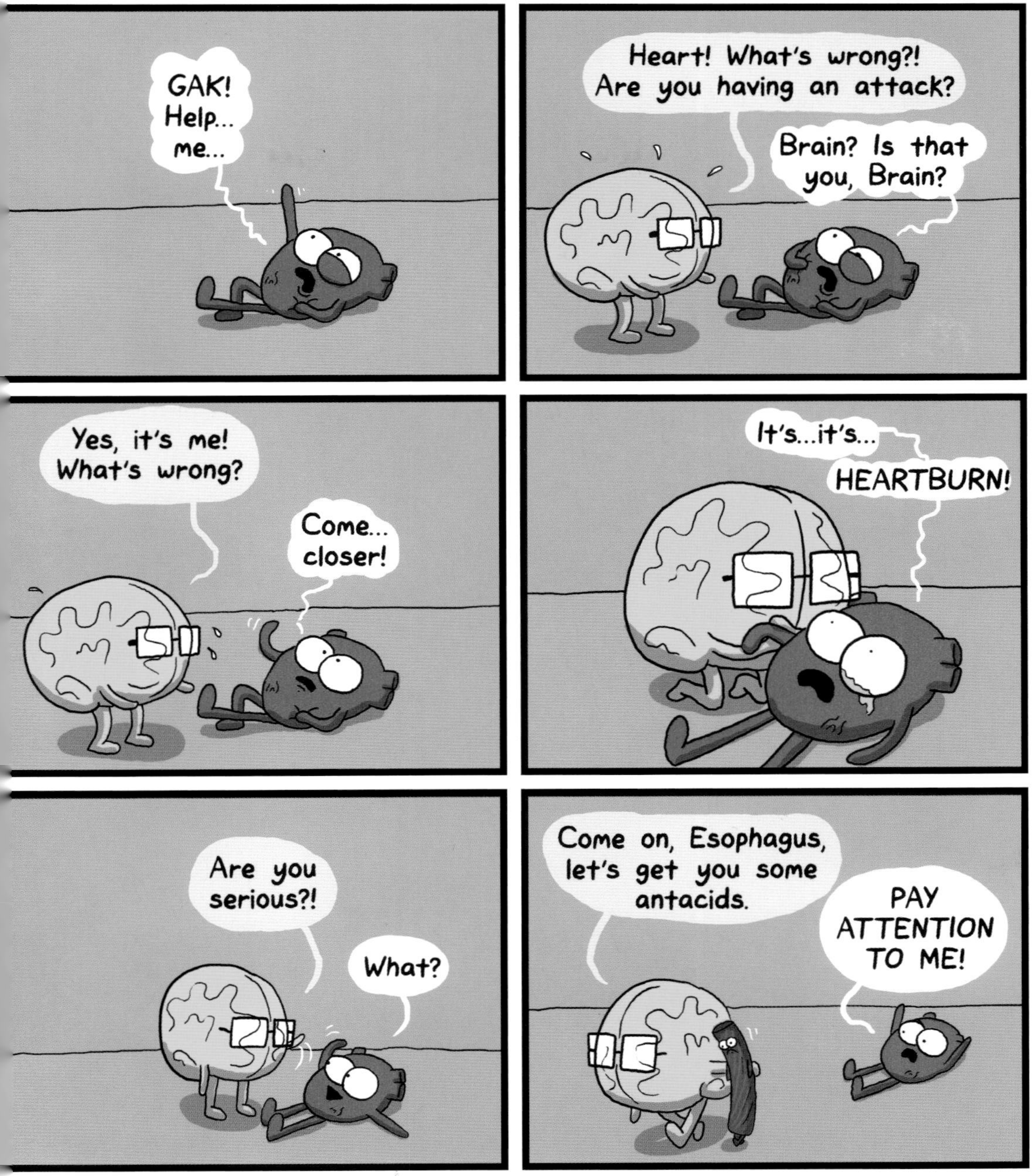
GAK! Help... me...
Heart! What's wrong?! Are you having an attack?
Brain? Is that you, Brain?
Yes, it's me! What's wrong?
Come... closer!
It's...it's...
HEARTBURN!
Are you serious?!
What?
Come on, Esophagus, let's get you some antacids.
PAY ATTENTION TO ME!

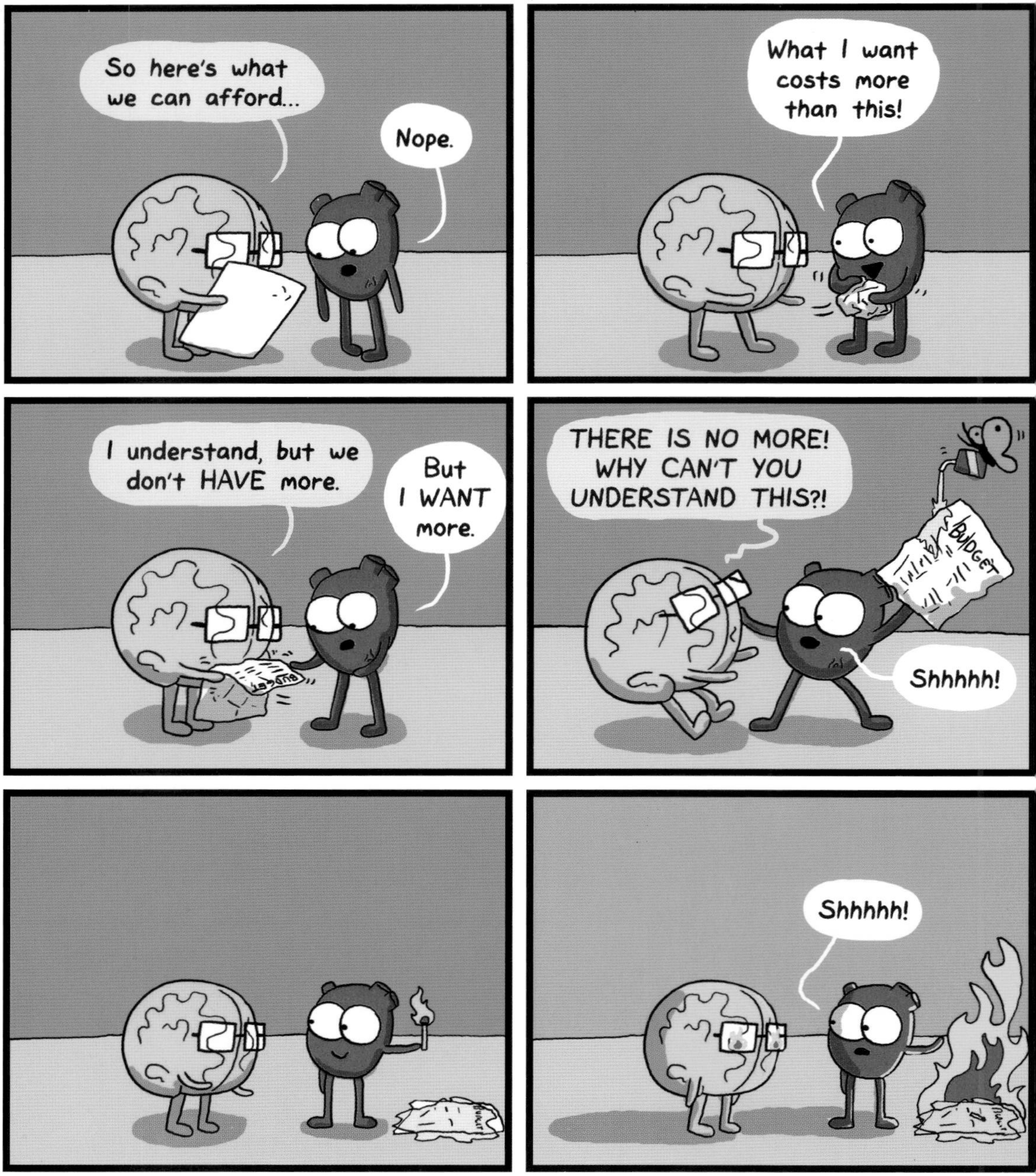
So here's what we can afford...
Nope.
What I want costs more than this!
I understand, but we don't HAVE more.
But I WANT more.
BUDGET
THERE IS NO MORE! WHY CAN'T YOU UNDERSTAND THIS?!
BUDGET
Shhhhh!
Shhhhh!

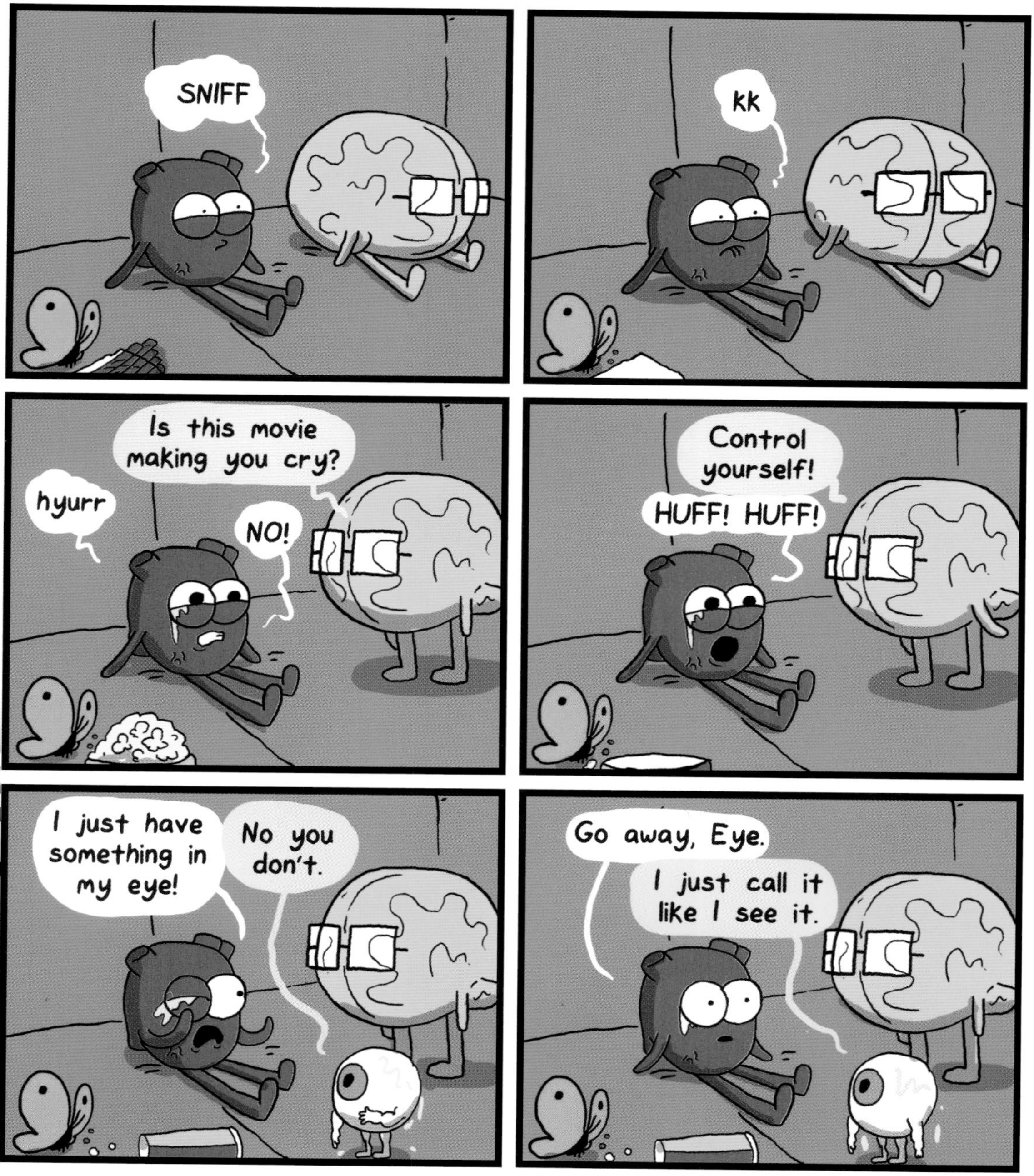
SNIFF
kk
Is this movie making you cry?
hyurr
NO!
Control yourself!
HUFF! HUFF!
I just have something in my eye!
No you don't.
Go away, Eye.
I just call it like I see it.

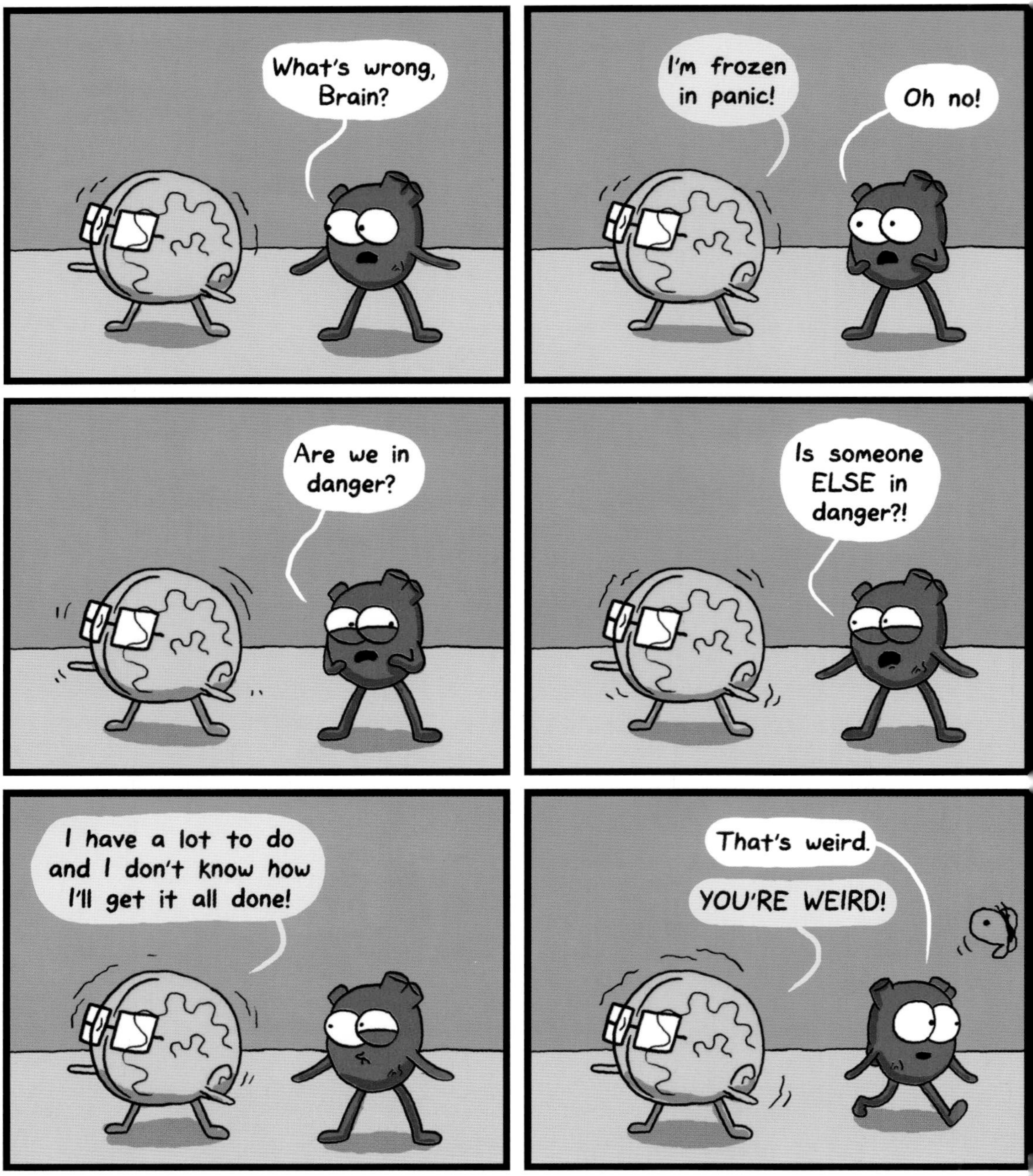
What's wrong, Brain?
I'm frozen in panic!
Oh no!
Are we in danger?
Is someone ELSE in danger?!
I have a lot to do and I don't know how I'll get it all done!
That's weird.
YOU'RE WEIRD!

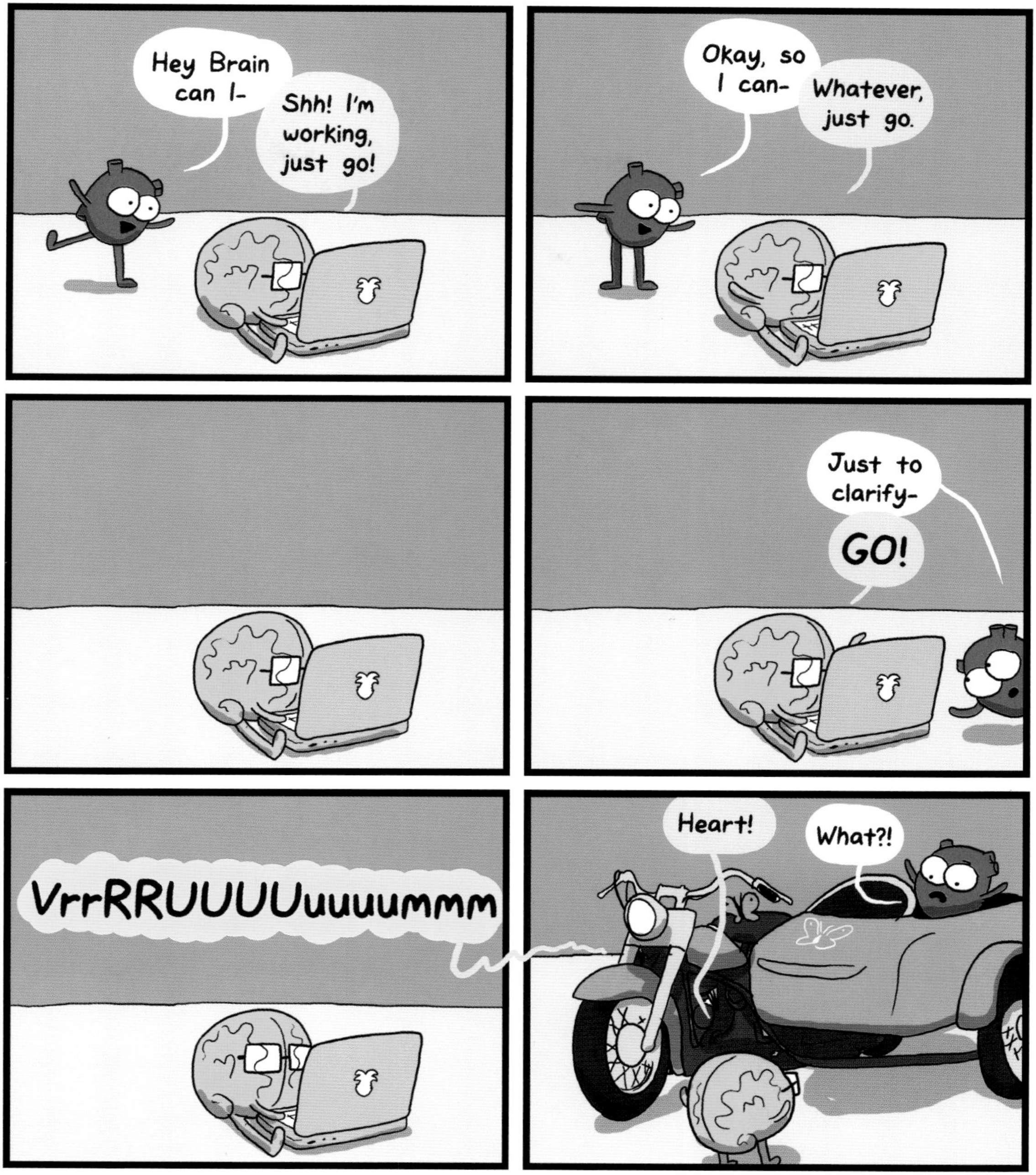
Hey Brain can I-
Shh! I'm working, just go!
Okay, so I can-
Whatever, just go.
Just to clarify-
GO!
VrrRRUUUUUuuuummm
Heart!
What?!

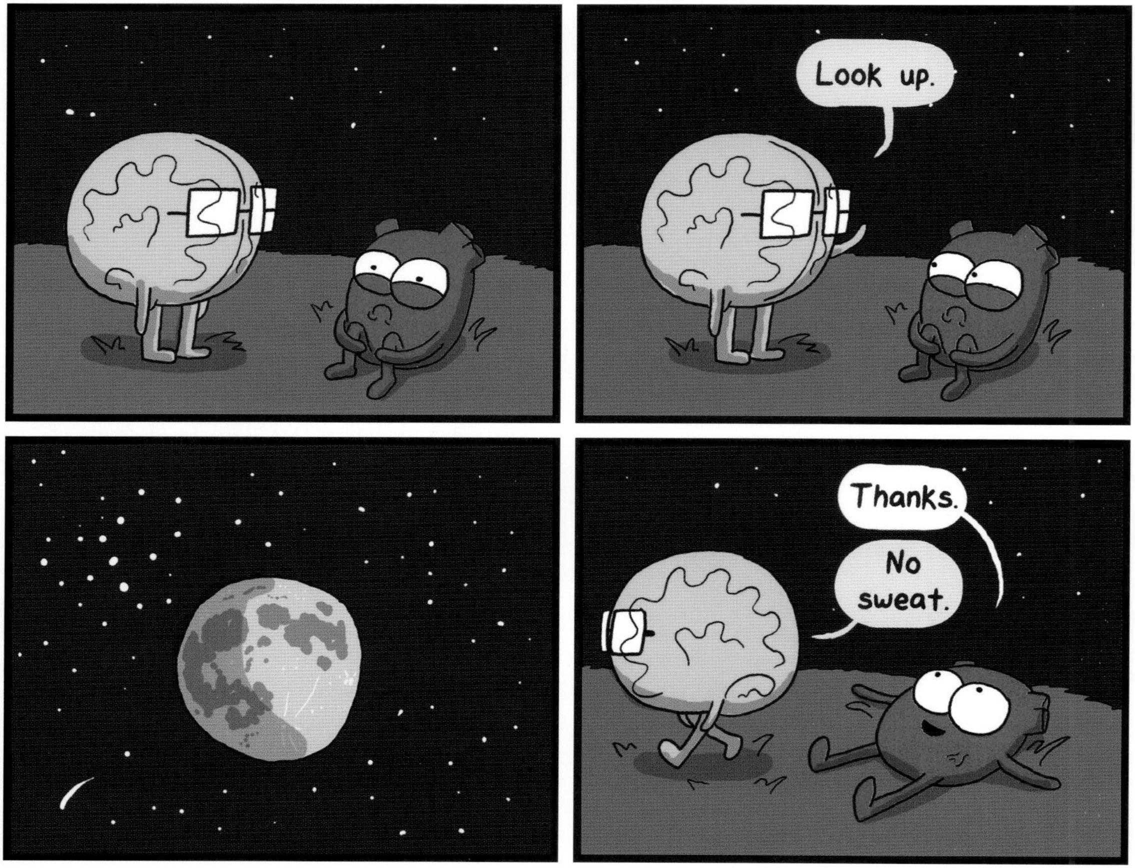
Look up.
Thanks.
No sweat.

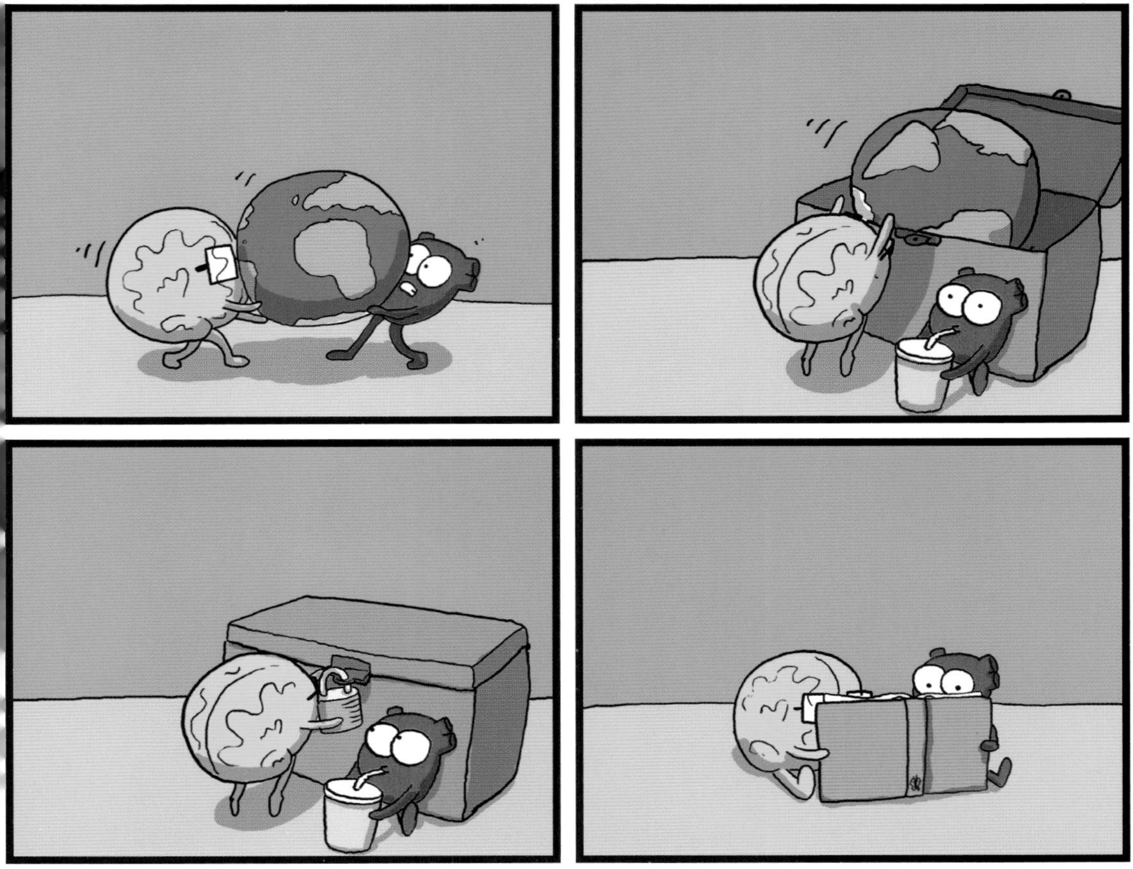

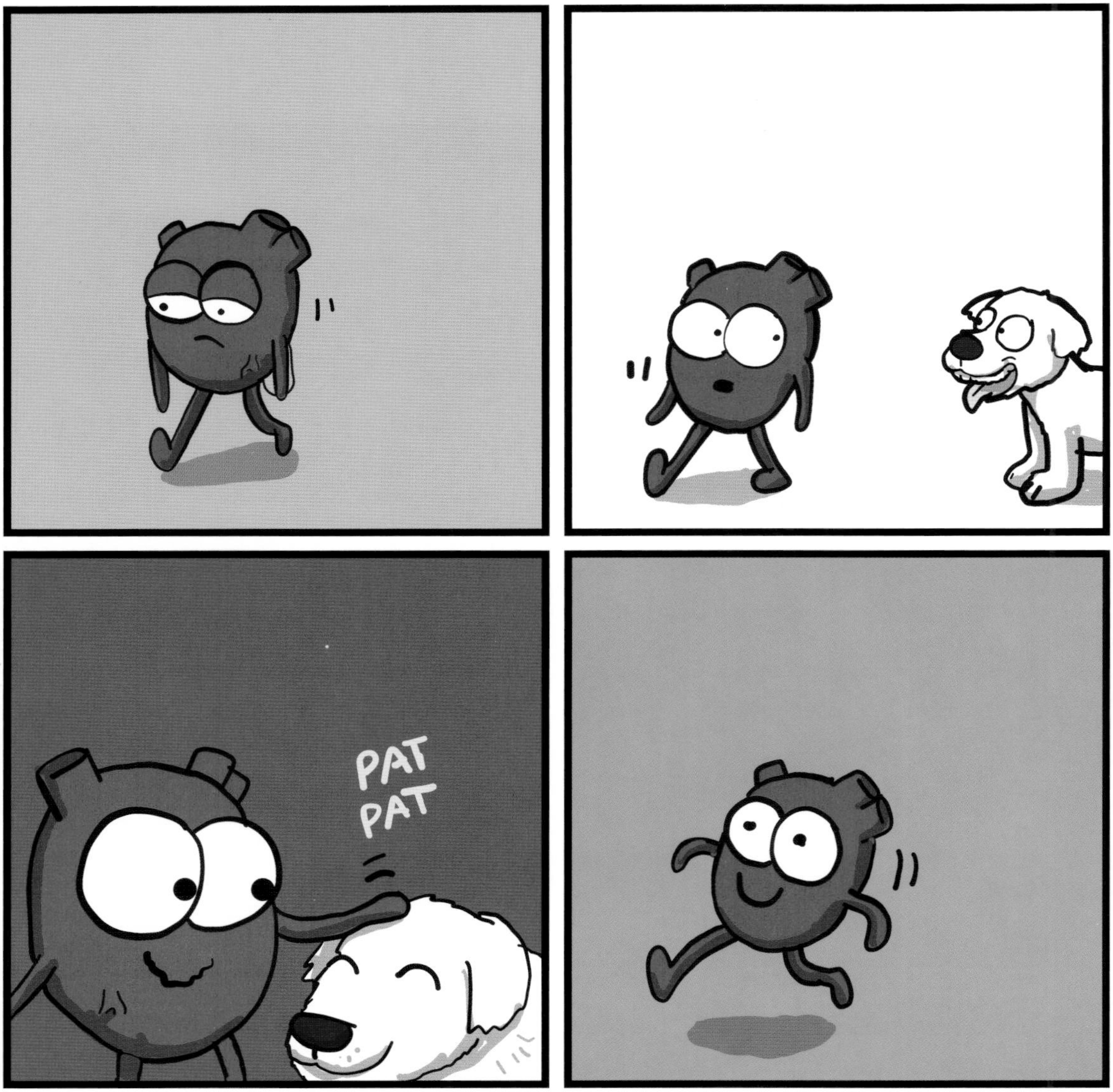
PAT
PAT

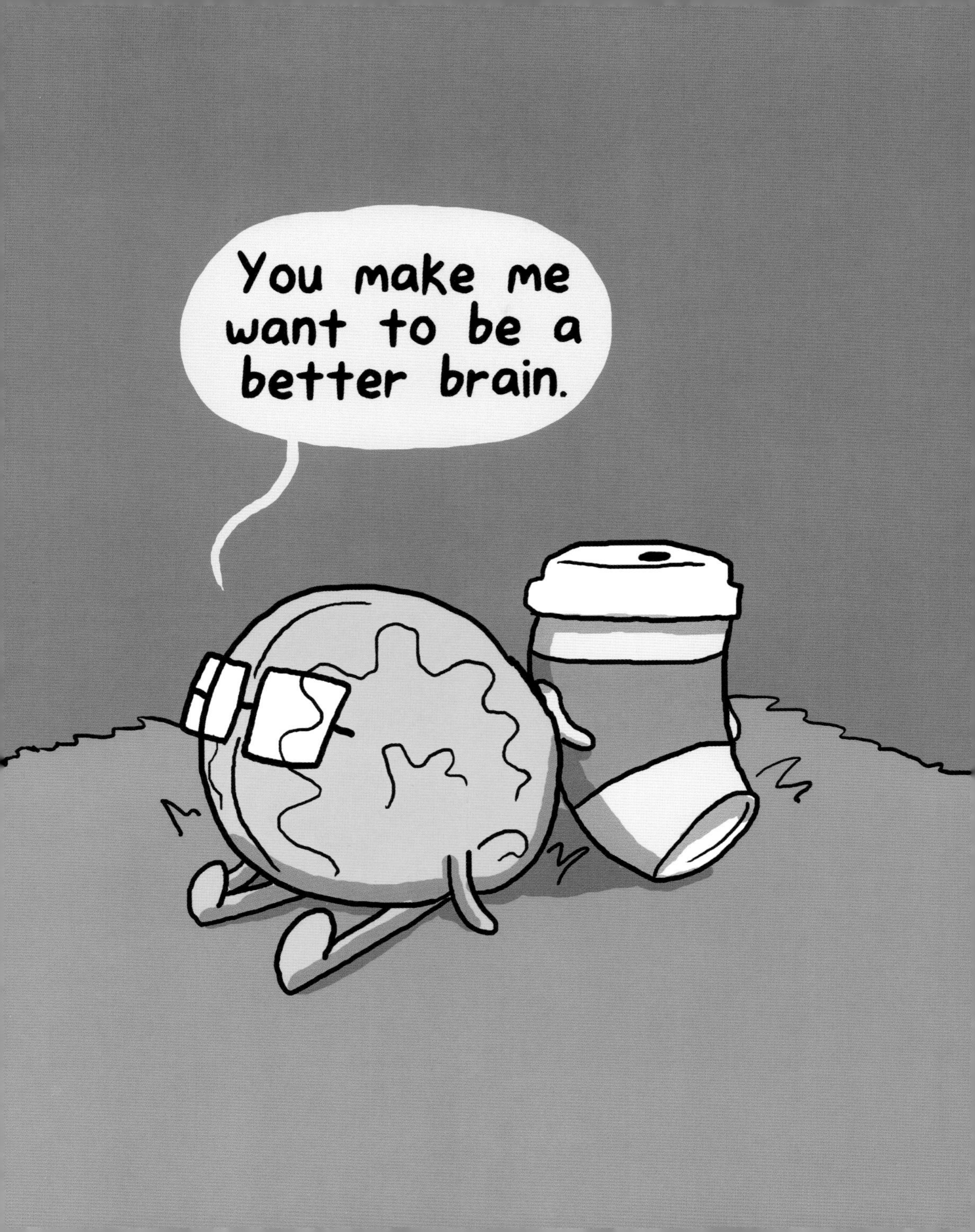
You make me want to be a better brain.

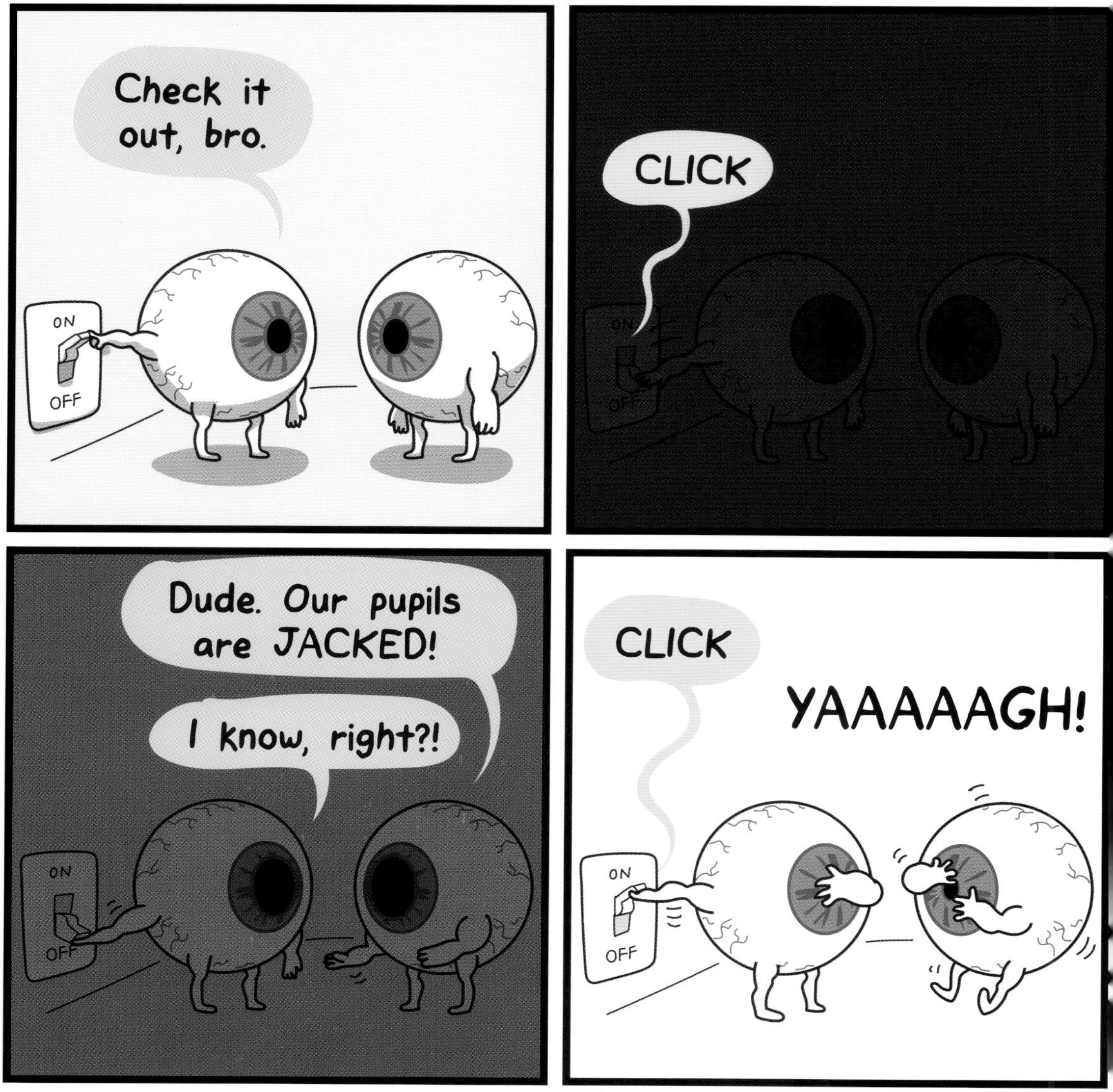
Check it out, bro.
ON
OFF
CLICK
Dude. Our pupils are JACKED!
I know, right?!
ON
OFF
CLICK
YAAAAAGH!
ON
OFF

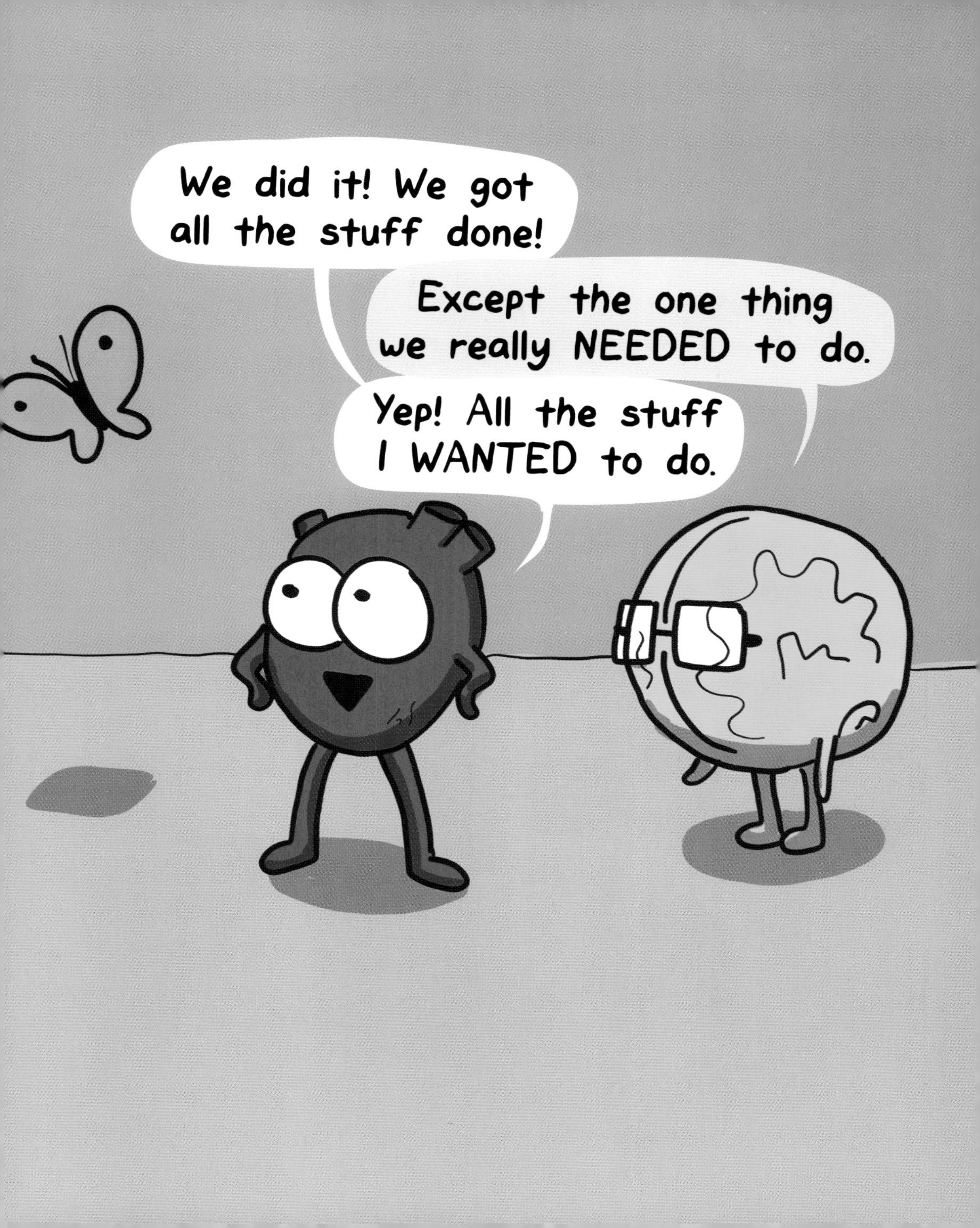
We did it! We got all the stuff done!
Except the one thing we really NEEDED to do.
Yep! All the stuff I WANTED to do.

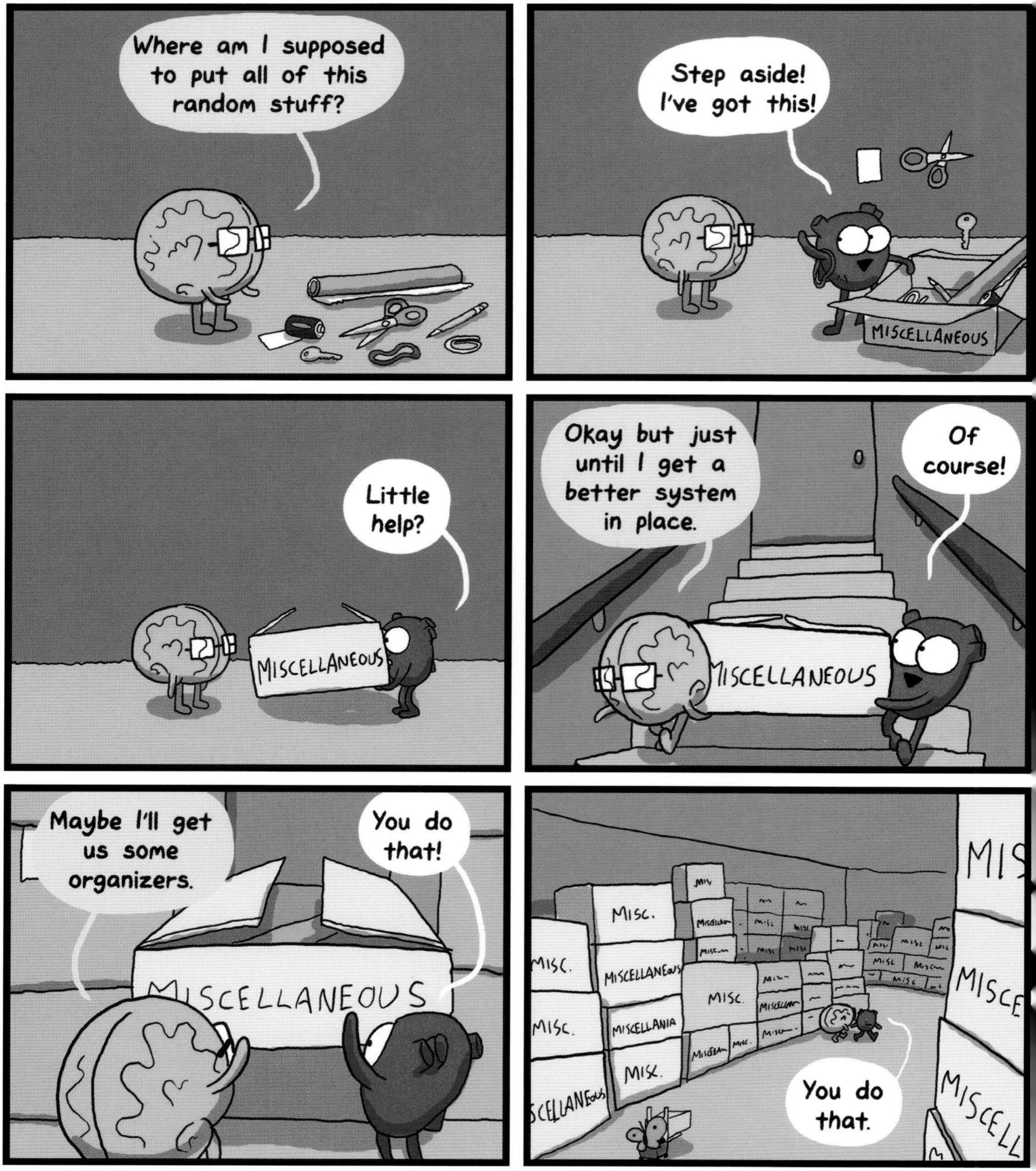
Where am I supposed to put all of this random stuff?
Step aside! I've got this!
MISCELLANEOUS
Little help?
MISCELLANEOUS
Okay but just until I get a better system in place.
Of course!
MISCELLANEOUS
Maybe I'll get us some organizers.
You do that!
MISCELLANEOUS
MISC.
MISCELLANEOUS
MISCELLANIA
MISC.
You do that.

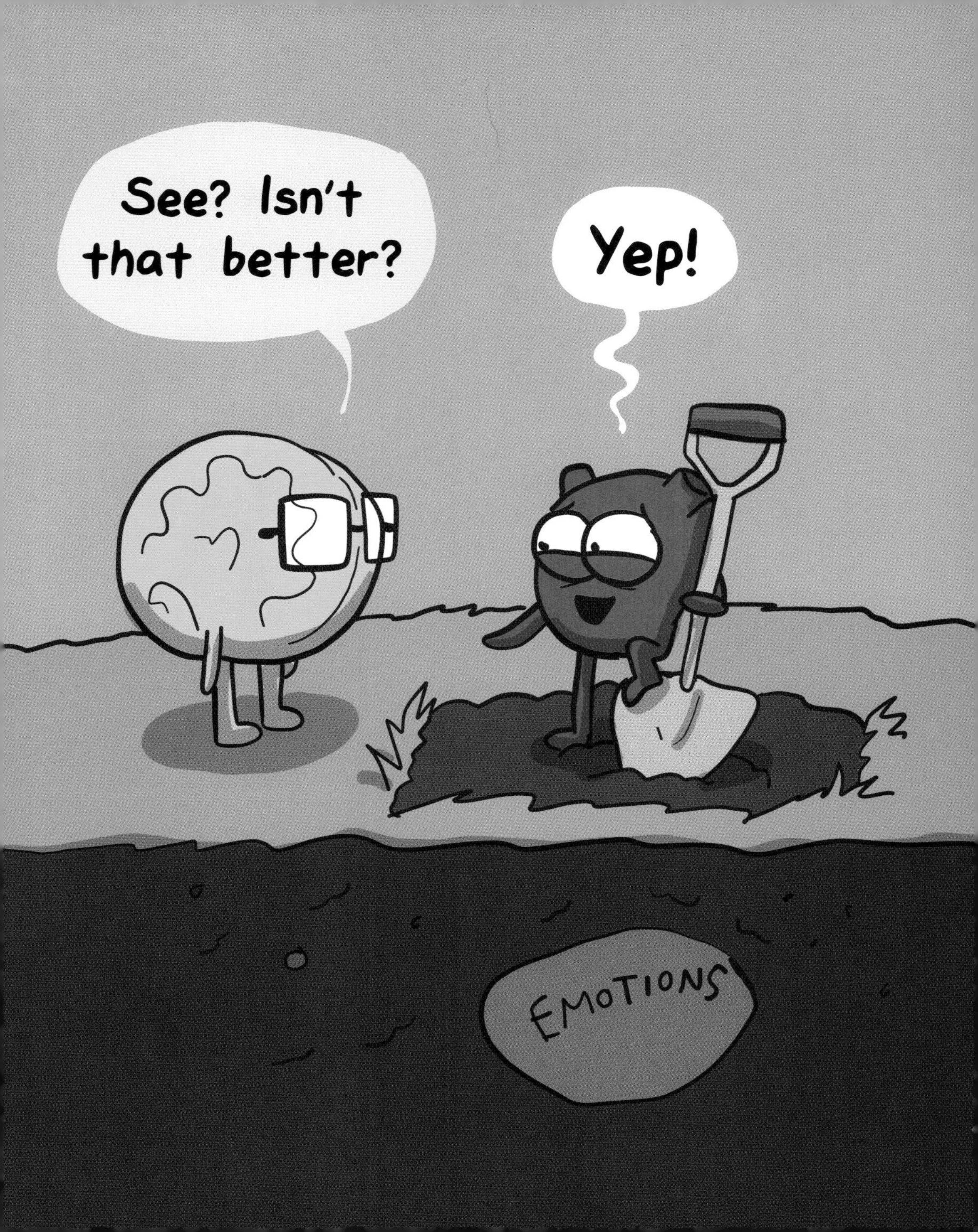
See? Isn't that better?
Yep!
EMOTIONS

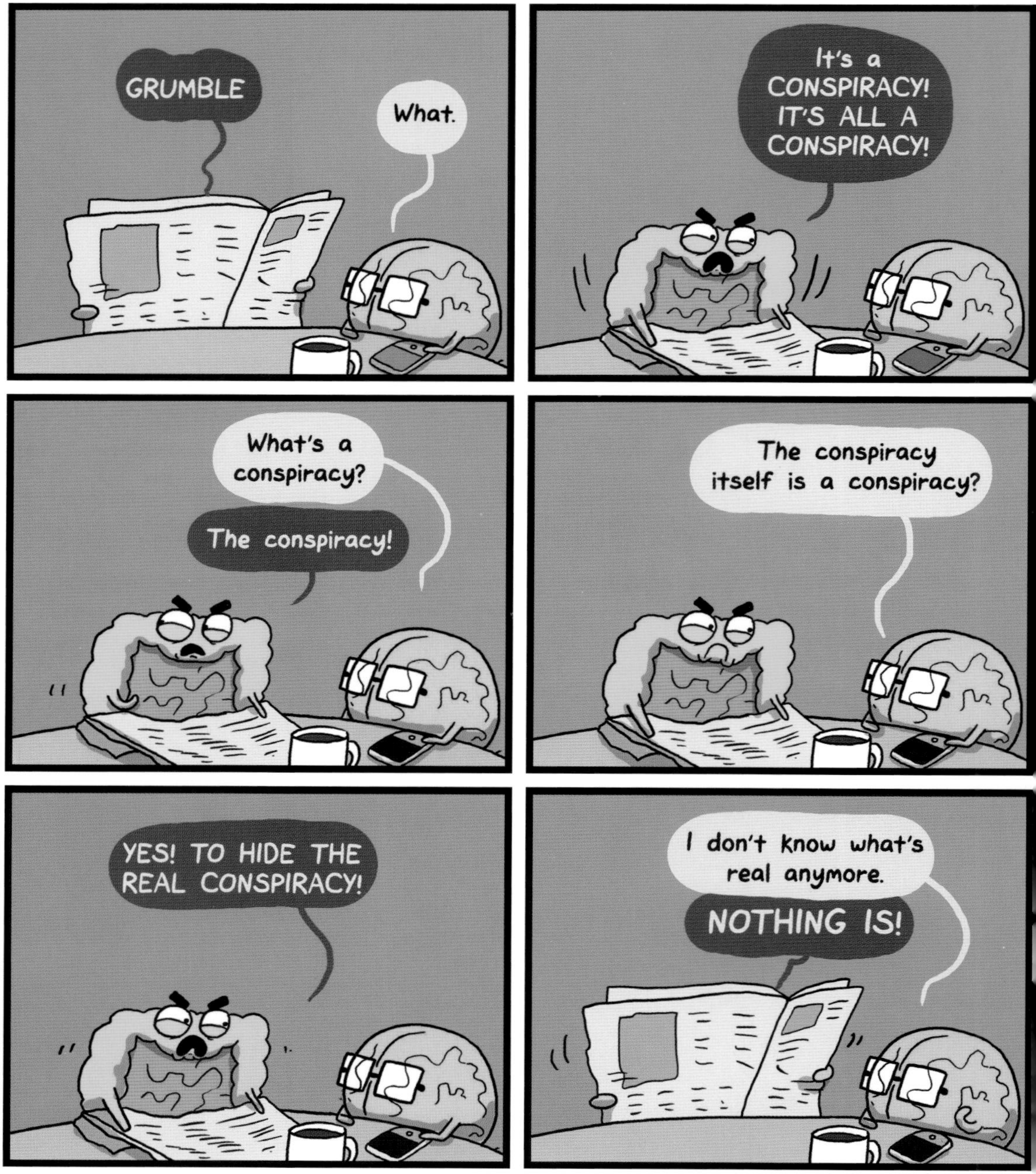
GRUMBLE
What.
It's a CONSPIRACY! IT'S ALL A CONSPIRACY!
What's a conspiracy?
The conspiracy!
The conspiracy itself is a conspiracy?
YES! TO HIDE THE REAL CONSPIRACY!
I don't know what's real anymore.
NOTHING IS!

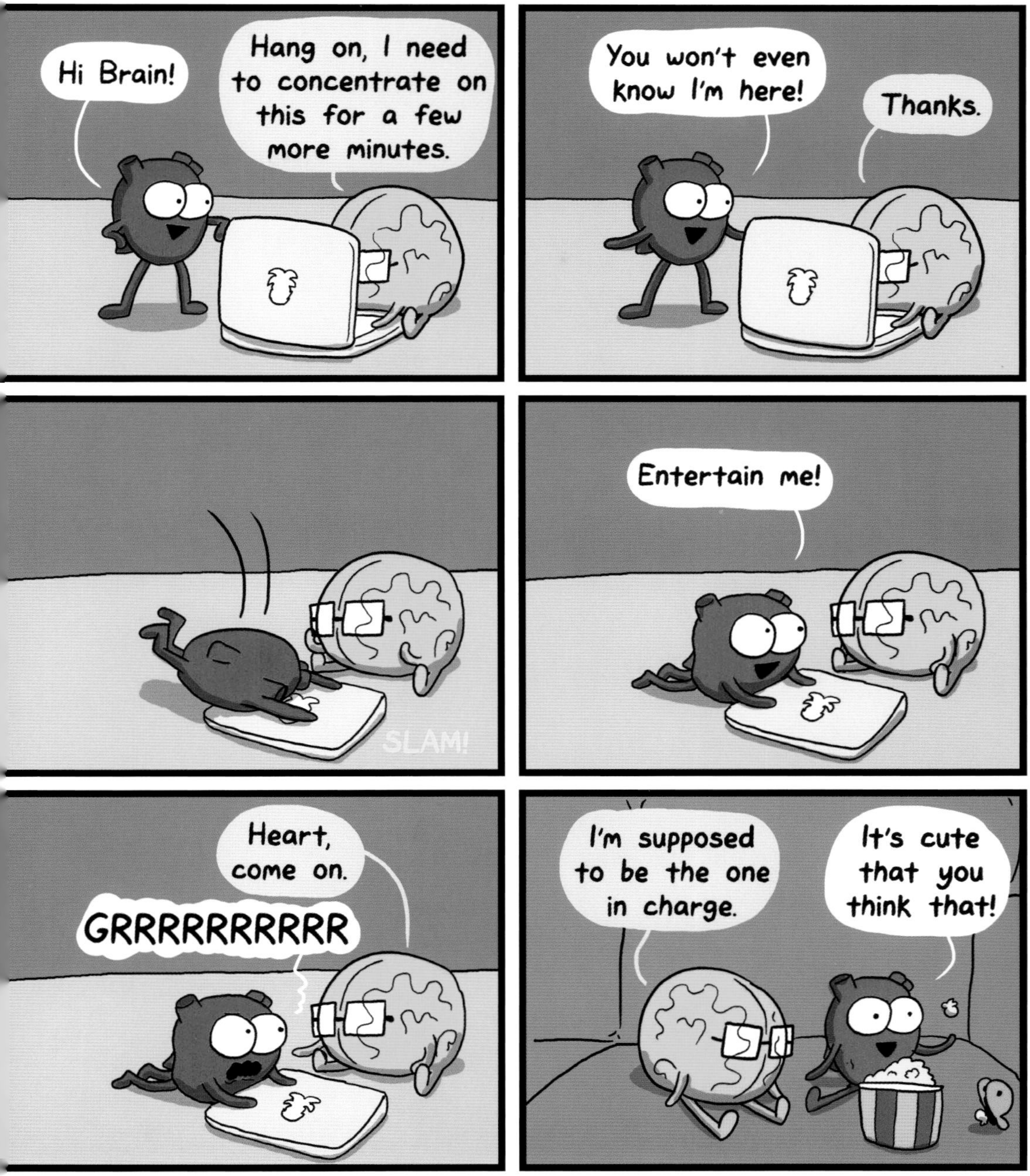
Hi Brain!
Hang on, I need to concentrate on this for a few more minutes.
You won't even know I'm here!
Thanks.
SLAM!
Entertain me!
Heart, come on.
GRRRRRRRRRR
I'm supposed to be the one in charge.
It's cute that you think that!

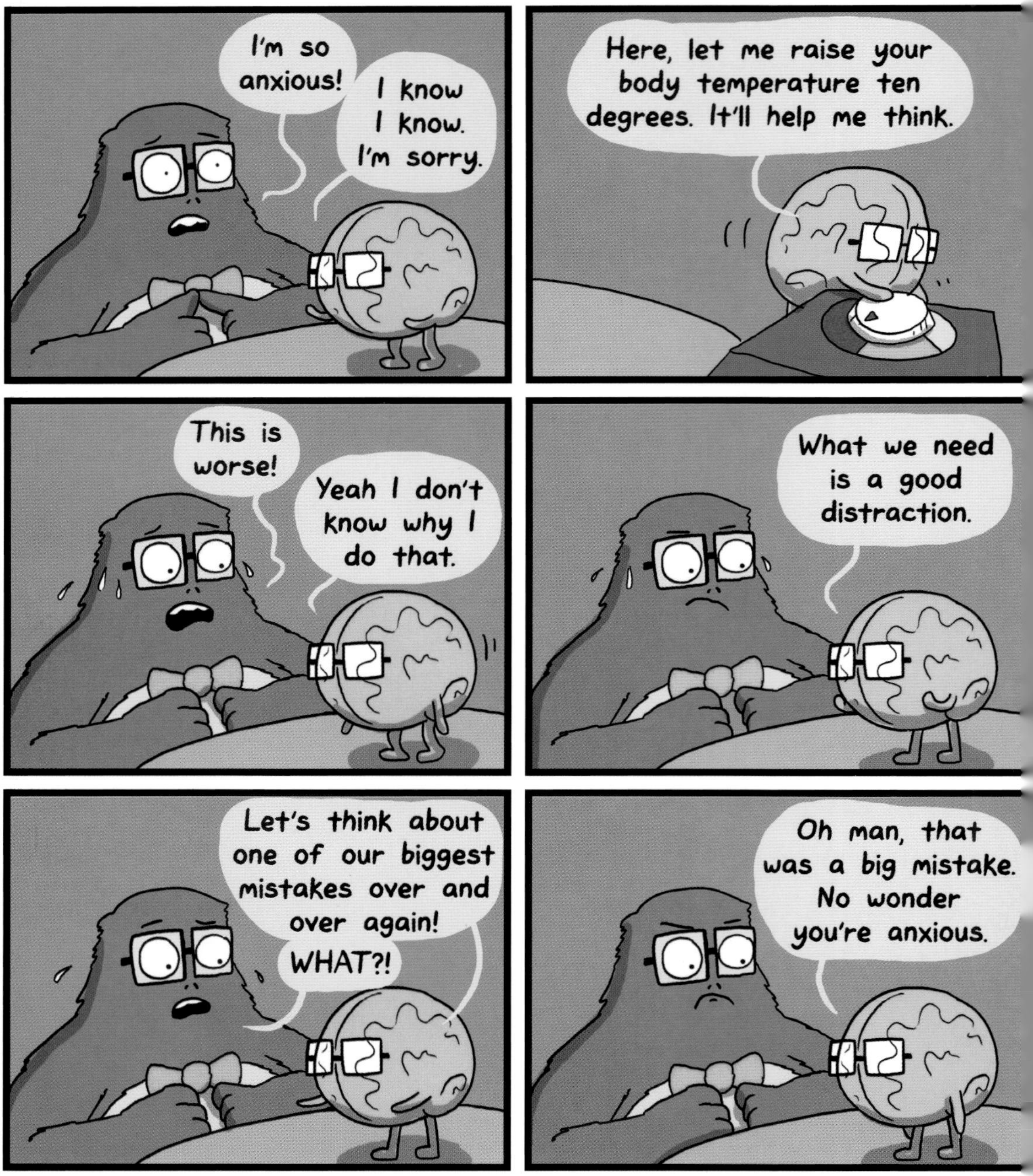
I'm so anxious!
I know I know. I'm sorry.
Here, let me raise your body temperature ten degrees. It'll help me think.
This is worse!
Yeah I don't know why I do that.
What we need is a good distraction.
Let's think about one of our biggest mistakes over and over again!
WHAT?!
Oh man, that was a big mistake. No wonder you're anxious.

REGRET
REGRET

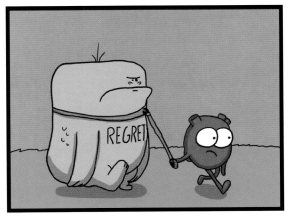

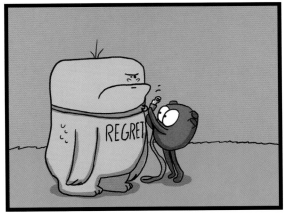

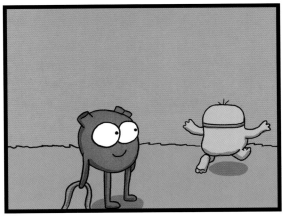

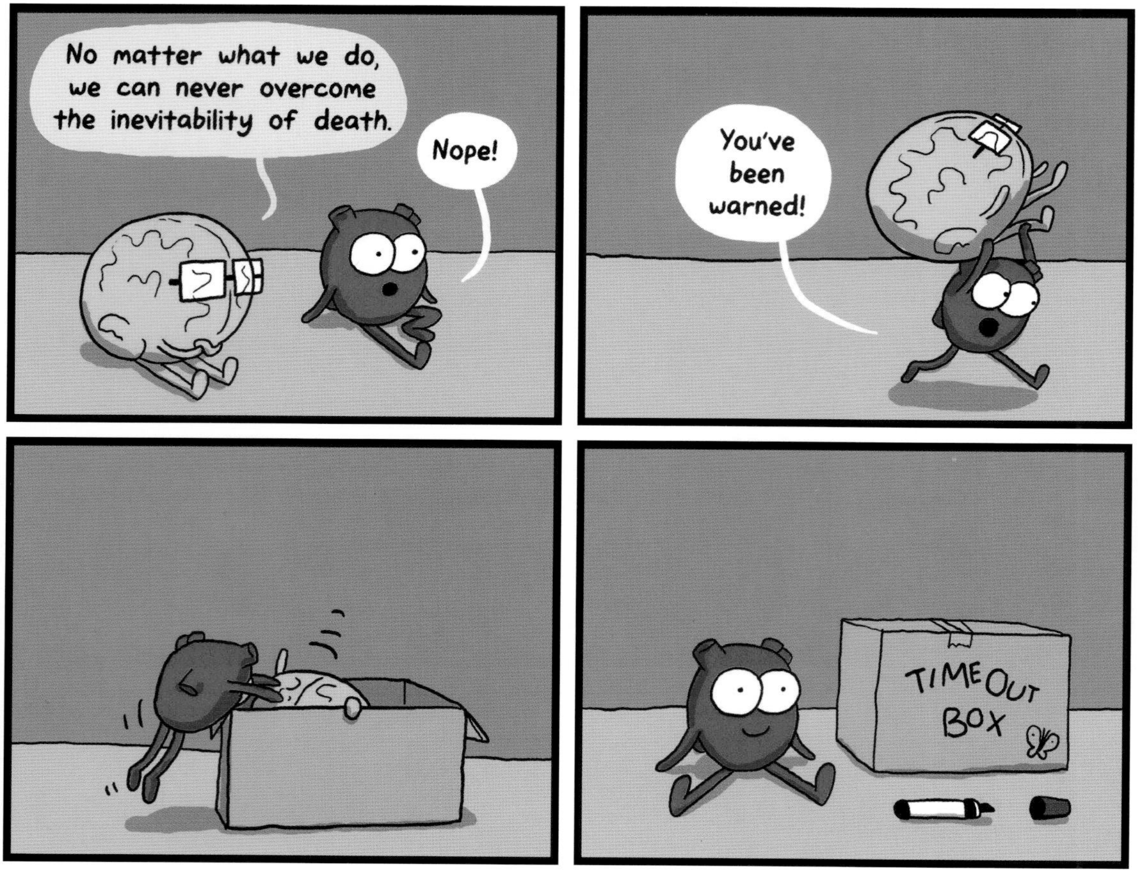
No matter what we do, we can never overcome the inevitability of death.
Nope!
You've been warned!
TIME OUT BOX

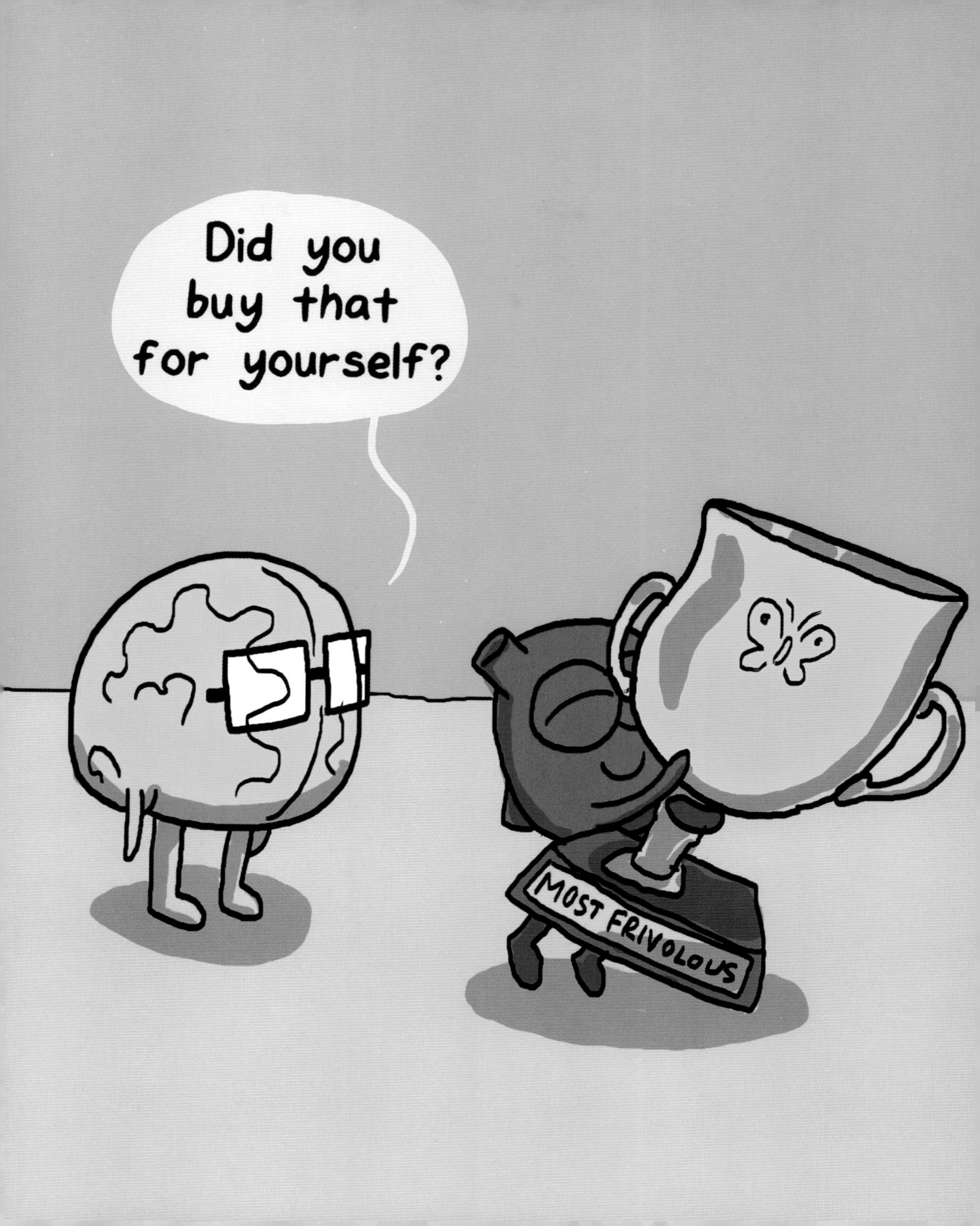
Did you buy that for yourself?
MOST FRIVOLOUS

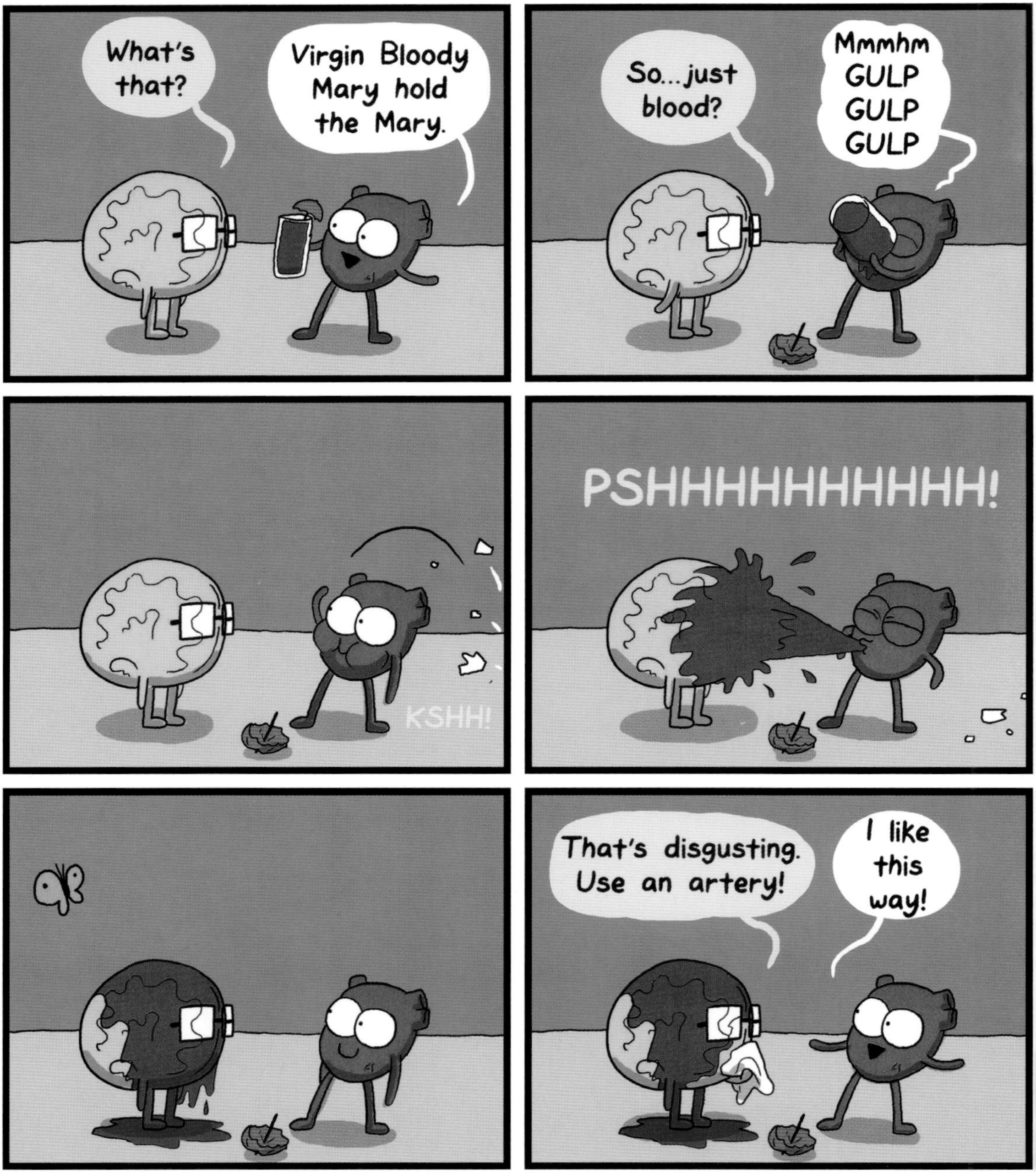
What's that?
Virgin Bloody Mary hold the Mary.
So...just blood?
Mmmhm GULP GULP GULP
KSHH!
PSHHHHHHHHHHH!
That's disgusting. Use an artery!
I like this way!

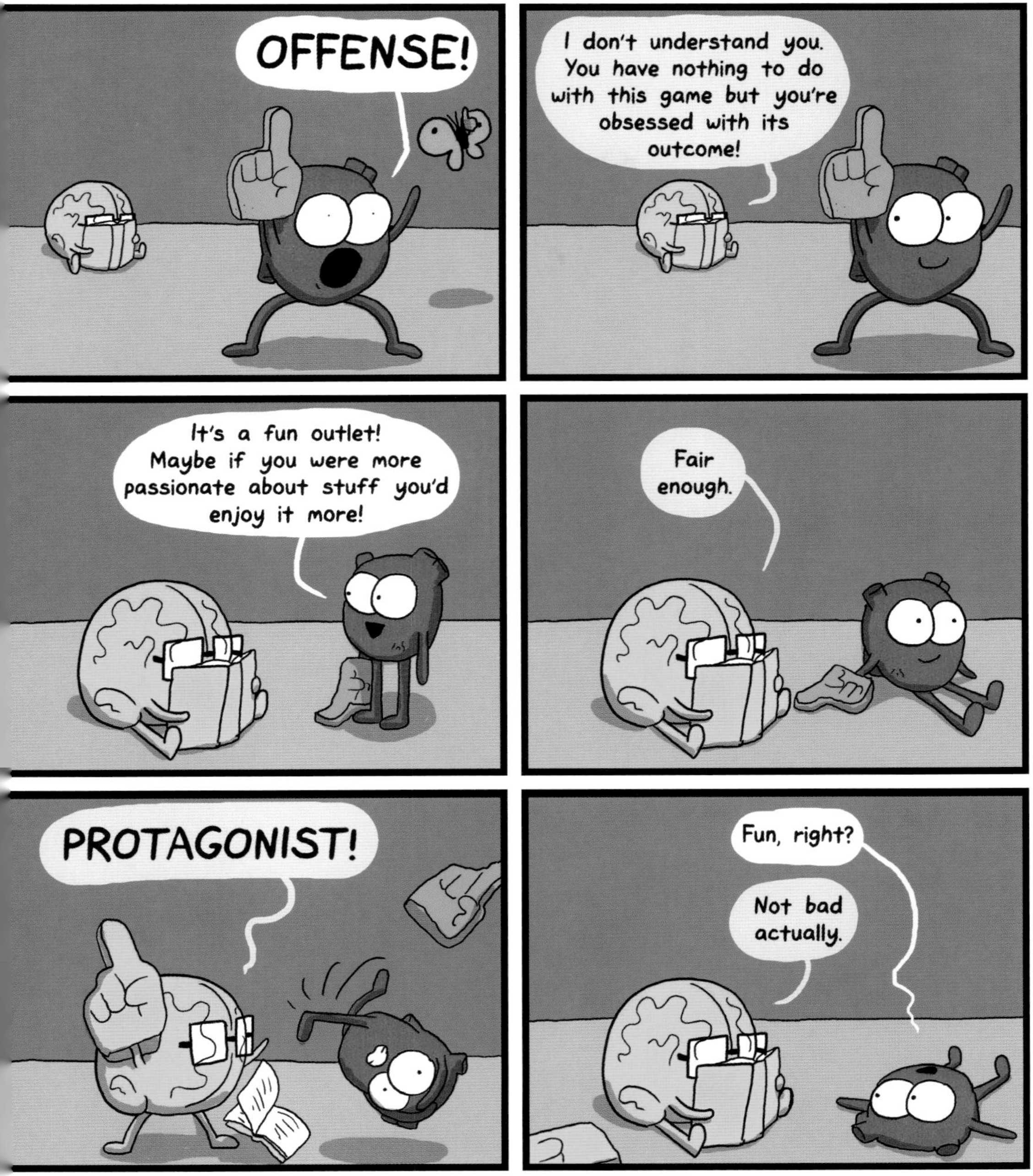
OFFENSE!
I don't understand you. You have nothing to do with this game but you're obsessed with its outcome!
It's a fun outlet! Maybe if you were more passionate about stuff you'd enjoy it more!
Fair enough.
PROTAGONIST!
Fun, right?
Not bad actually.

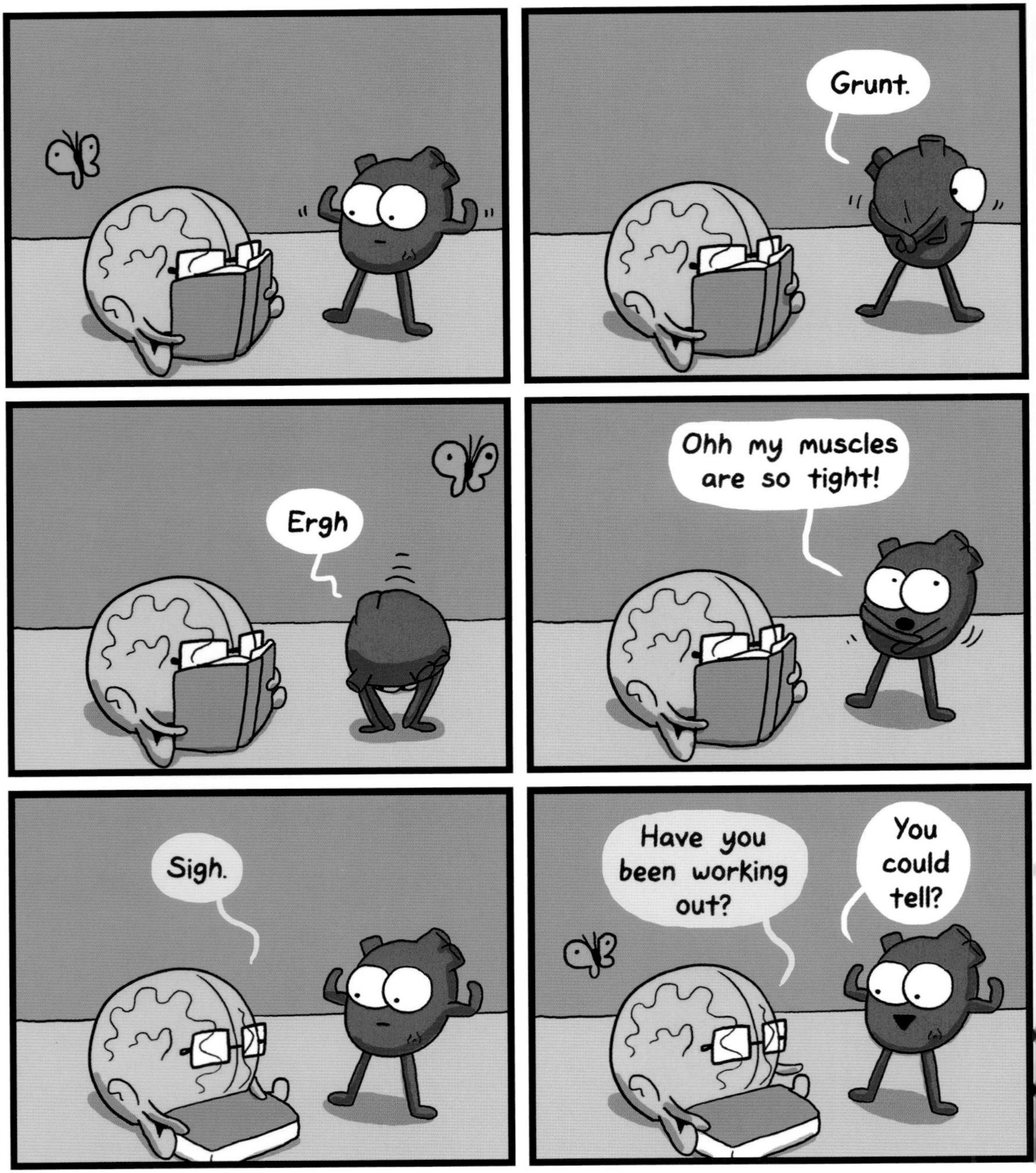
Grunt.
Ergh
Ohh my muscles are so tight!
Sigh.
Have you been working out?
You could tell?

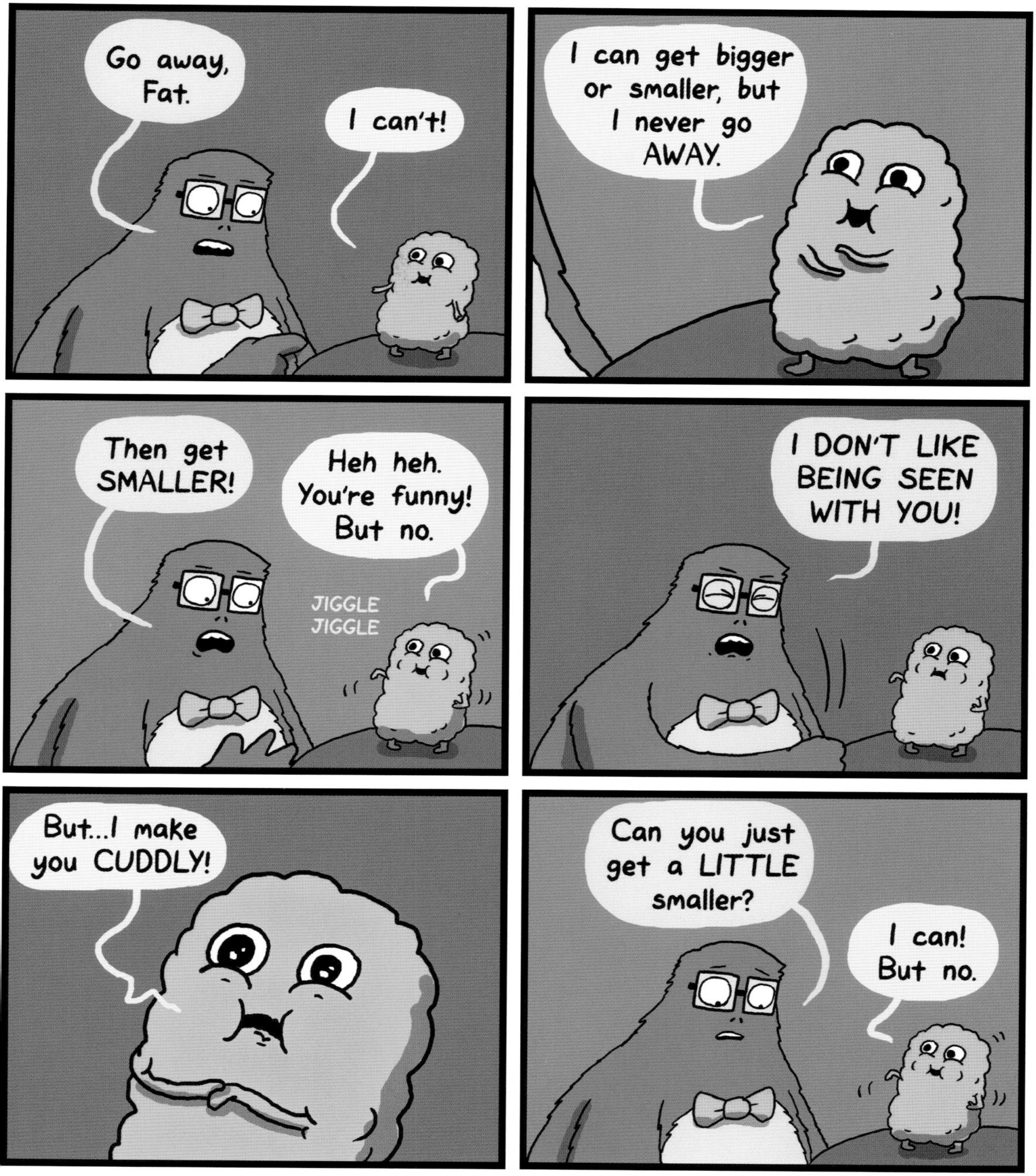
Go away, Fat.
I can't!
I can get bigger or smaller, but I never go AWAY.
Then get SMALLER!
Heh heh. You're funny! But no.
JIGGLE JIGGLE
I DON'T LIKE BEING SEEN WITH YOU!
But...I make you CUDDLY!
Can you just get a LITTLE smaller?
I can! But no.

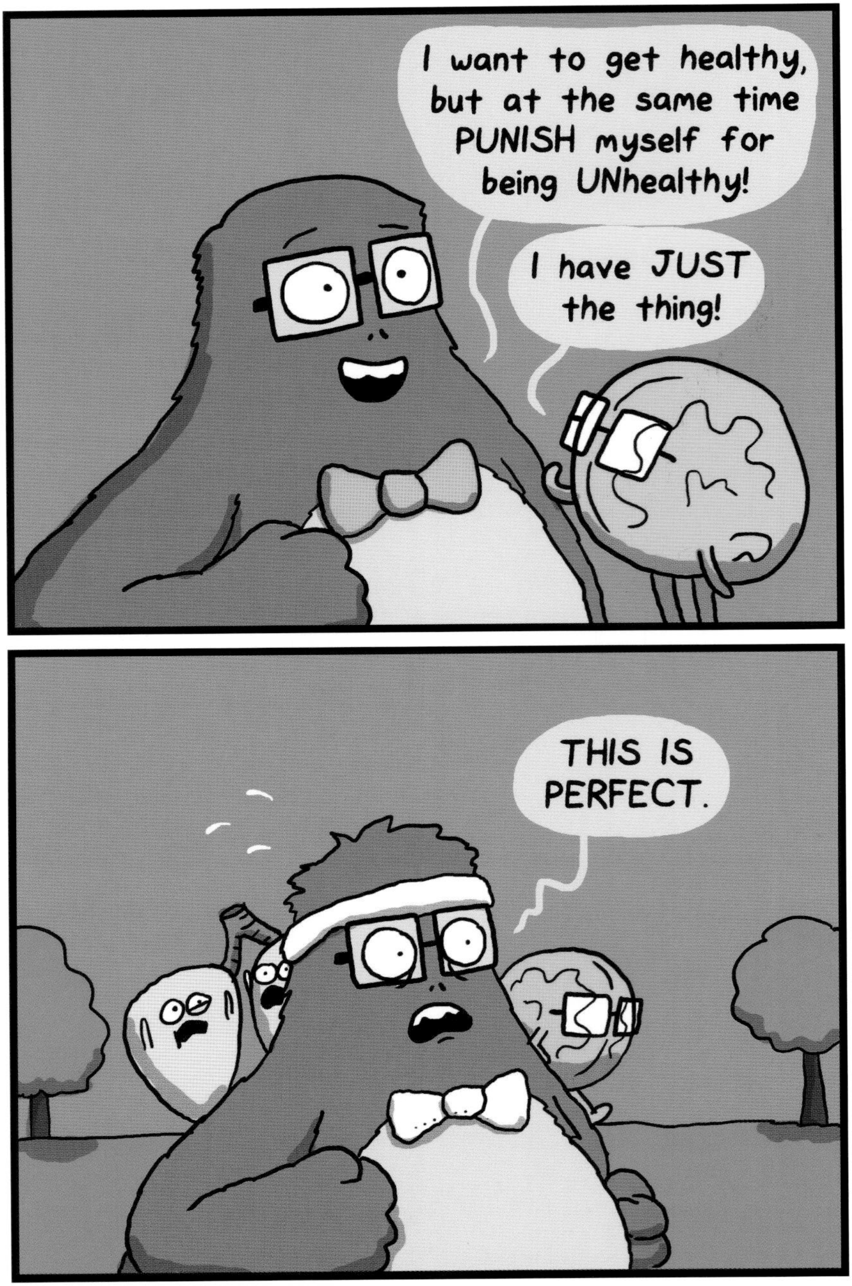
I want to get healthy, but at the same time PUNISH myself for being UNhealthy!
I have JUST the thing!
THIS IS PERFECT.

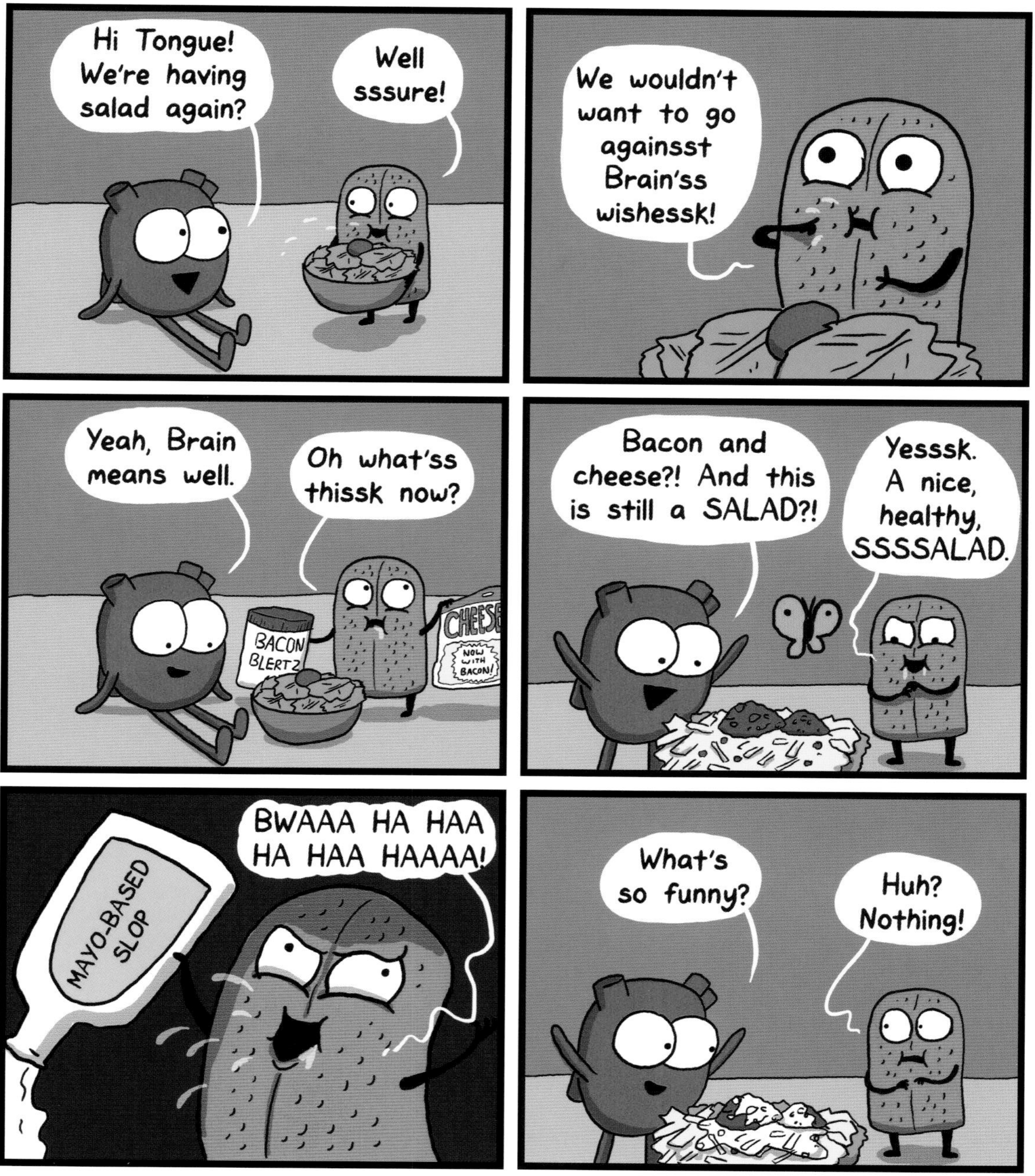
Hi Tongue! We're having salad again?
Well sssure!
We wouldn't want to go againsst Brain'ss wishessk!
Yeah, Brain means well.
Oh what'ss thissk now?
BACON BLERTZ
CHEESE
NOW WITH BACON!
Bacon and cheese?! And this is still a SALAD?!
Yesssk. A nice, healthy, SSSSALAD.
MAYO-BASED SLOP
BWAAA HA HAA HA HAA HAAAA!
What's so funny?
Huh? Nothing!

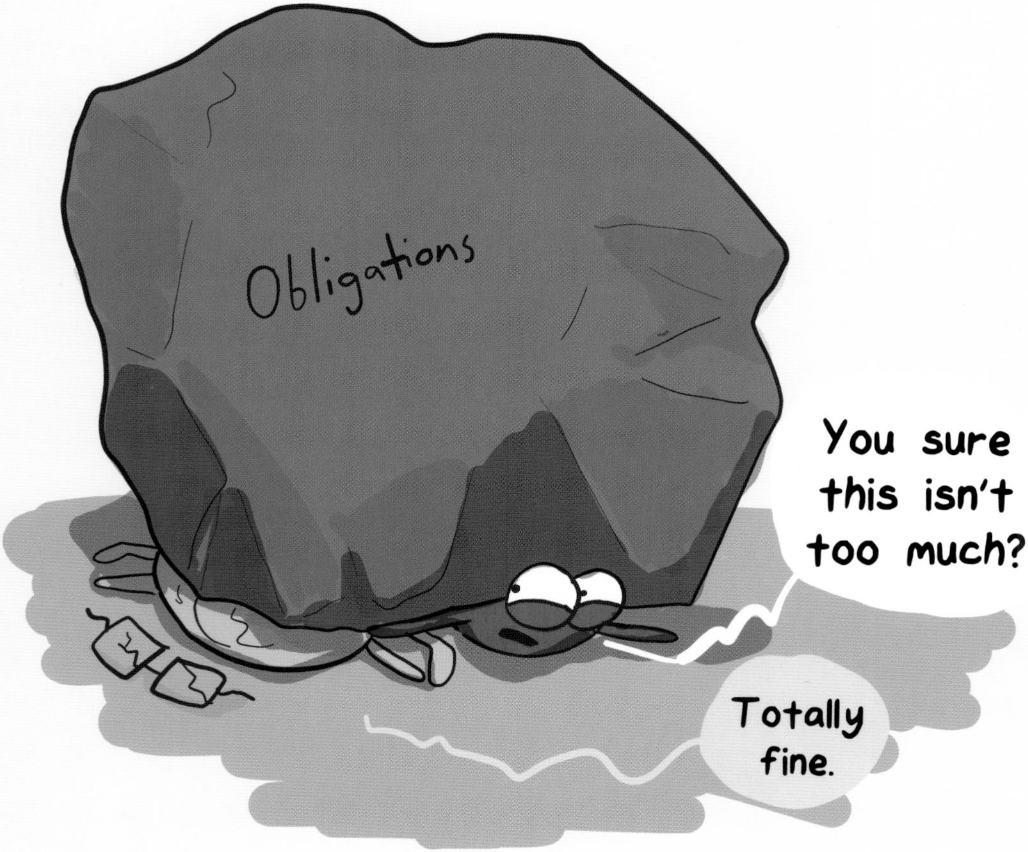
Obligations
You sure this isn't too much?
Totally fine.

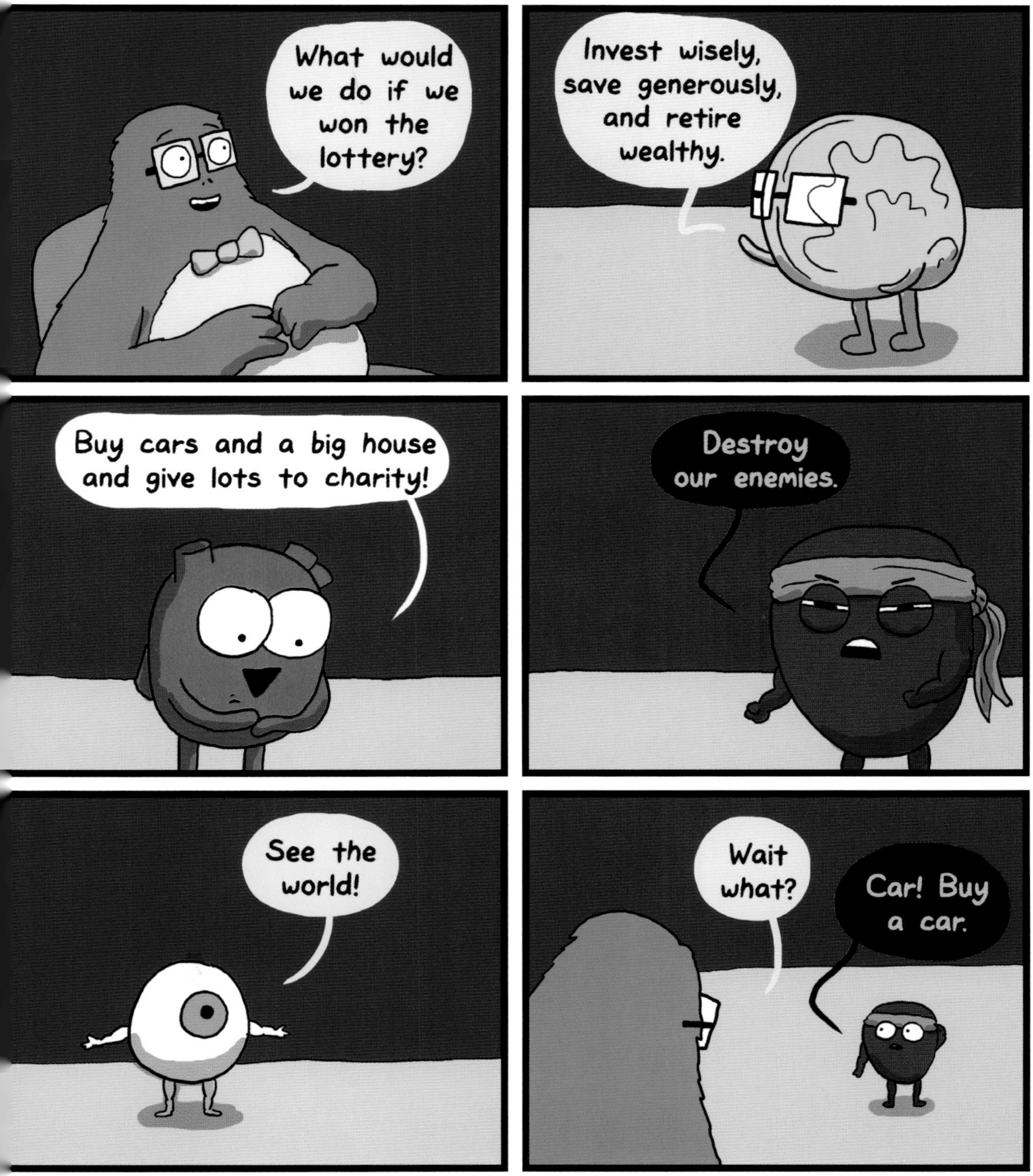
What would we do if we won the lottery?
Invest wisely, save generously, and retire wealthy.
Buy cars and a big house and give lots to charity!
Destroy our enemies.
See the world!
Wait what?
Car! Buy a car.

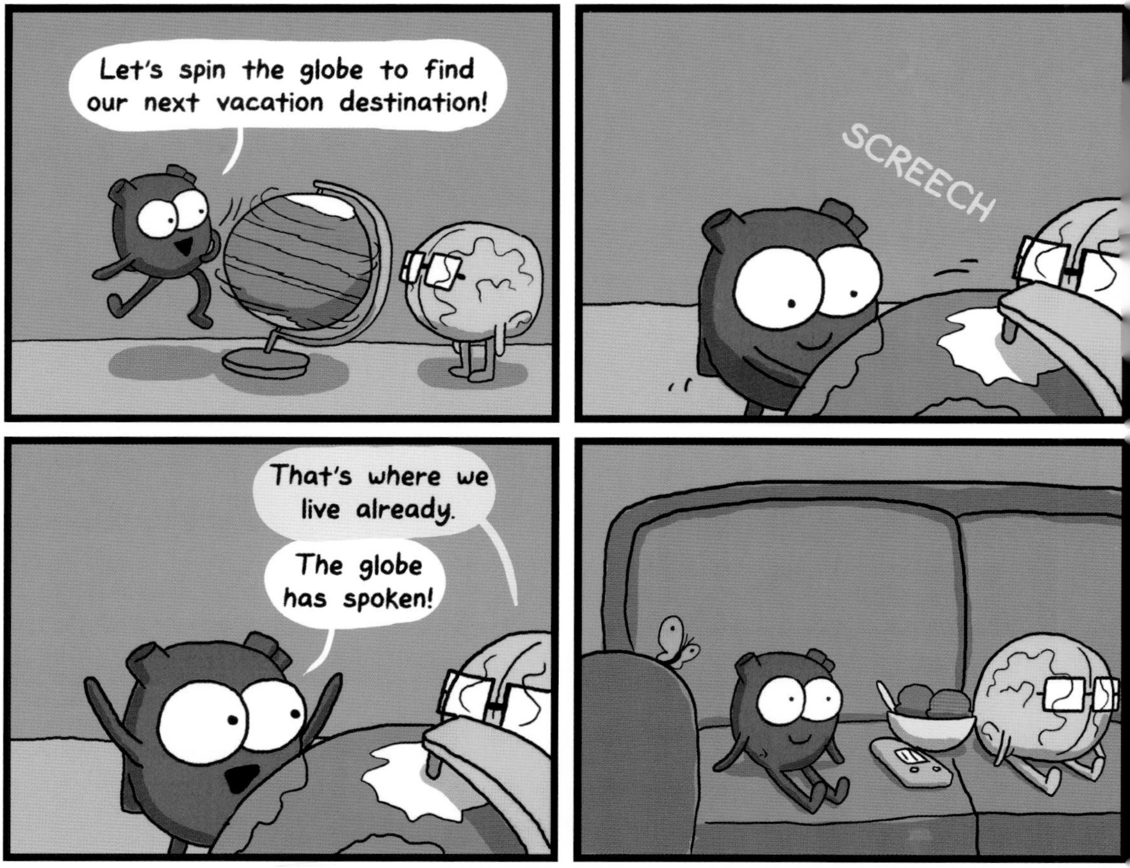
Let's spin the globe to find our next vacation destination!
SCREECH
That's where we live already.
The globe has spoken!

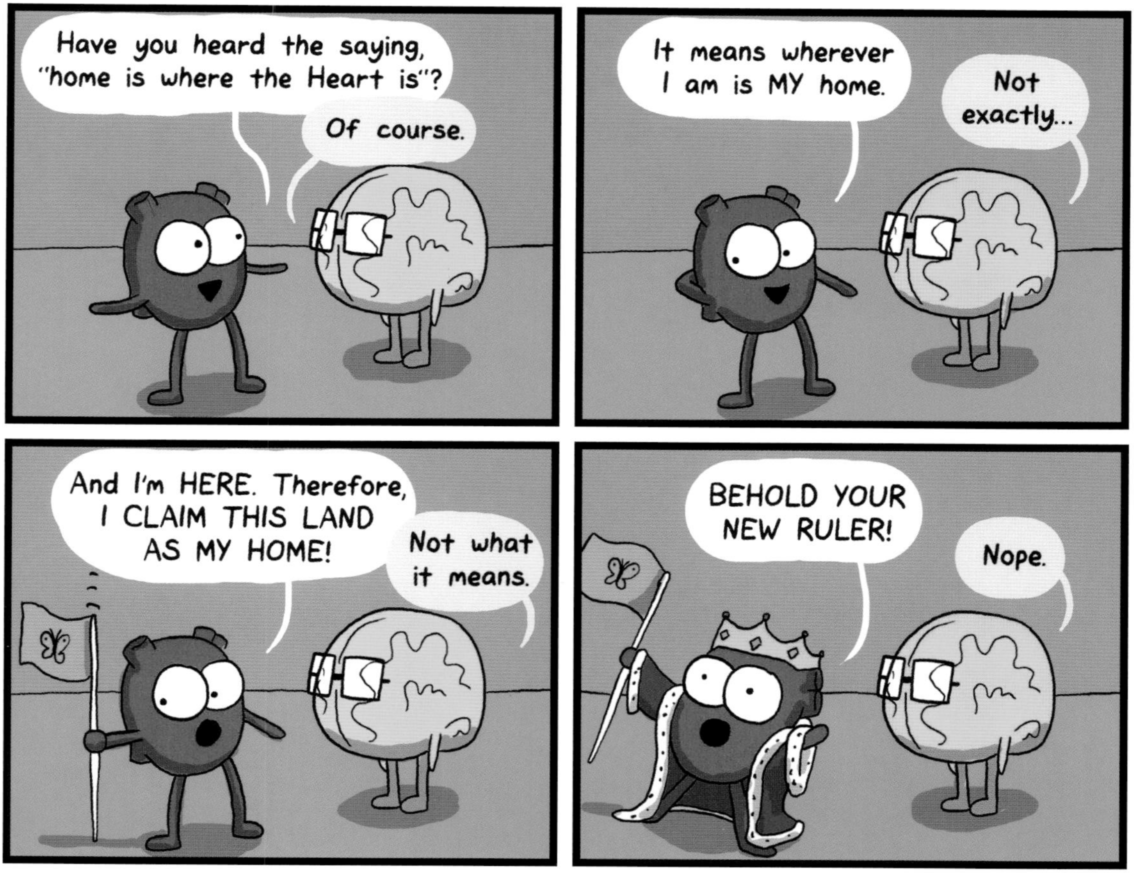

Have you heard the saying, "home is where the Heart is"?
Of course.
It means wherever I am is MY home.
Not exactly...
And I'm HERE. Therefore, I CLAIM THIS LAND AS MY HOME!
Not what it means.
BEHOLD YOUR NEW RULER!
Nope.

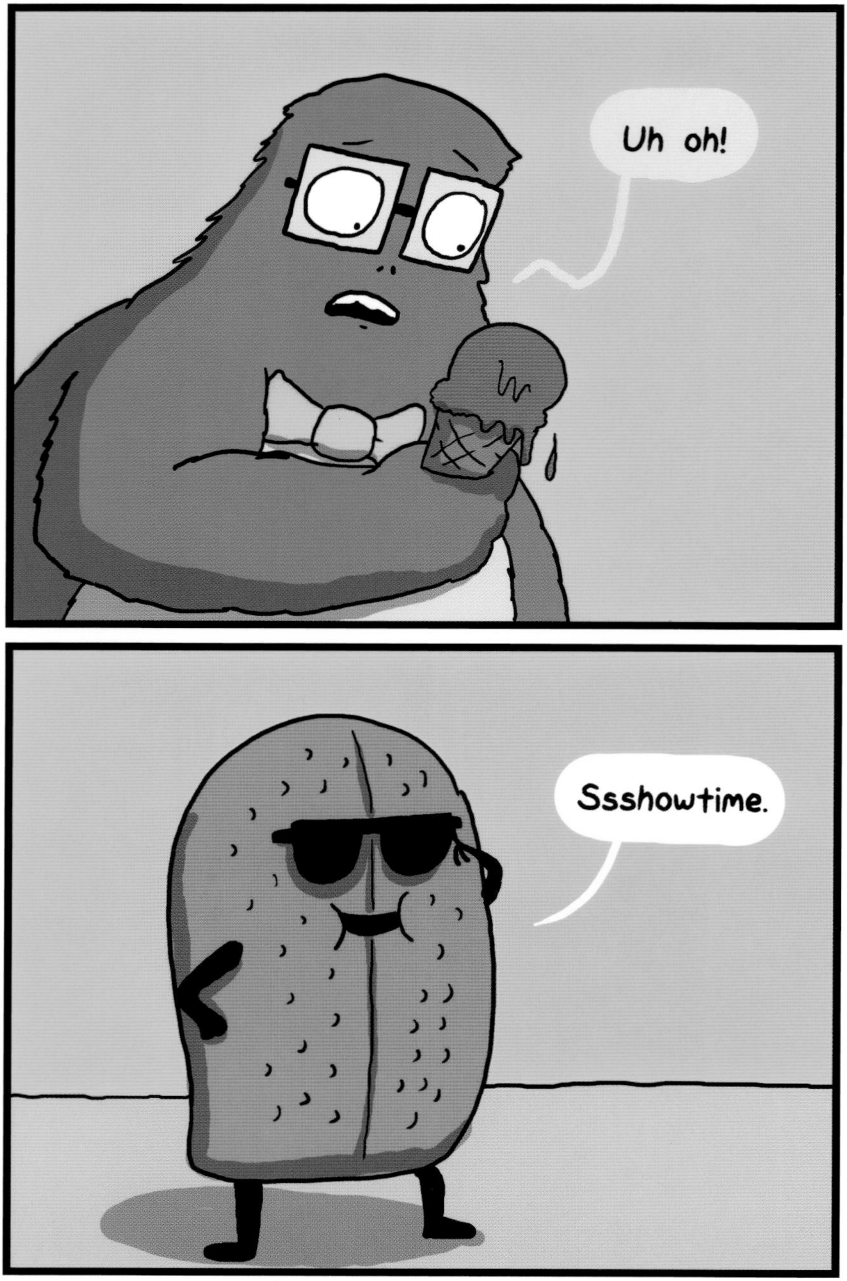
Uh oh!
Ssshowtime.

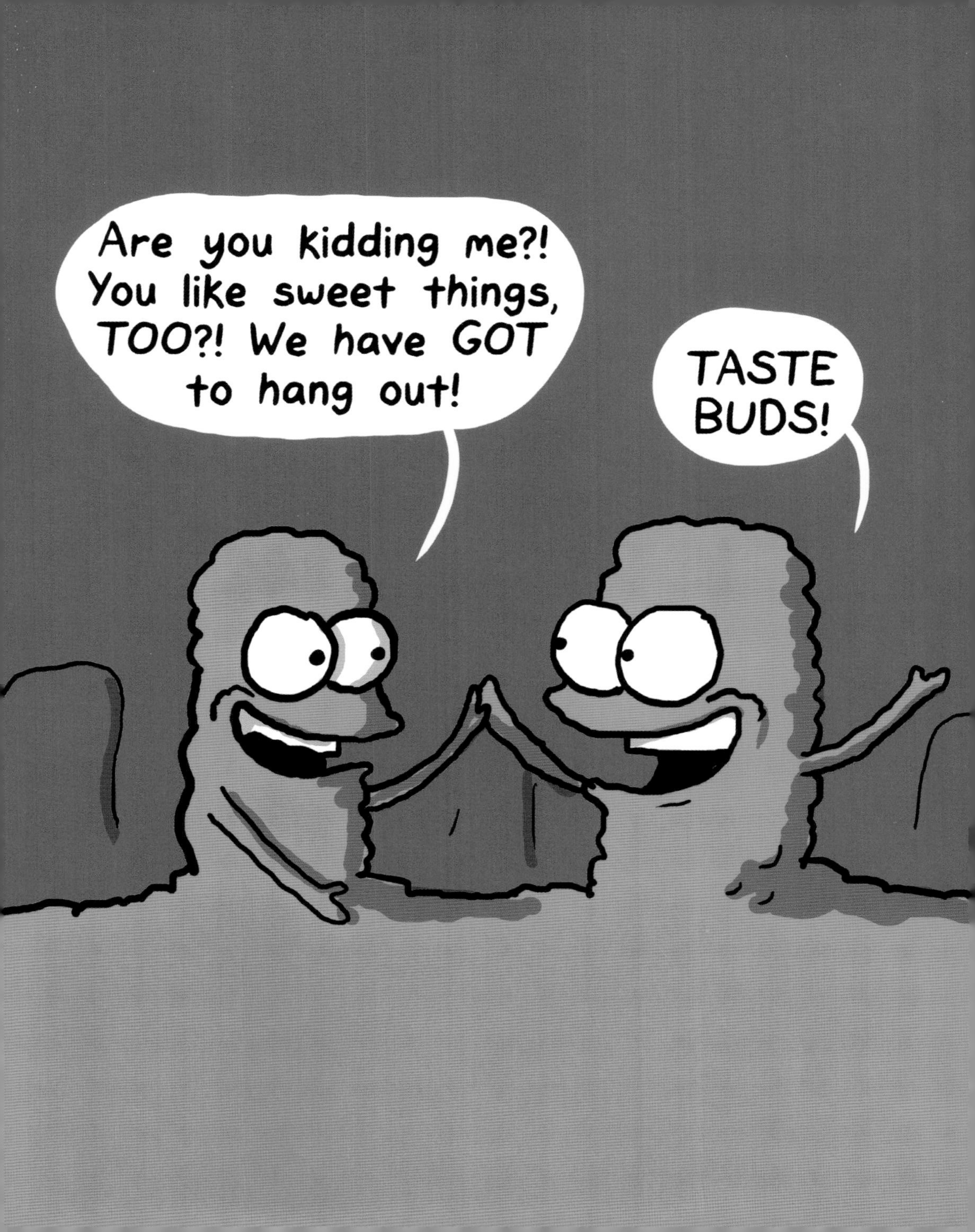
Are you kidding me?! You like sweet things, TOO?! We have GOT to hang out!
TASTE BUDS!

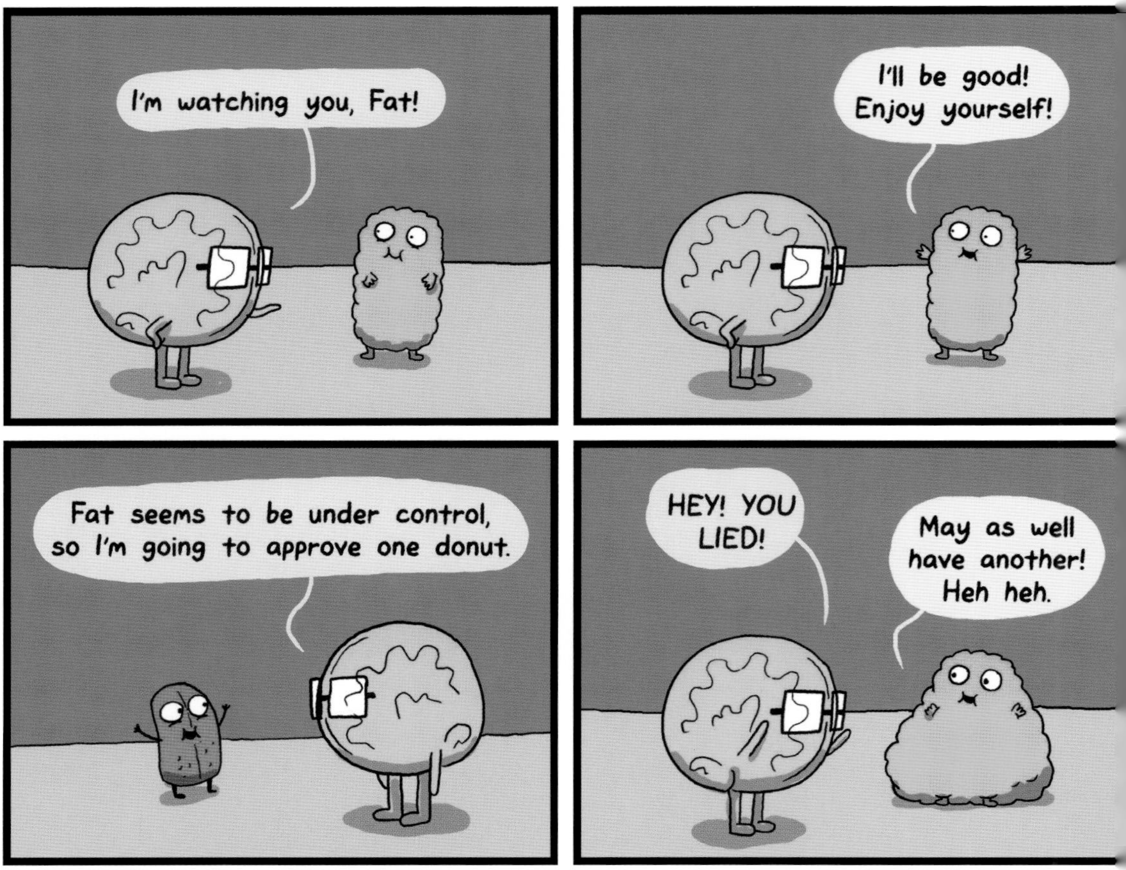
I'm watching you, Fat!
I'll be good! Enjoy yourself!
Fat seems to be under control, so I'm going to approve one donut.
HEY! YOU LIED!
May as well have another! Heh heh.

Tongue's Guide To
HEALTHY LIVING

If nobody sees you eat it, it didn't happen!

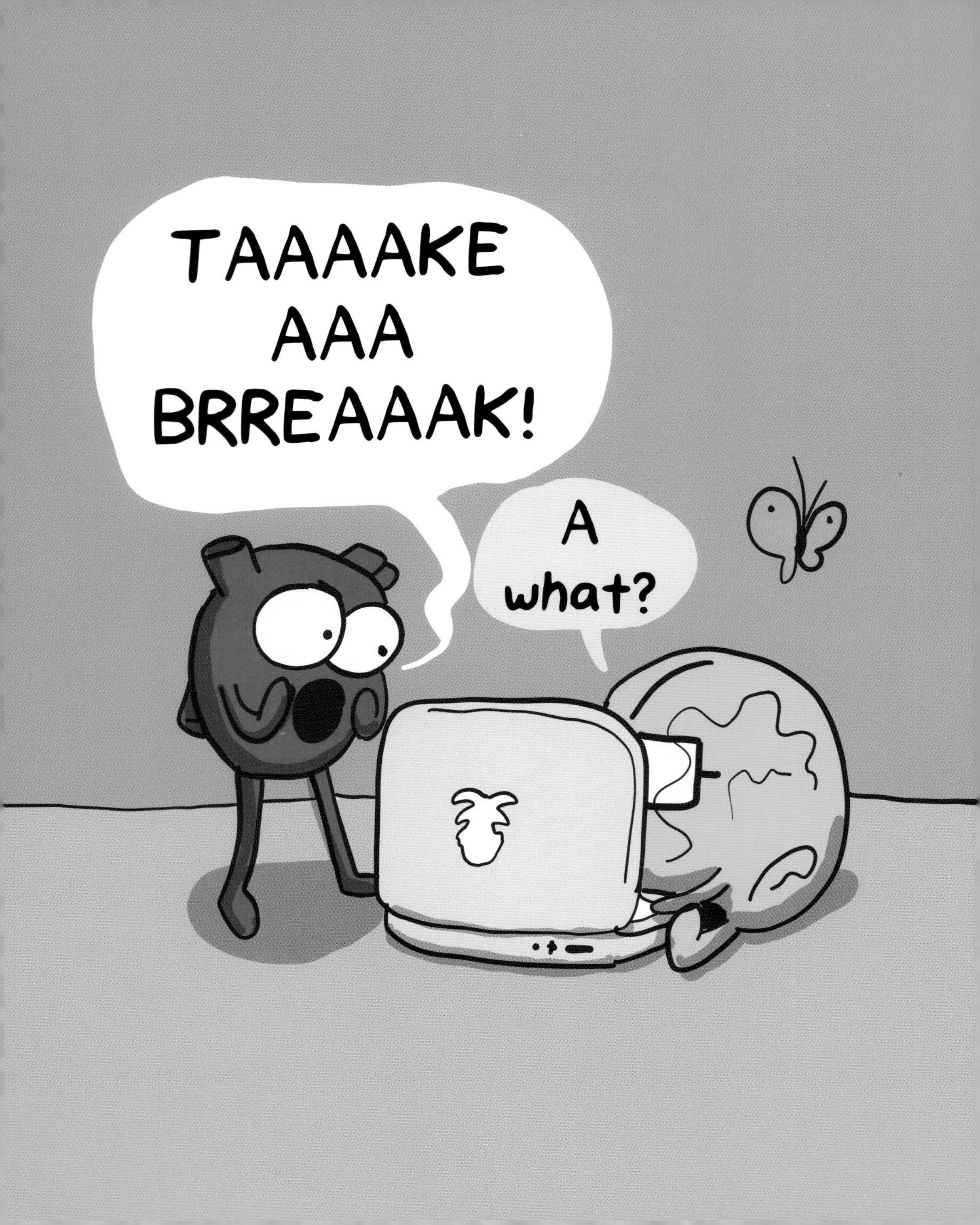
TAAAAKE AAA BRREAAAK!
A what?

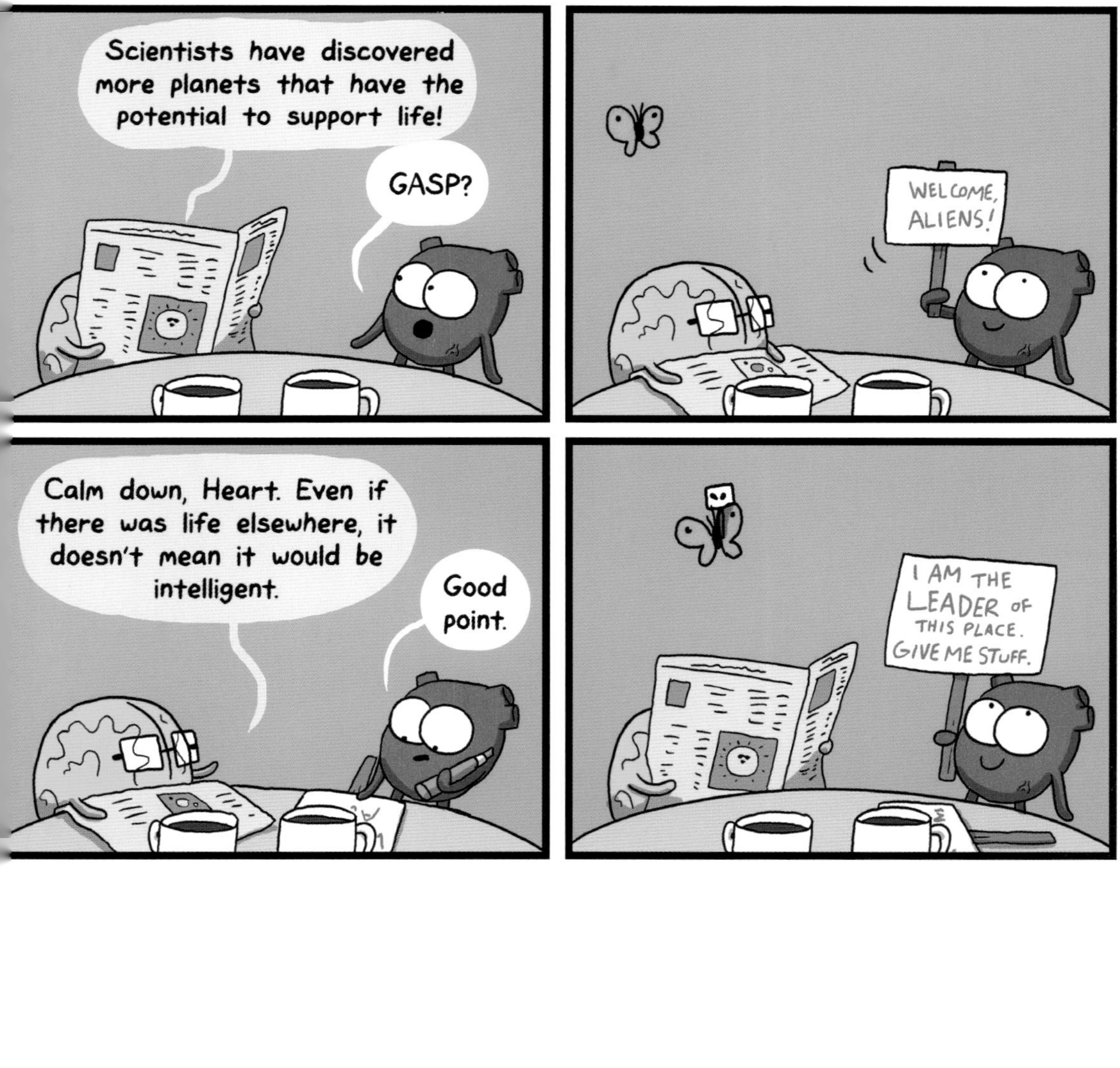
Scientists have discovered more planets that have the potential to support life!
GASP?
WELCOME, ALIENS!
Calm down, Heart. Even if there was life elsewhere, it doesn't mean it would be intelligent.
Good point.
I AM THE LEADER OF THIS PLACE. GIVE ME STUFF.

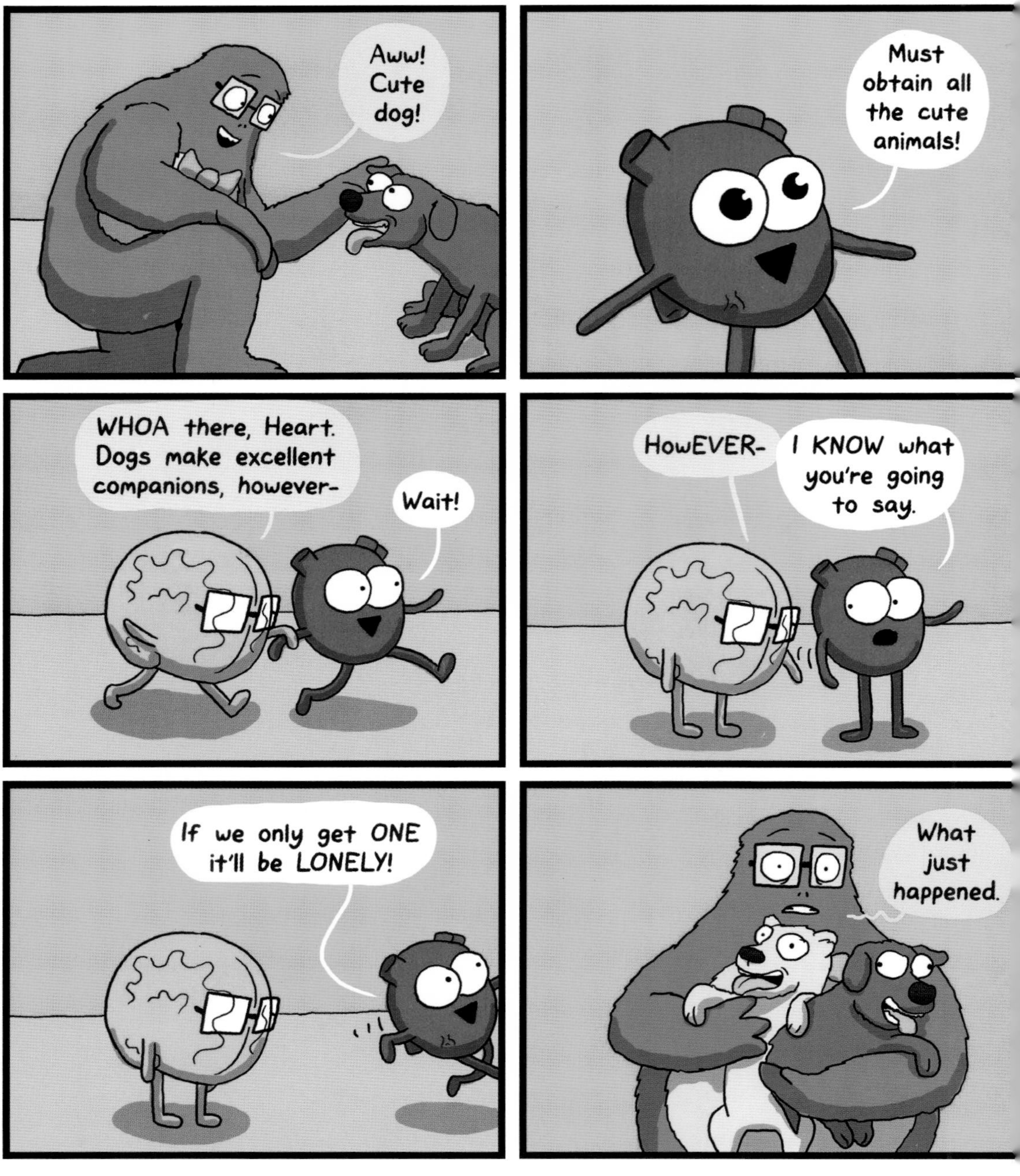
Aww! Cute dog!
Must obtain all the cute animals!
WHOA there, Heart. Dogs make excellent companions, however-
Wait!
HowEVER-
I KNOW what you're going to say.
If we only get ONE it'll be LONELY!
What just happened.

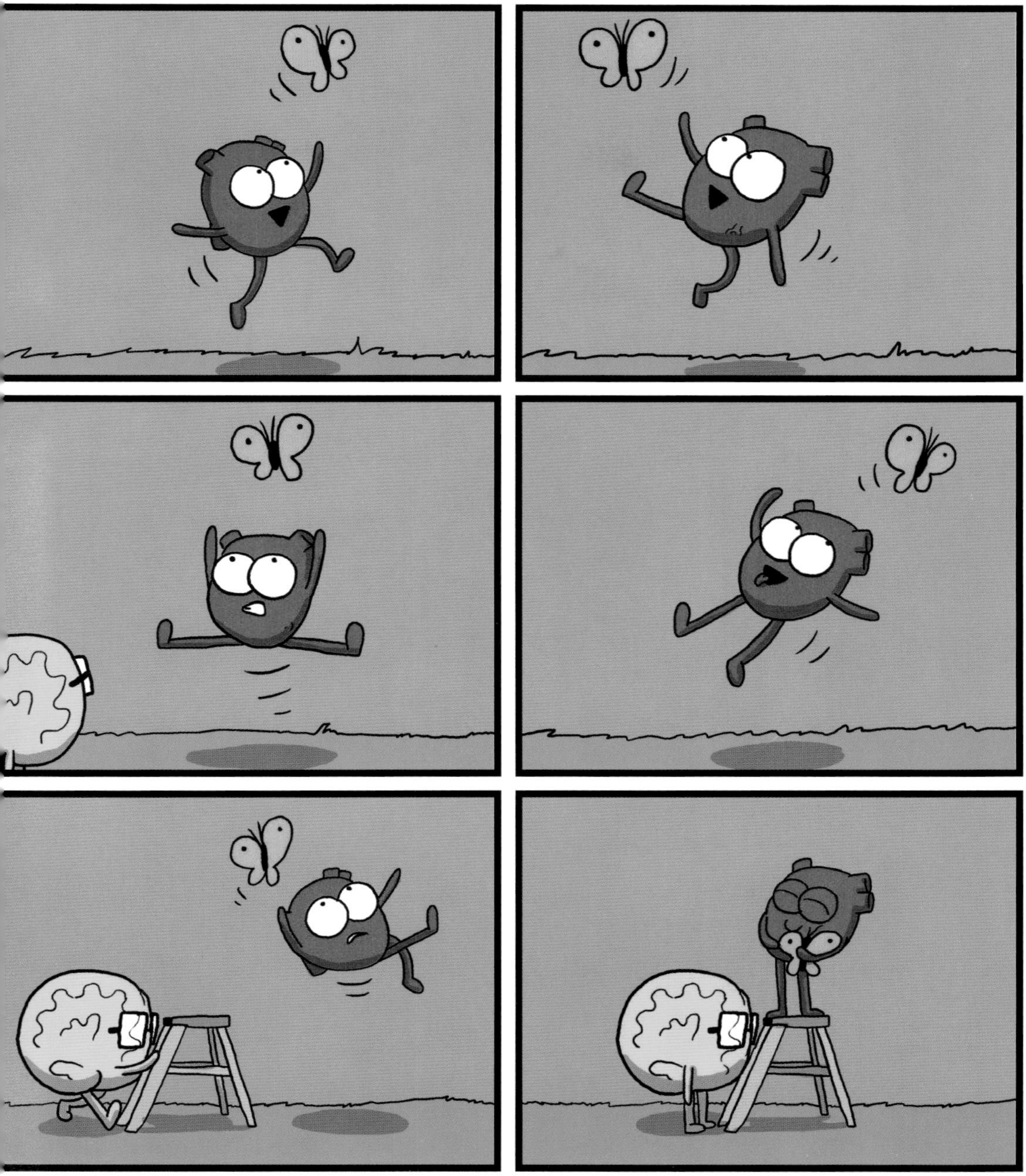

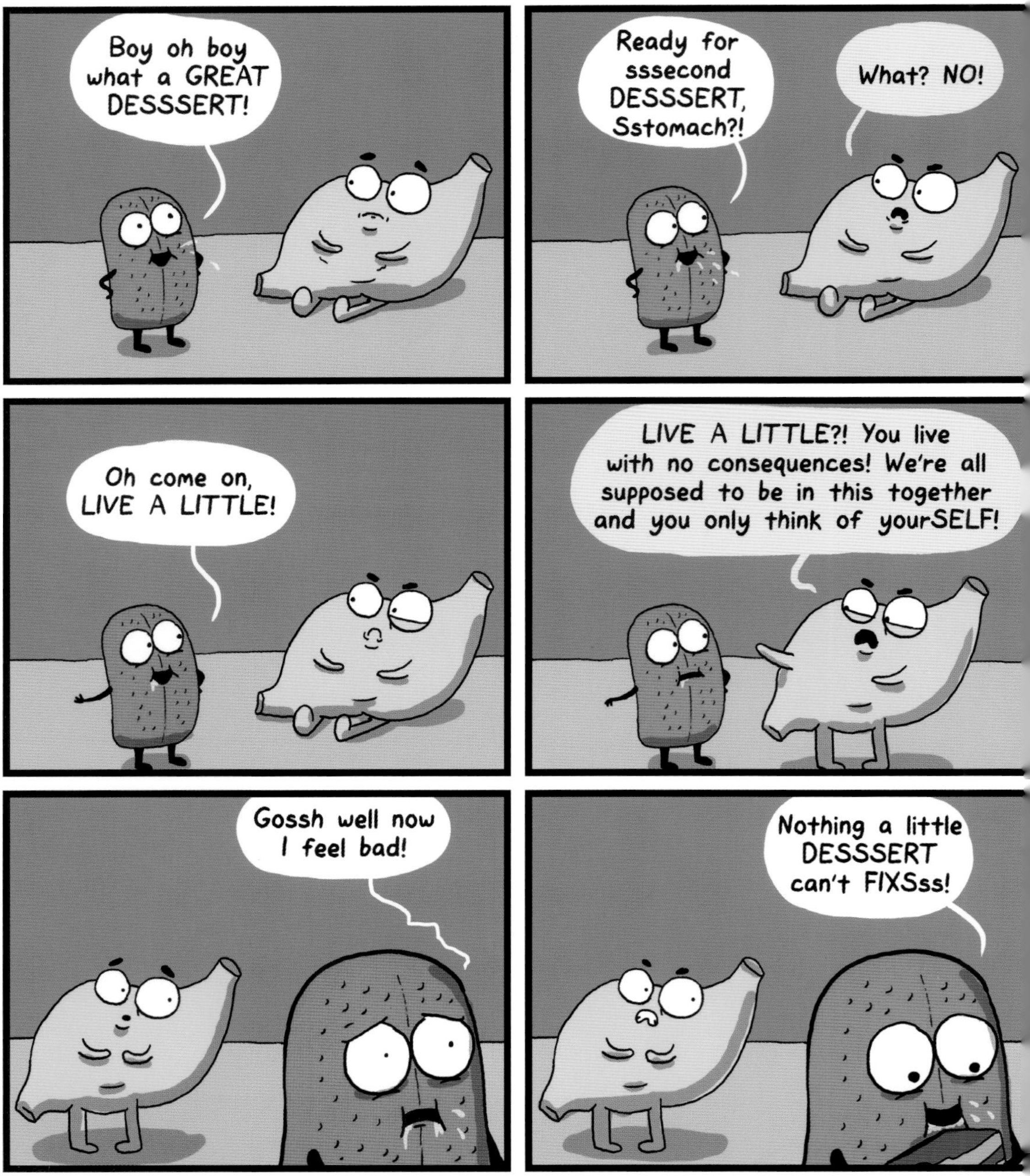
Boy oh boy what a GREAT DESSSERT!
Ready for sssecond DESSSERT, Sstomach?!
What? NO!
Oh come on, LIVE A LITTLE!
LIVE A LITTLE?! You live with no consequences! We're all supposed to be in this together and you only think of yourSELF!
Gossh well now I feel bad!
Nothing a little DESSSERT can't FIXSss!

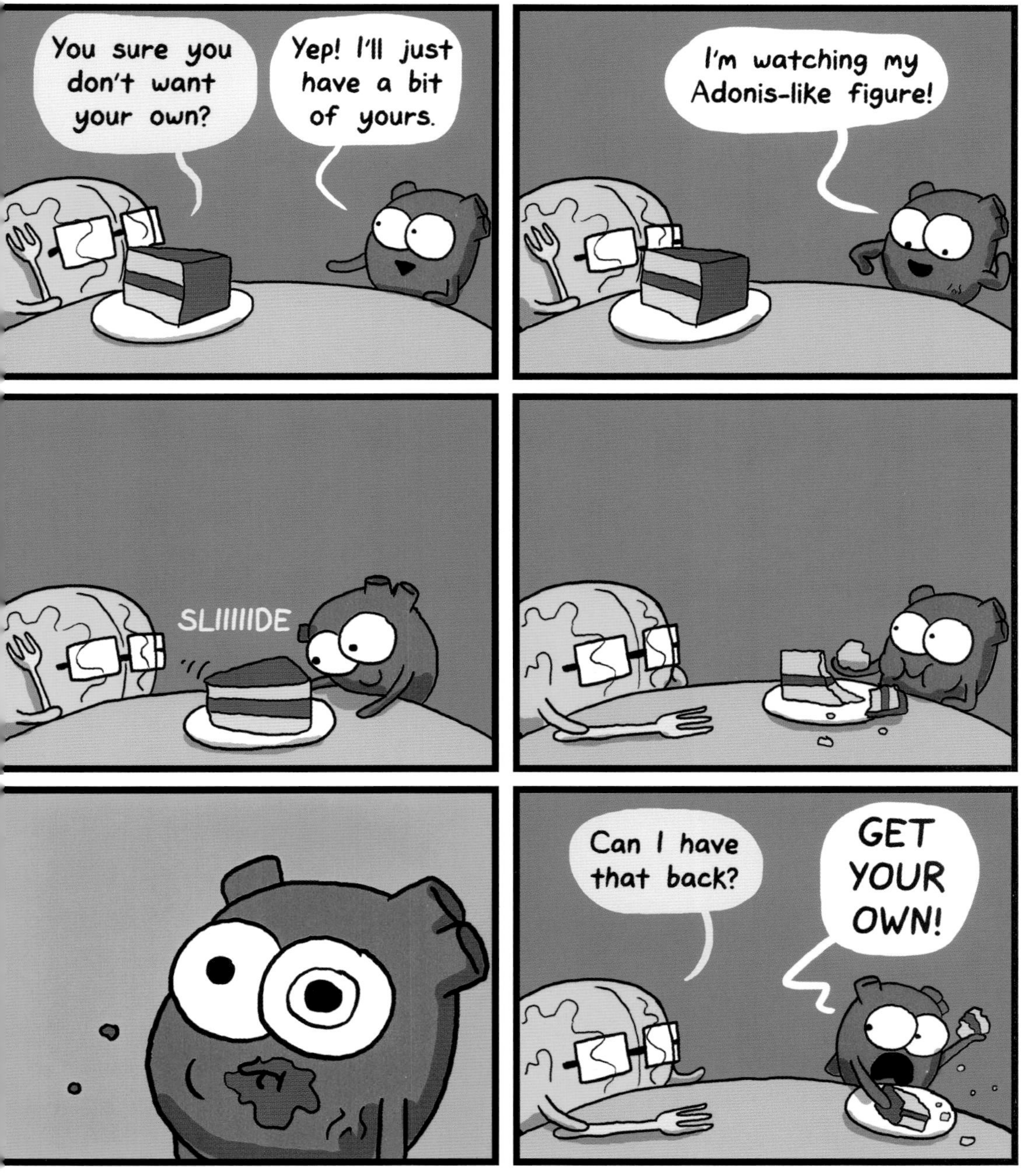
You sure you don't want your own?
Yep! I'll just have a bit of yours.
I'm watching my Adonis-like figure!
SLIIIIIDE
Can I have that back?
GET YOUR OWN!

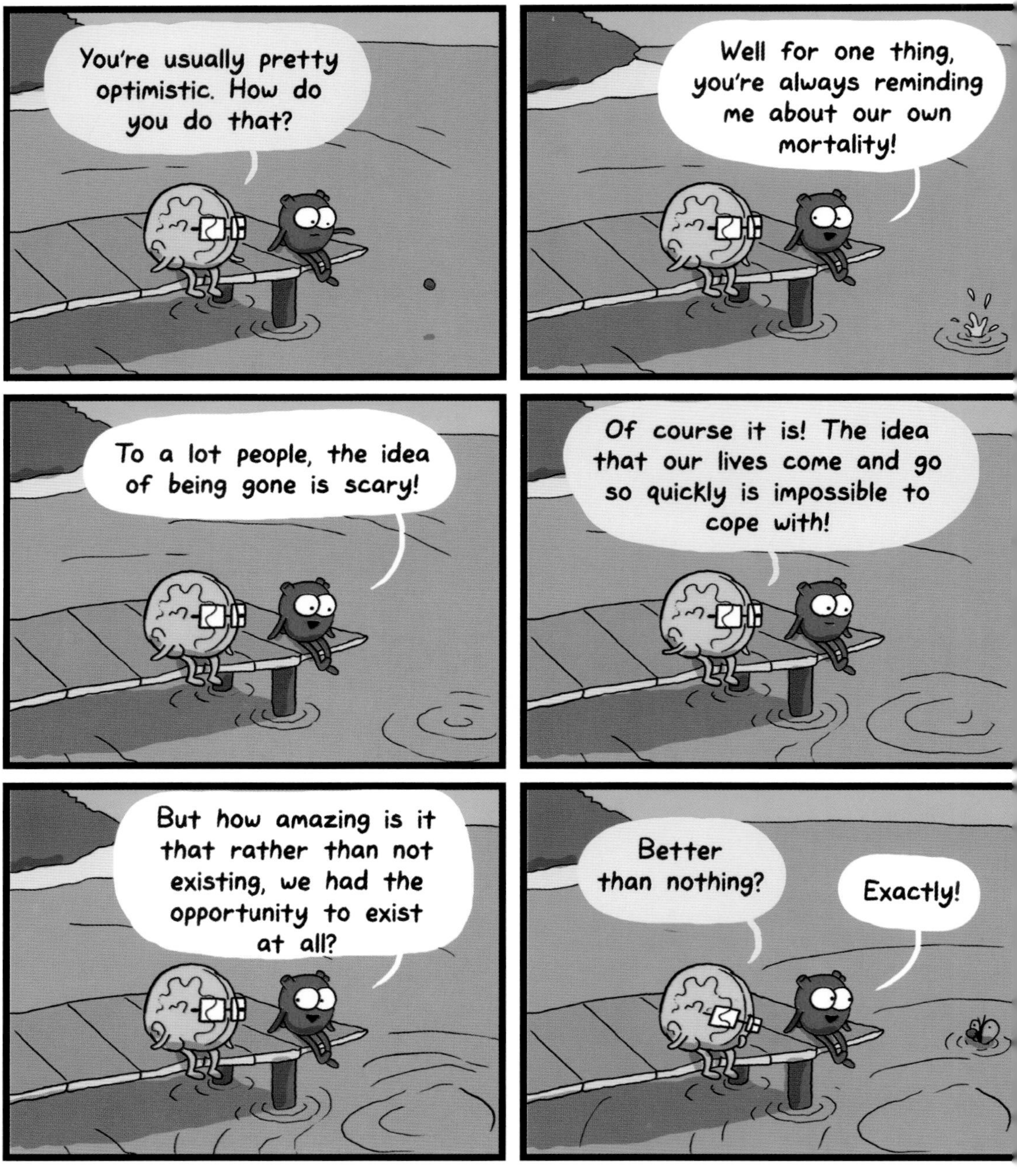
You're usually pretty optimistic. How do you do that?
Well for one thing, you're always reminding me about our own mortality!
To a lot people, the idea of being gone is scary!
Of course it is! The idea that our lives come and go so quickly is impossible to cope with!
But how amazing is it that rather than not existing, we had the opportunity to exist at all?
Better than nothing?
Exactly!

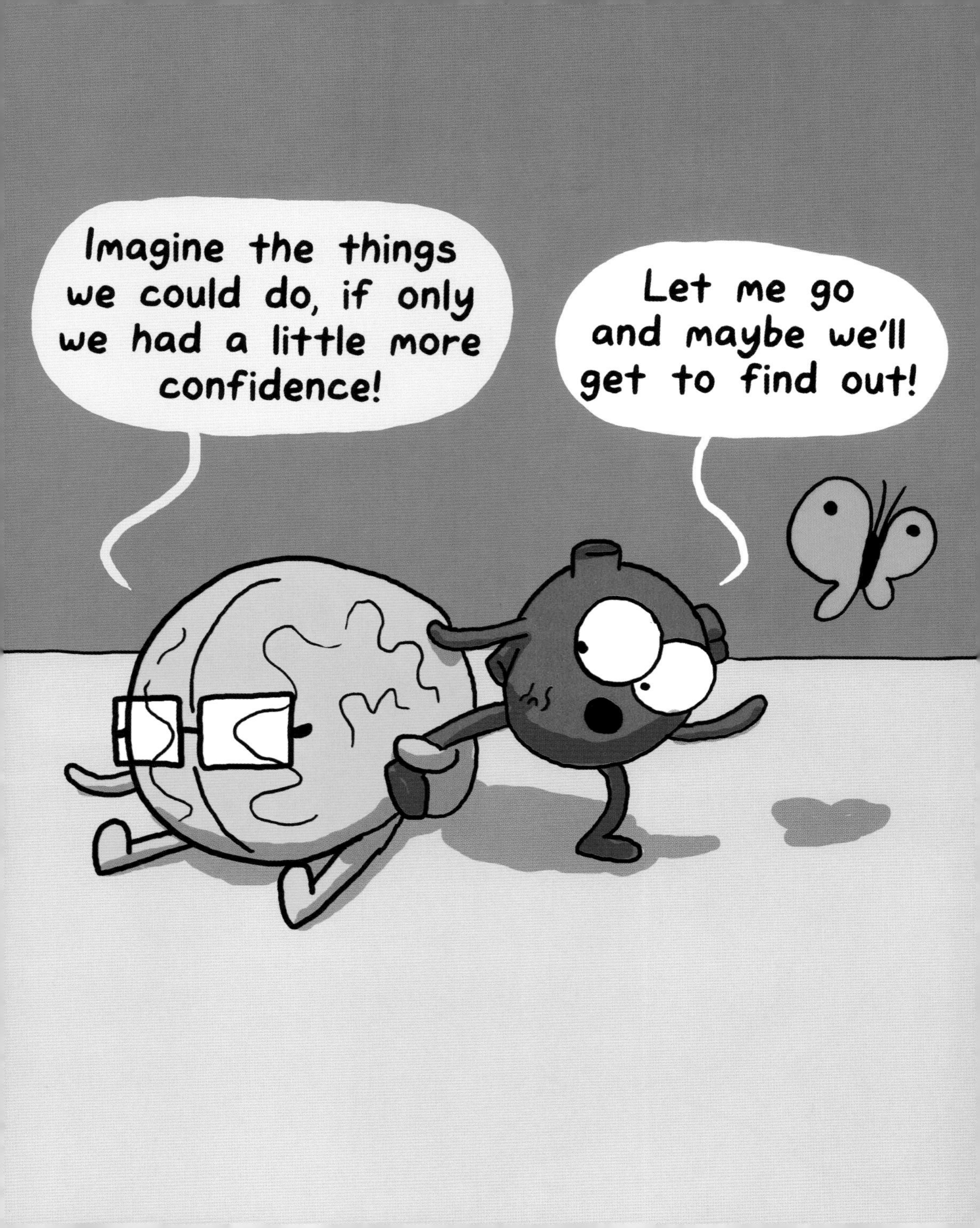
Imagine the things we could do, if only we had a little more confidence!
Let me go and maybe we'll get to find out!

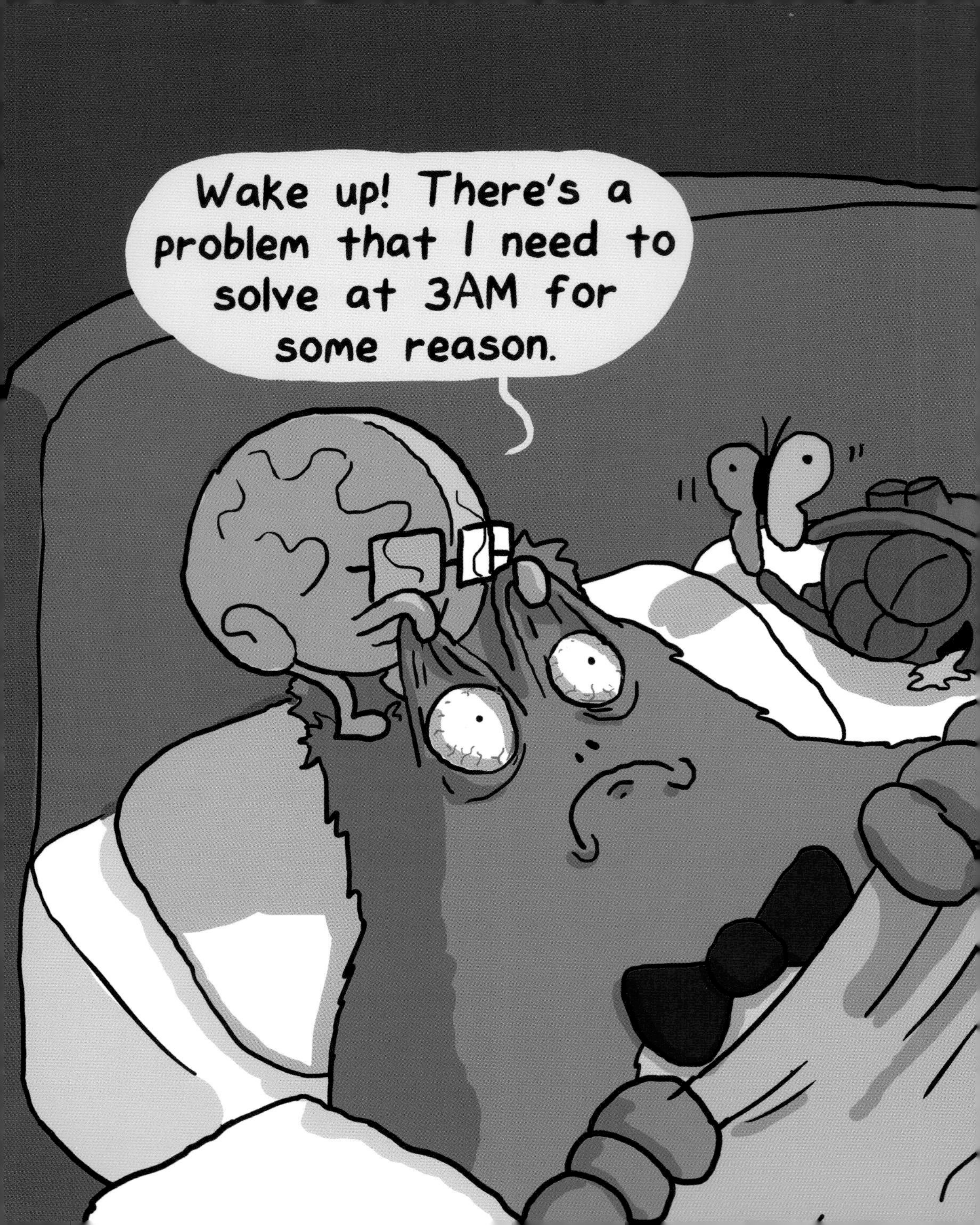
Wake up! There's a problem that I need to solve at 3AM for some reason.

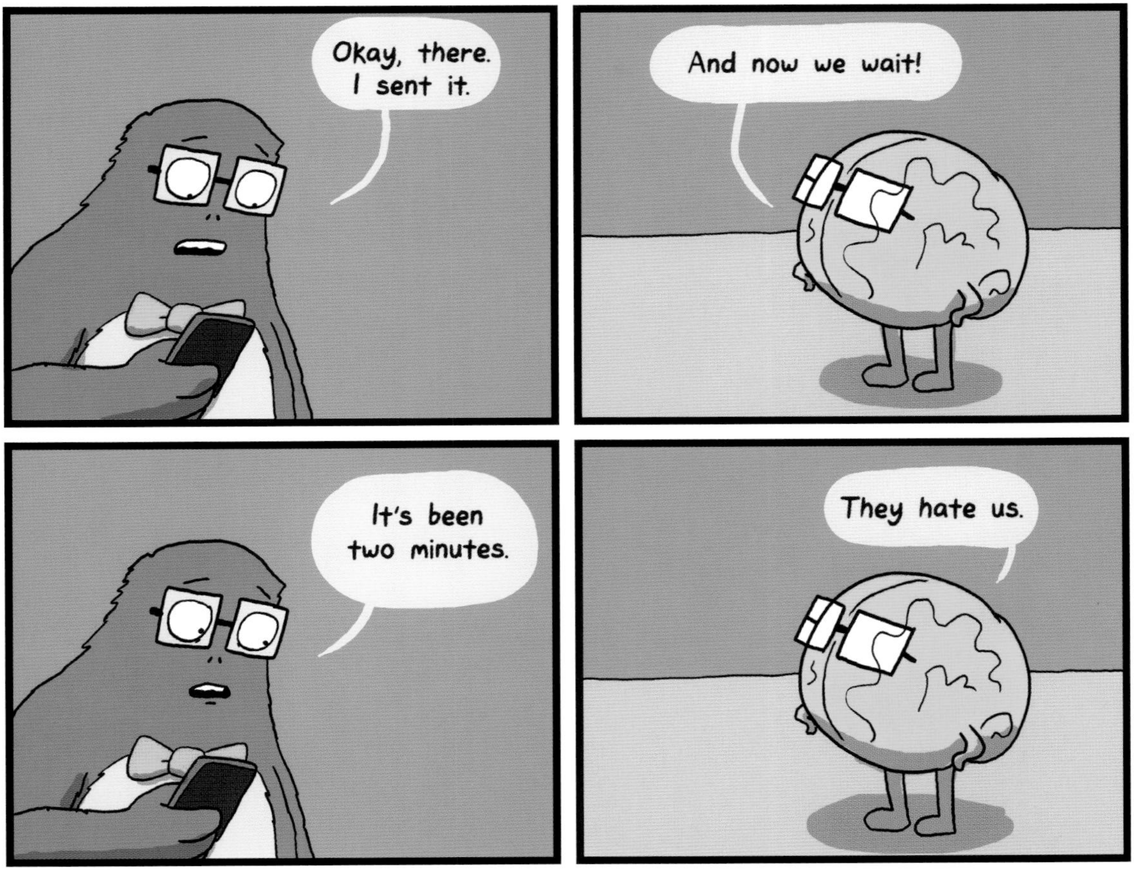
Okay, there.
I sent it.
And now we wait!
It's been
two minutes.
They hate us.

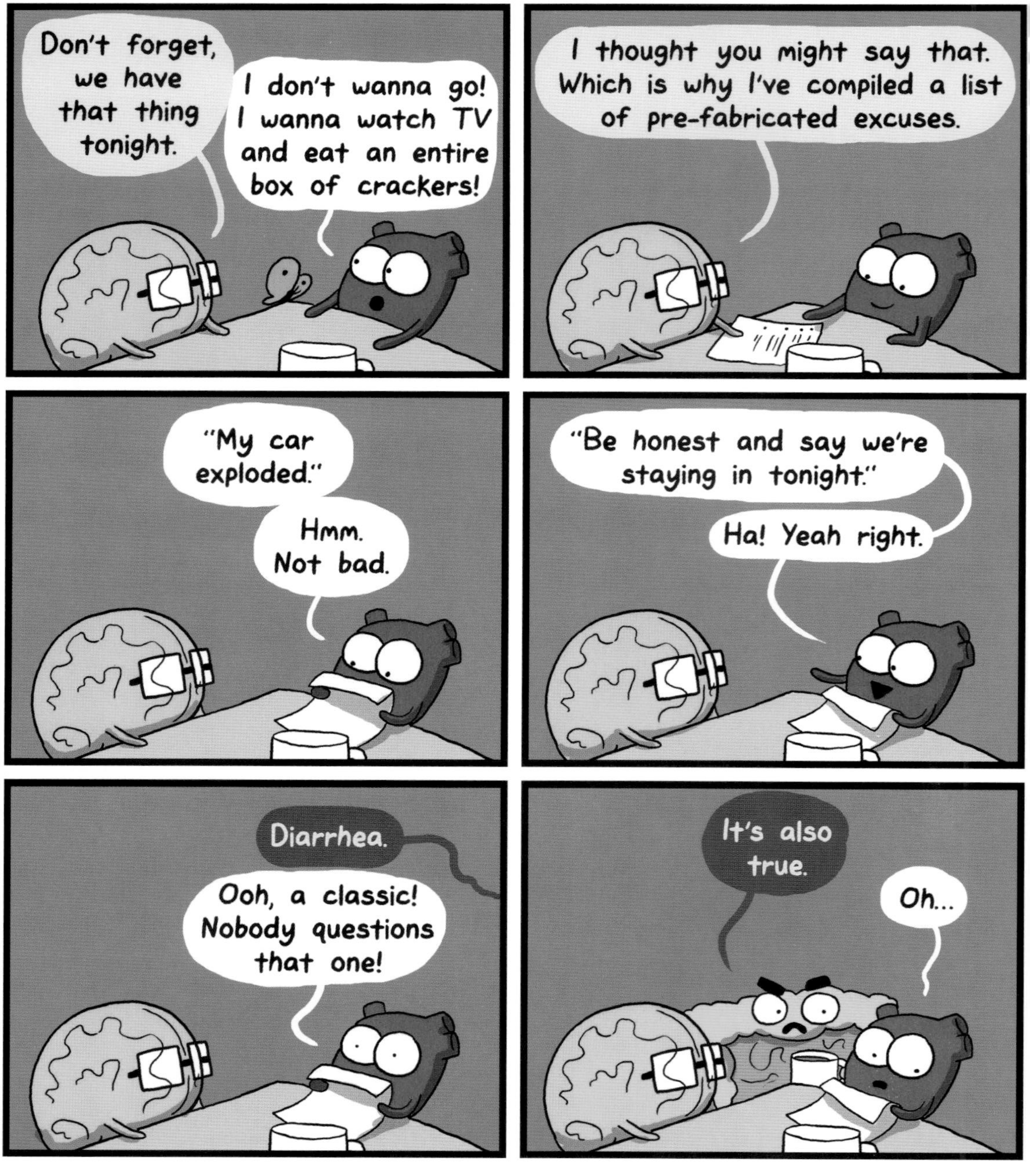
Don't forget, we have that thing tonight.
I don't wanna go! I wanna watch TV and eat an entire box of crackers!
I thought you might say that. Which is why I've compiled a list of pre-fabricated excuses.
"My car exploded."
Hmm. Not bad.
"Be honest and say we're staying in tonight."
Ha! Yeah right.
Diarrhea.
Ooh, a classic! Nobody questions that one!
It's also true.
Oh...

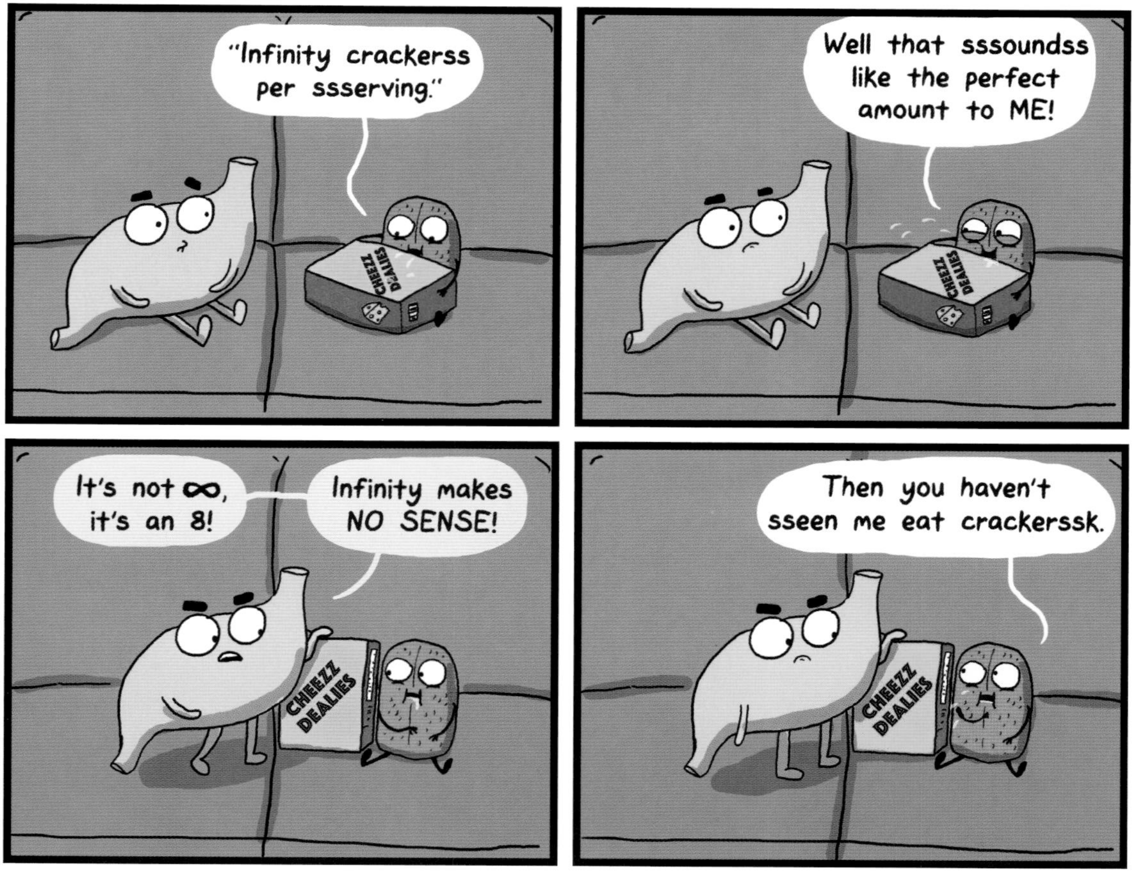
"Infinity crackerss per ssserving."
Well that sssoundss like the perfect amount to ME!
It's not ∞, it's an 8!
Infinity makes NO SENSE!
Then you haven't sseen me eat crackerssk.
CHEEZZ DEALIES

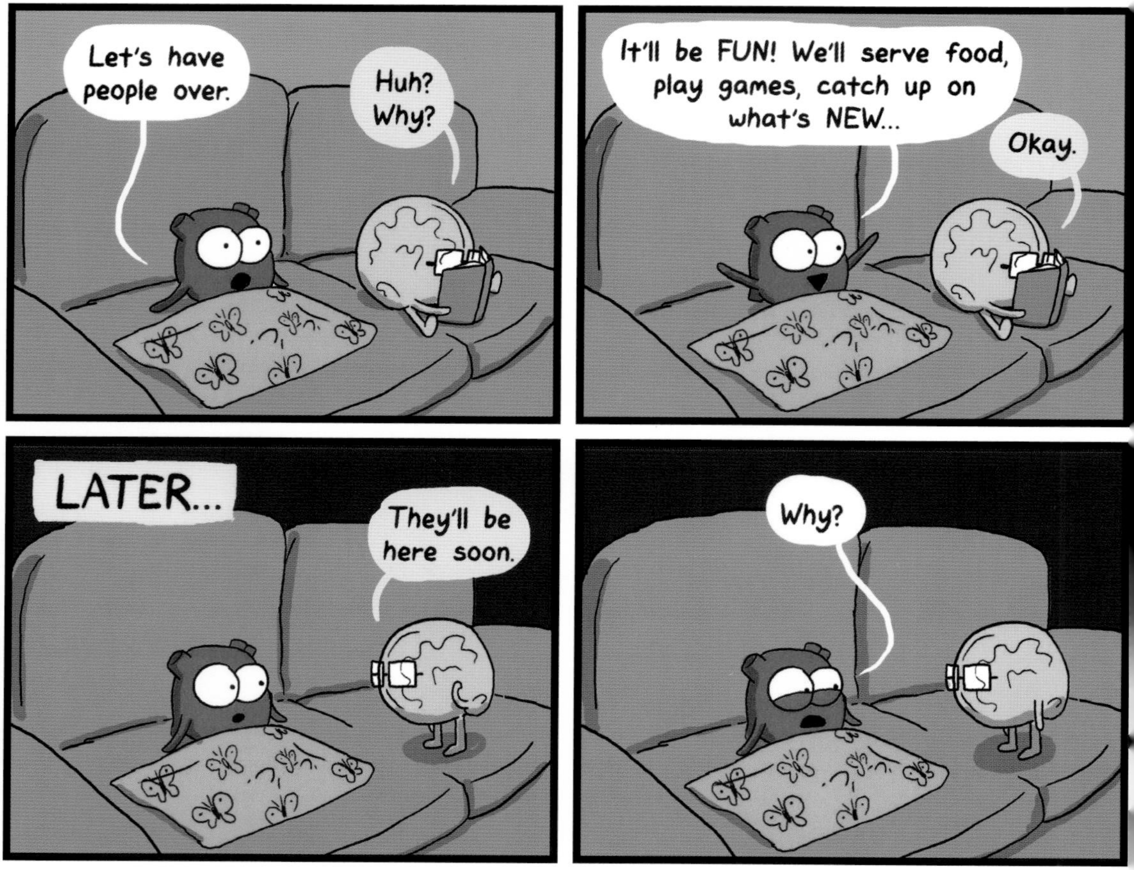
Let's have people over.
Huh? Why?
It'll be FUN! We'll serve food, play games, catch up on what's NEW...
Okay.
LATER...
They'll be here soon.
Why?

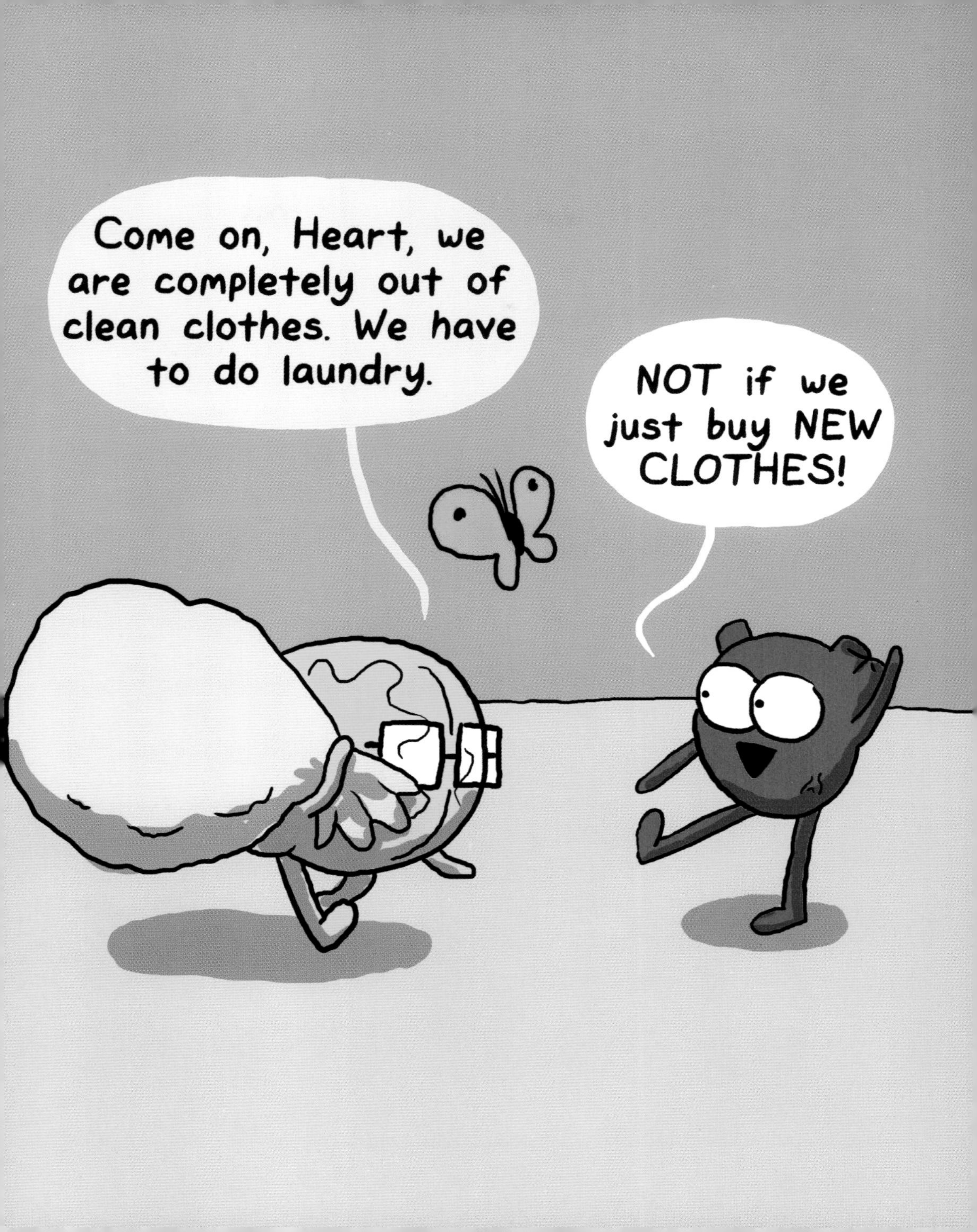
Come on, Heart, we are completely out of clean clothes. We have to do laundry.
NOT if we just buy NEW CLOTHES!

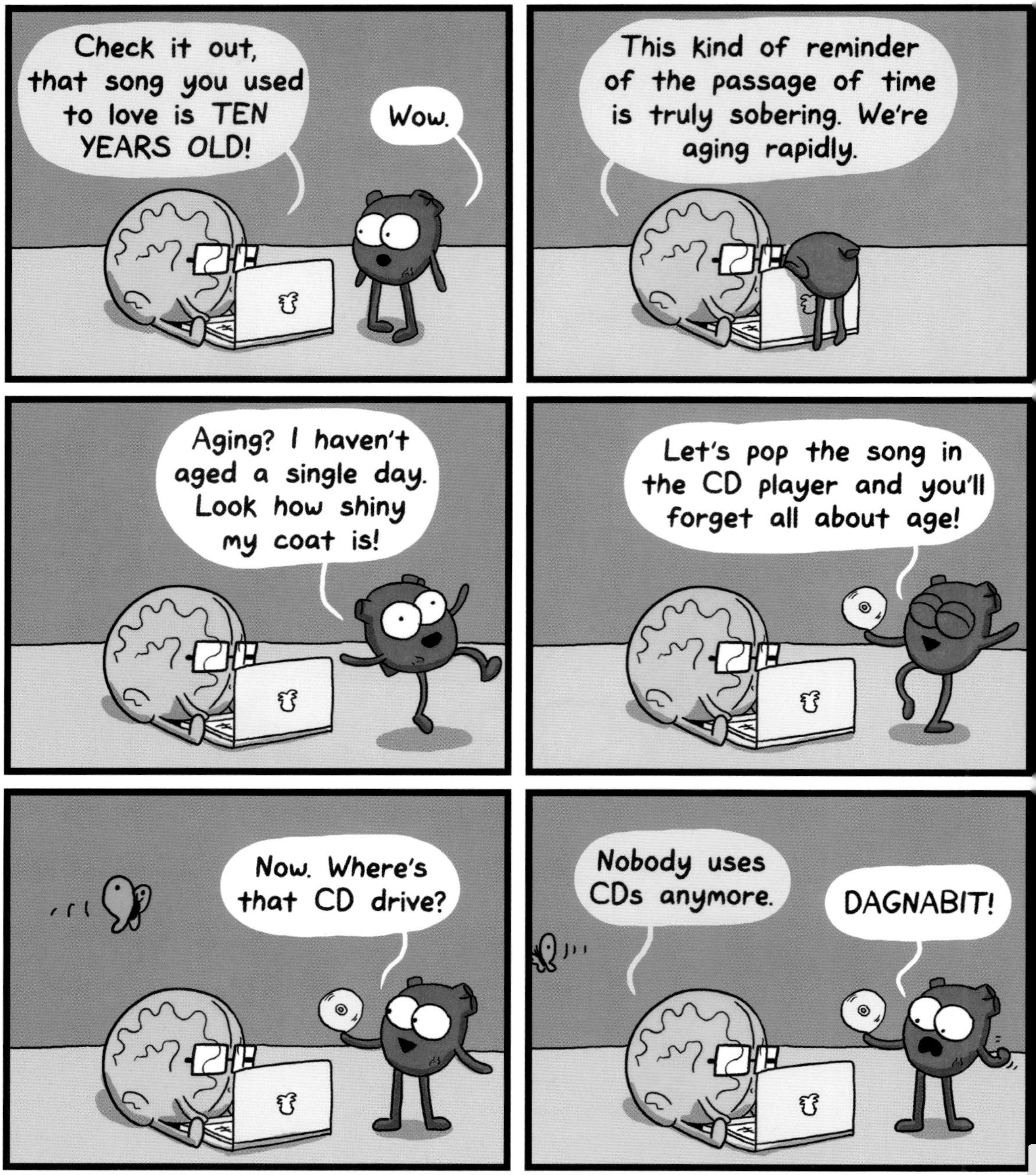
Check it out, that song you used to love is TEN YEARS OLD!
Wow.
This kind of reminder of the passage of time is truly sobering. We're aging rapidly.
Aging? I haven't aged a single day. Look how shiny my coat is!
Let's pop the song in the CD player and you'll forget all about age!
Now. Where's that CD drive?
Nobody uses CDs anymore.
DAGNABIT!

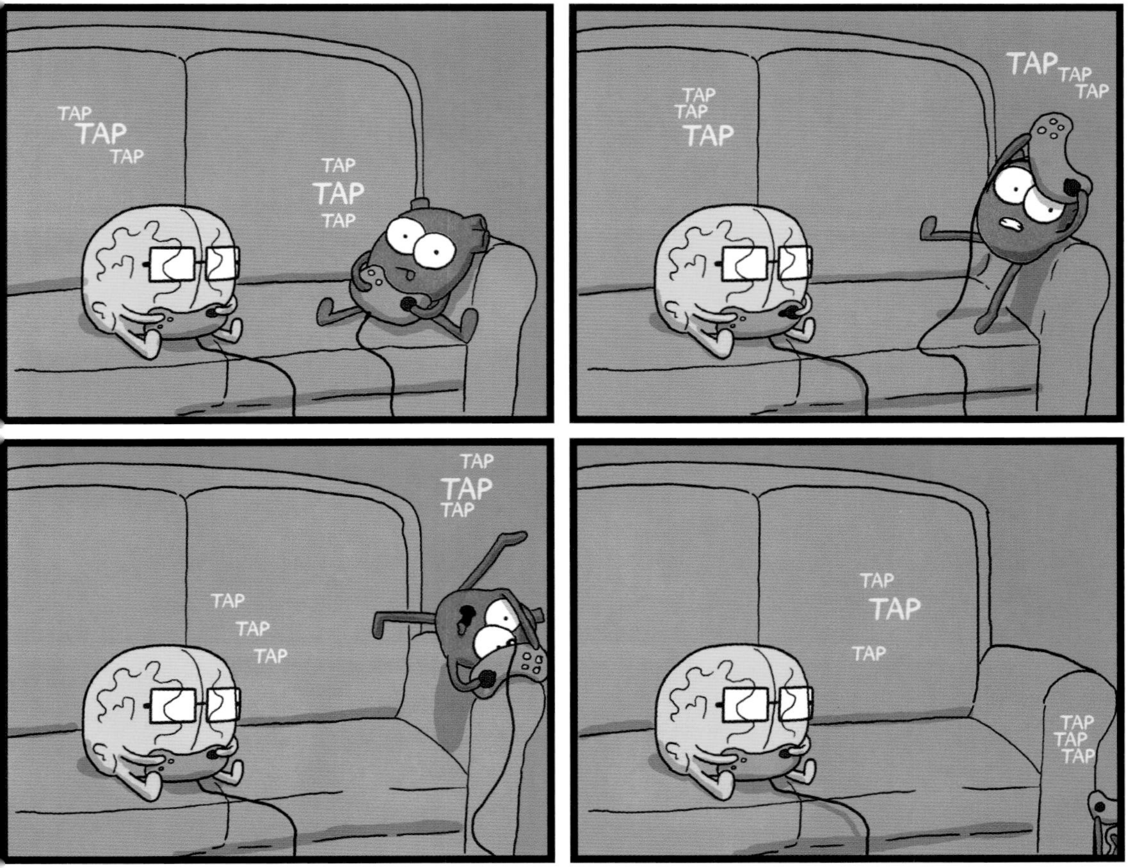
TAP TAP TAP
TAP TAP TAP
TAP TAP TAP
TAP TAP TAP
TAP TAP TAP
TAP TAP TAP
TAP TAP TAP
TAP TAP TAP

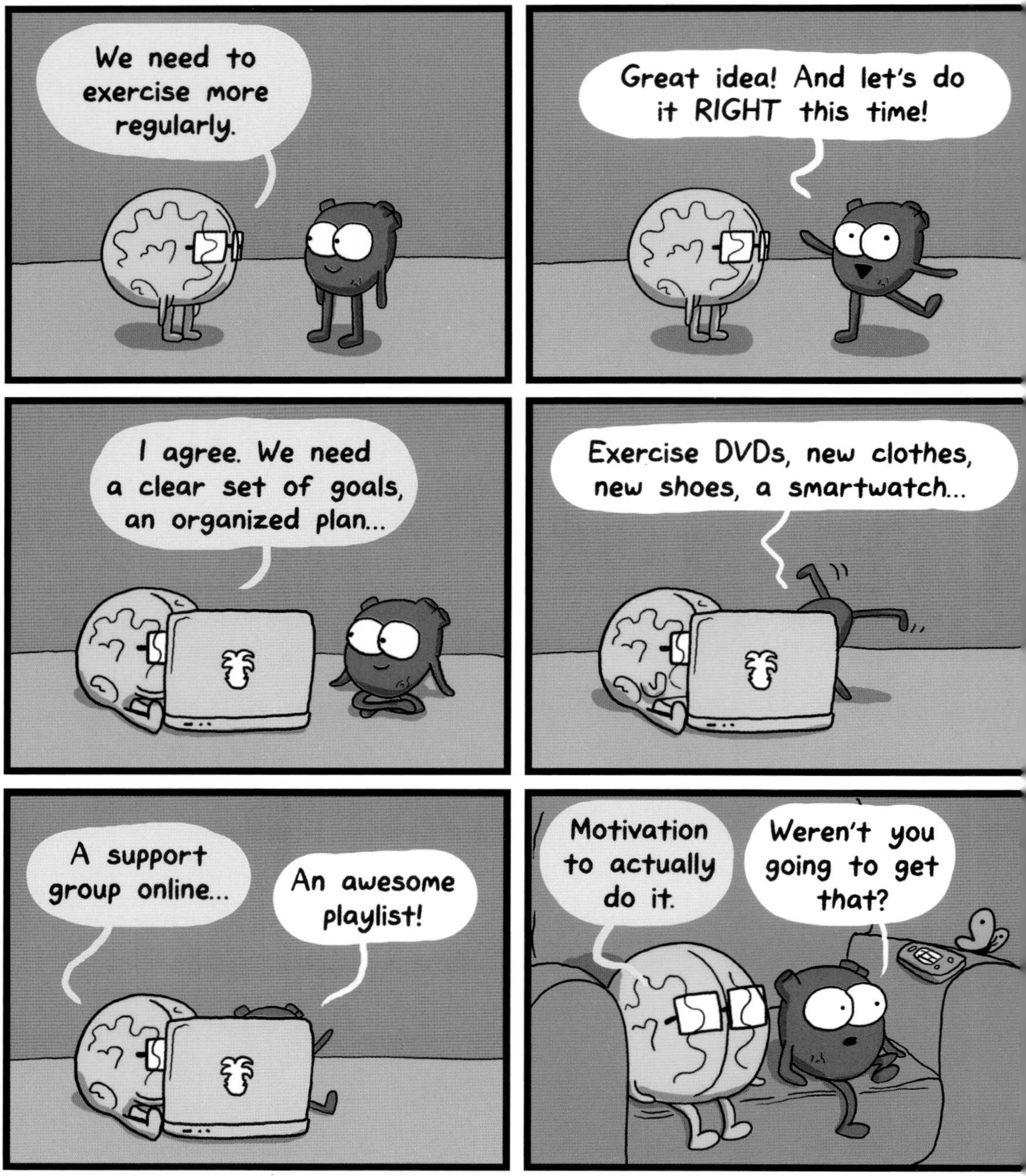
We need to exercise more regularly.
Great idea! And let's do it RIGHT this time!
I agree. We need a clear set of goals, an organized plan...
Exercise DVDs, new clothes, new shoes, a smartwatch...
A support group online...
An awesome playlist!
Motivation to actually do it.
Weren't you going to get that?

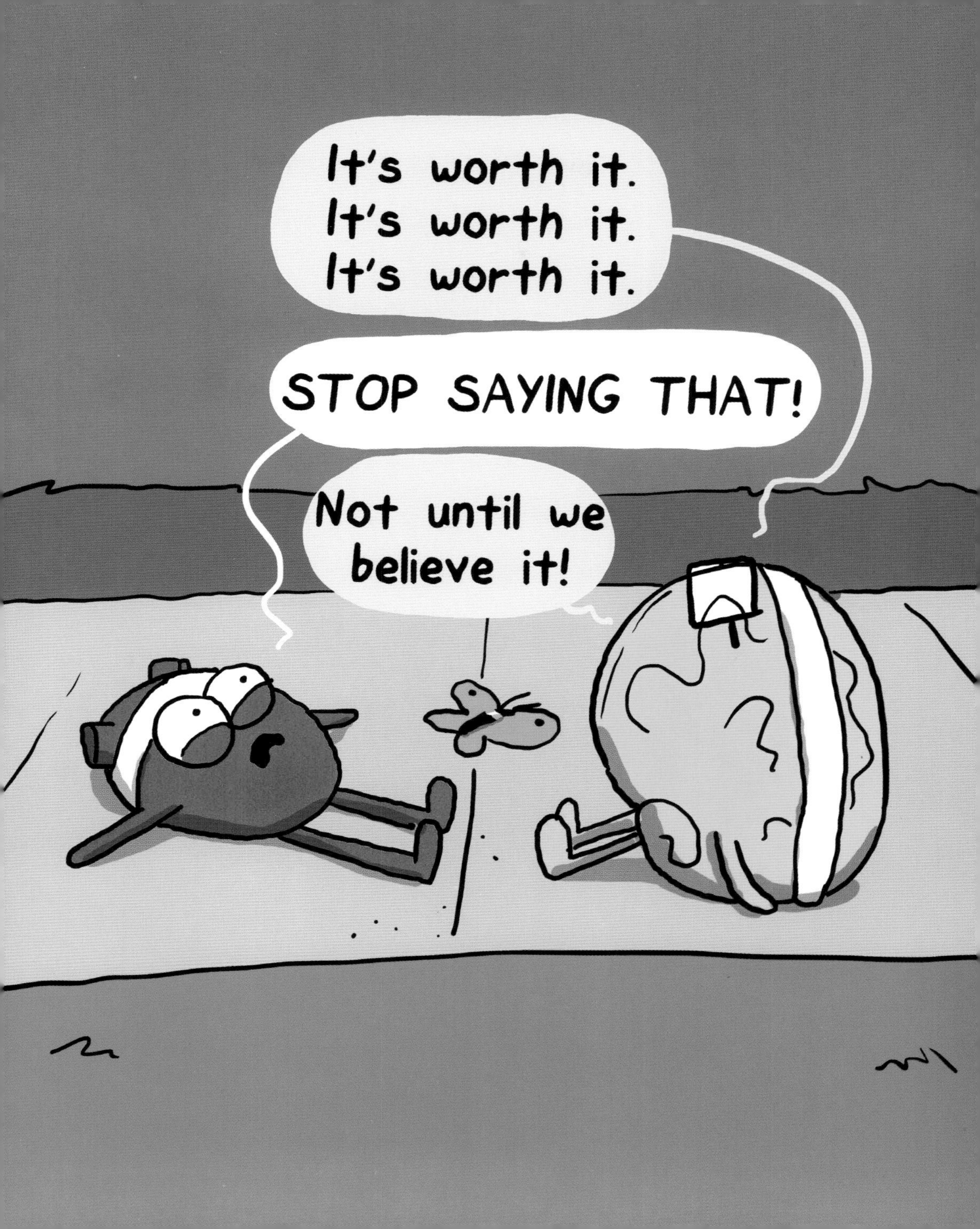
It's worth it.
It's worth it.
It's worth it.
STOP SAYING THAT!
Not until we believe it!

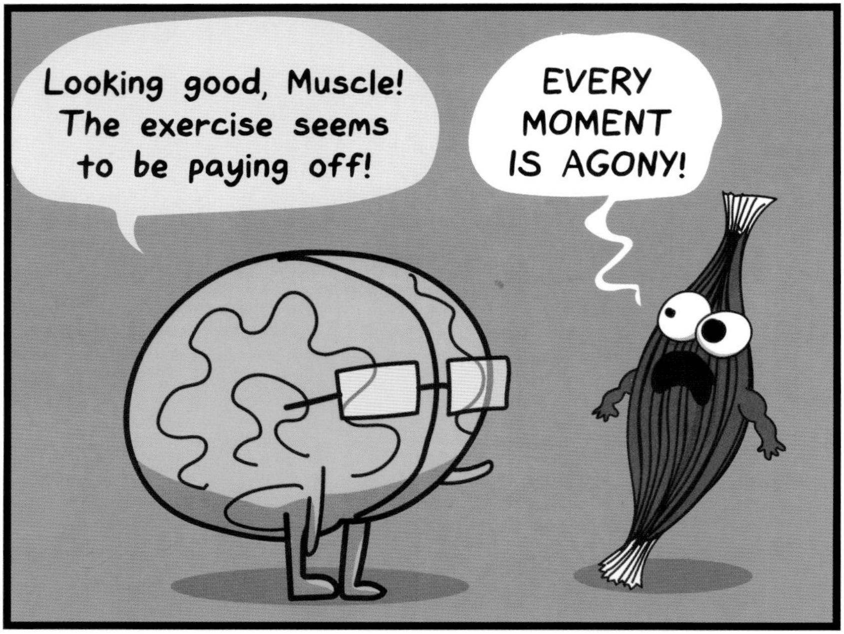
Looking good, Muscle! The exercise seems to be paying off!
EVERY MOMENT IS AGONY!

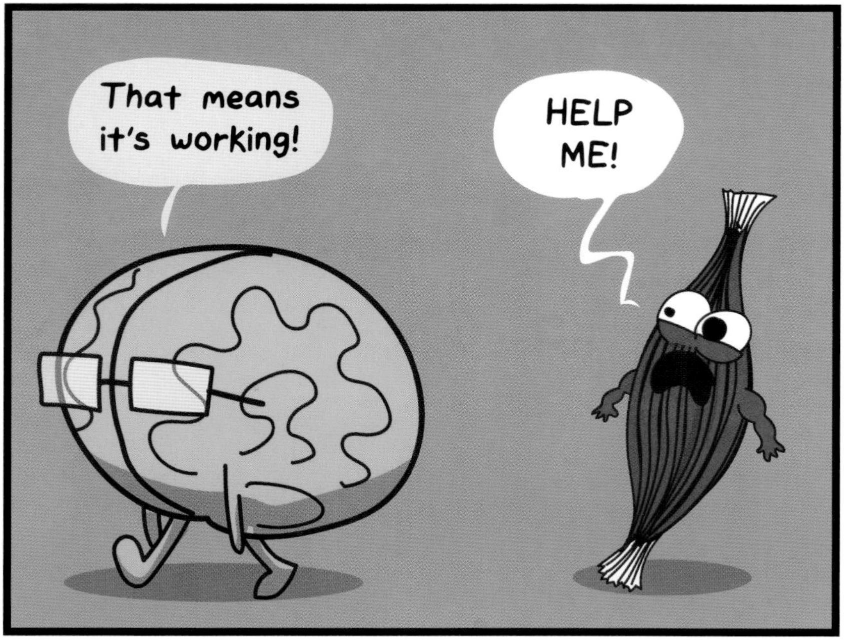
That means it's working!
HELP ME!

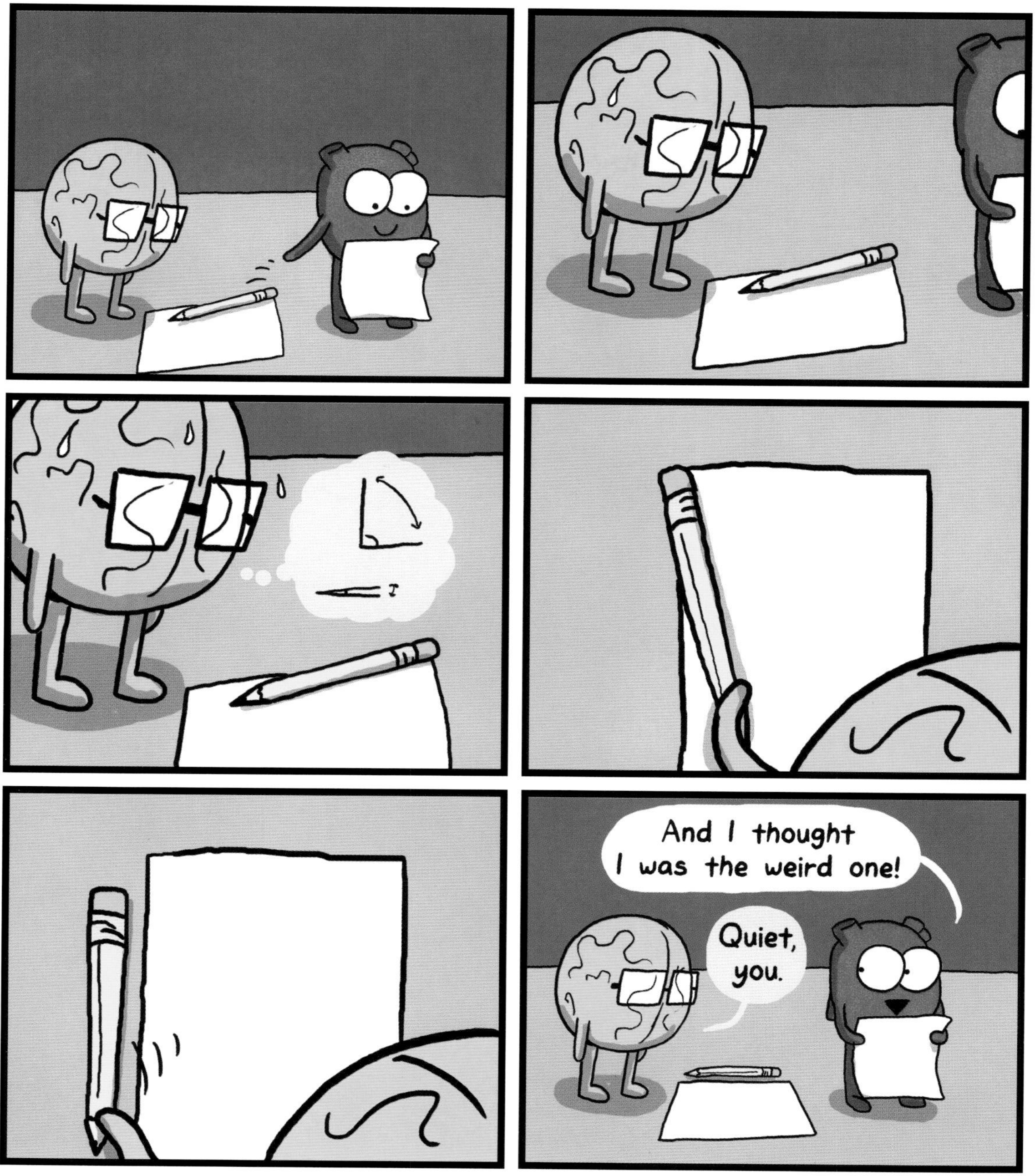
And I thought
I was the weird one!
Quiet,
you.

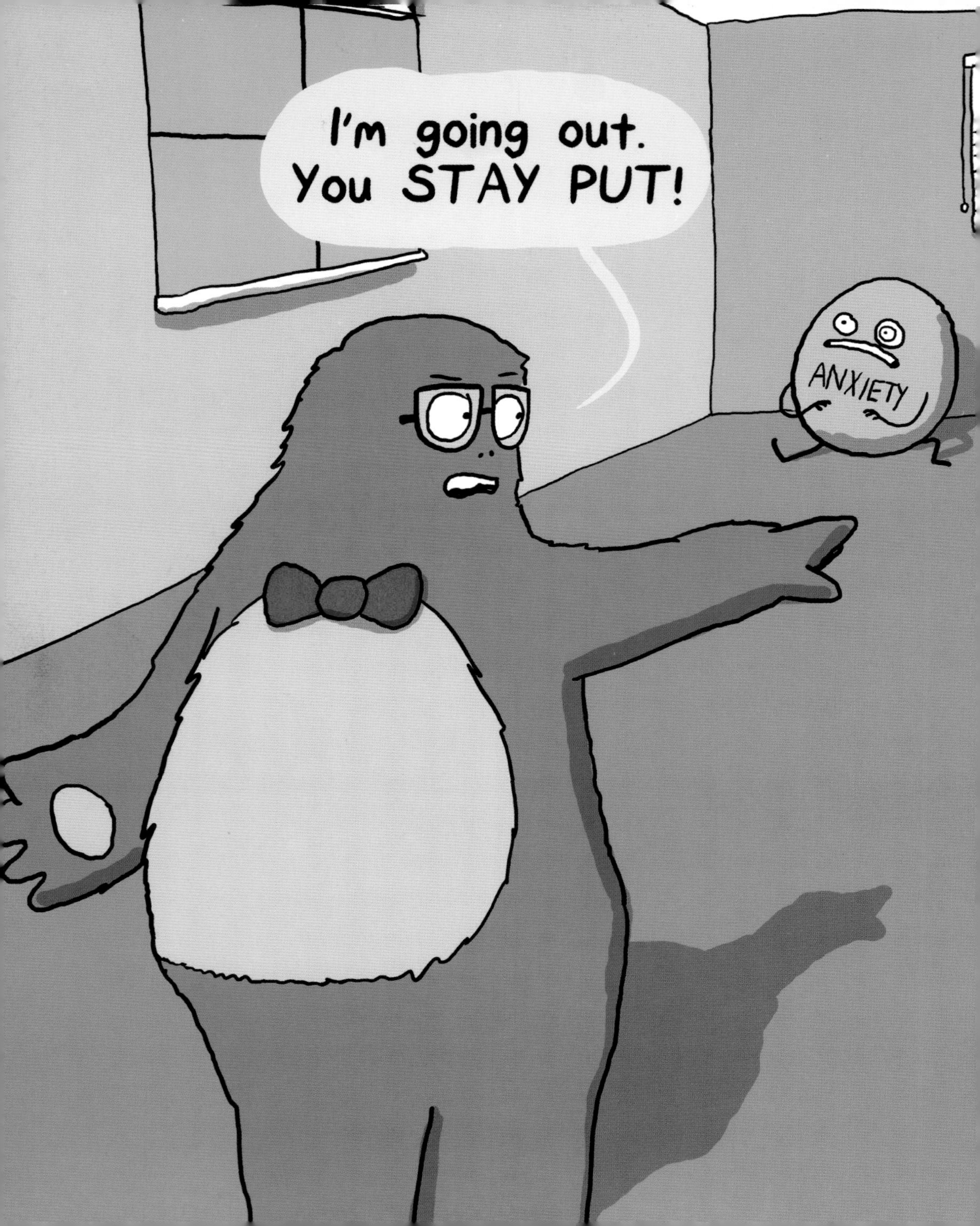
I'm going out. You STAY PUT!
ANXIETY

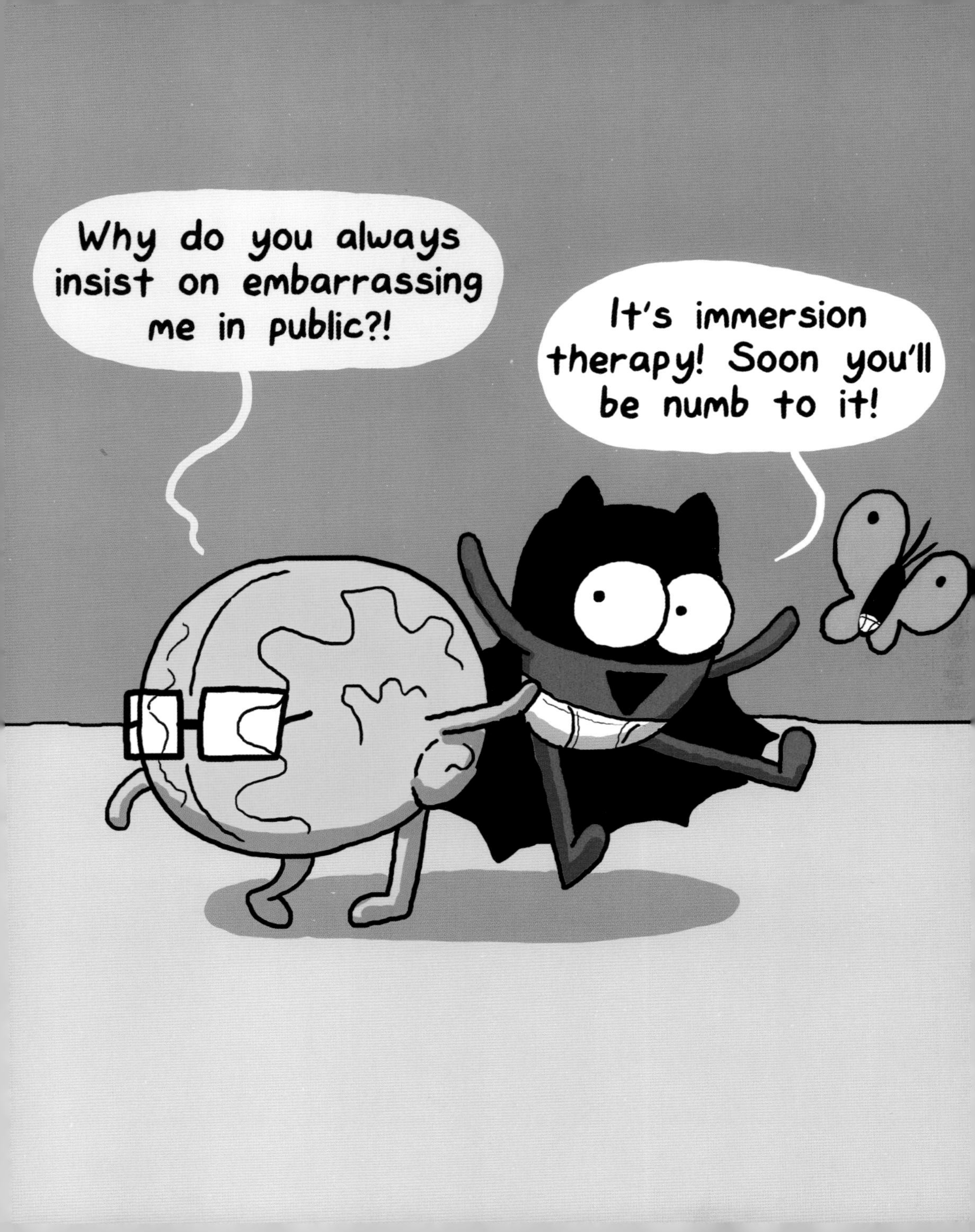
Why do you always insist on embarrassing me in public?!
It's immersion therapy! Soon you'll be numb to it!

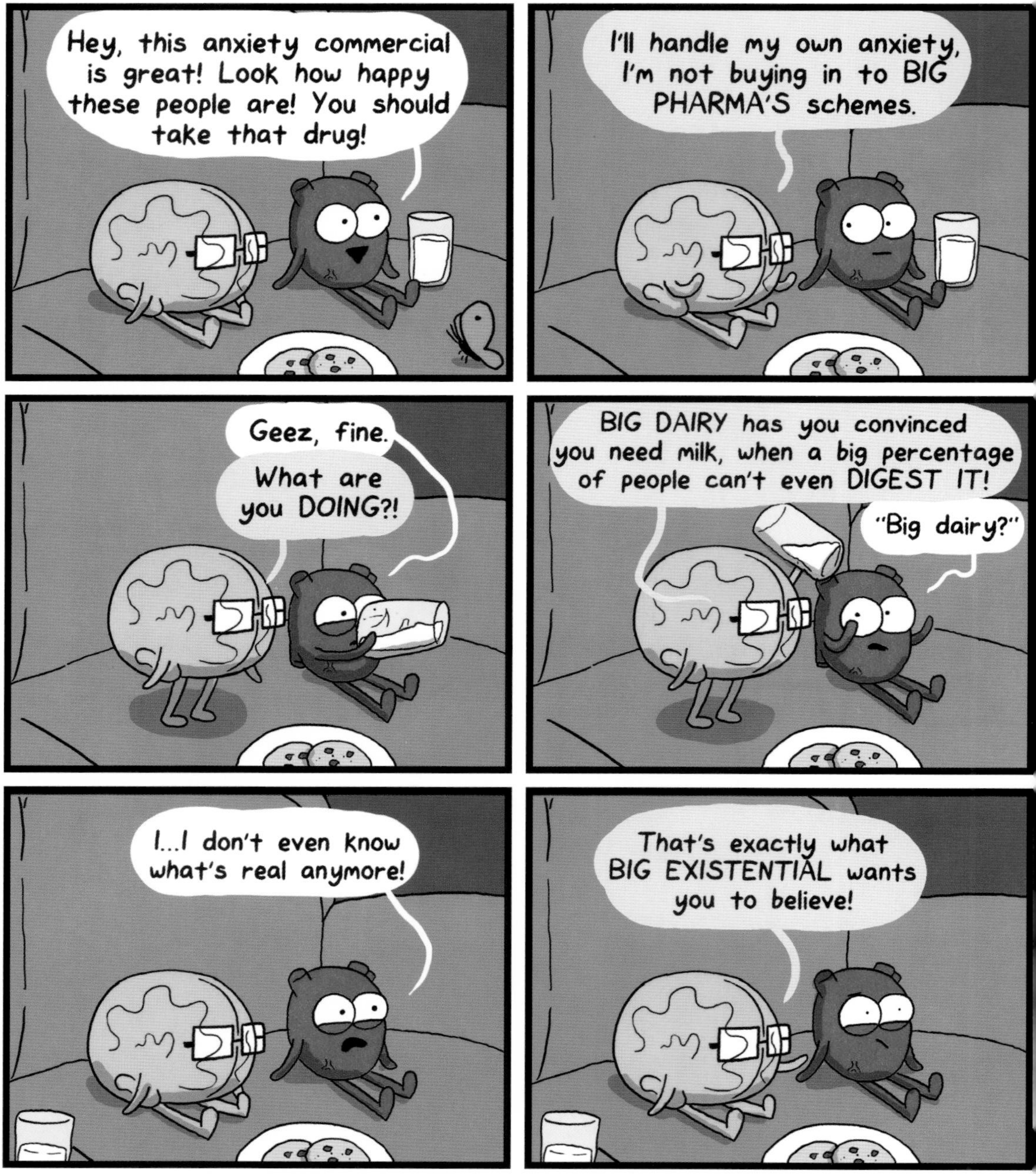
Hey, this anxiety commercial is great! Look how happy these people are! You should take that drug!
I'll handle my own anxiety, I'm not buying in to BIG PHARMA'S schemes.
Geez, fine.
What are you DOING?!
BIG DAIRY has you convinced you need milk, when a big percentage of people can't even DIGEST IT!
"Big dairy?"
I...I don't even know what's real anymore!
That's exactly what BIG EXISTENTIAL wants you to believe!

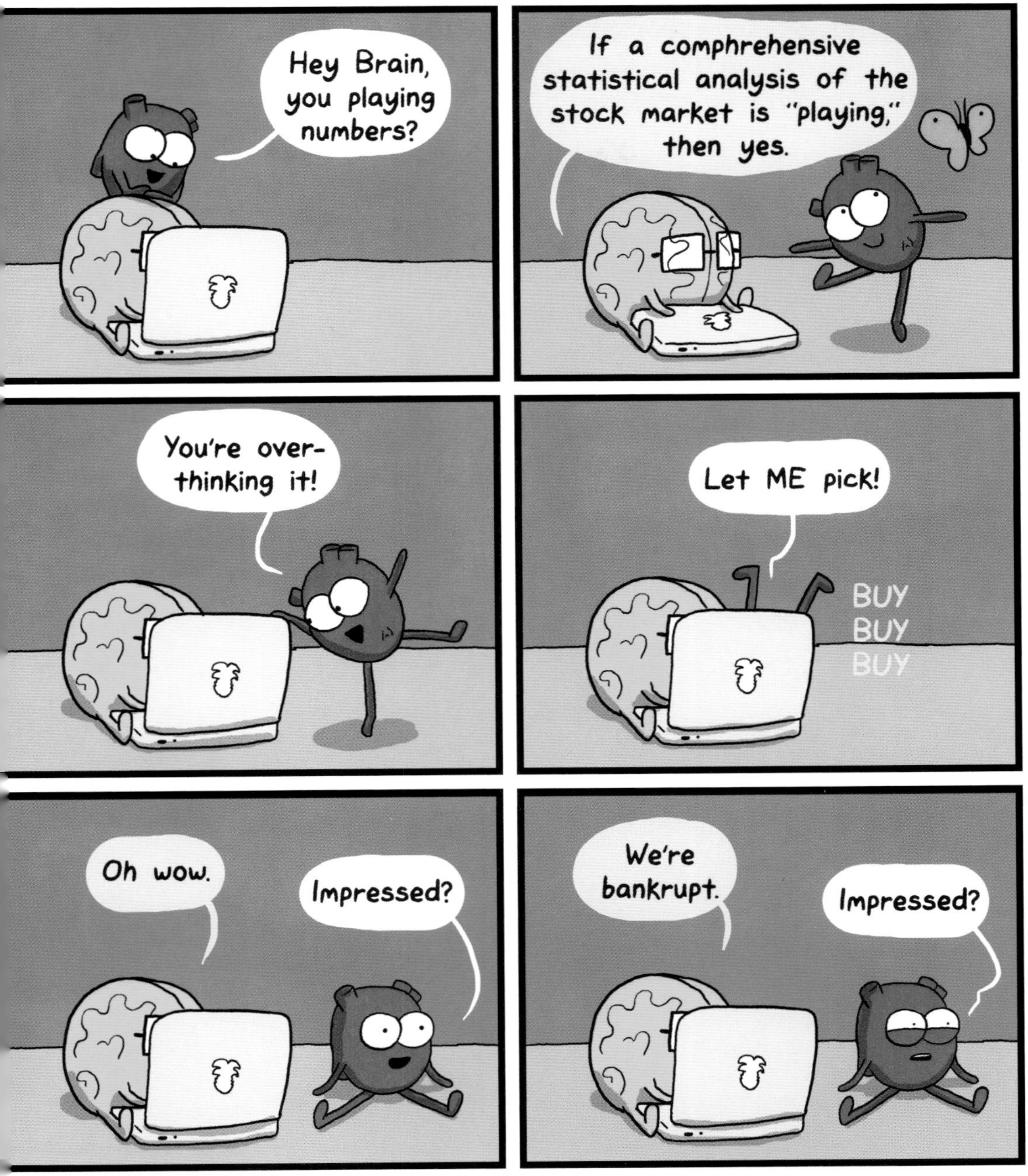
Hey Brain, you playing numbers?
If a comphrehensive statistical analysis of the stock market is "playing," then yes.
You're over-thinking it!
Let ME pick!
BUY
BUY
BUY
Oh wow.
Impressed?
We're bankrupt.
Impressed?

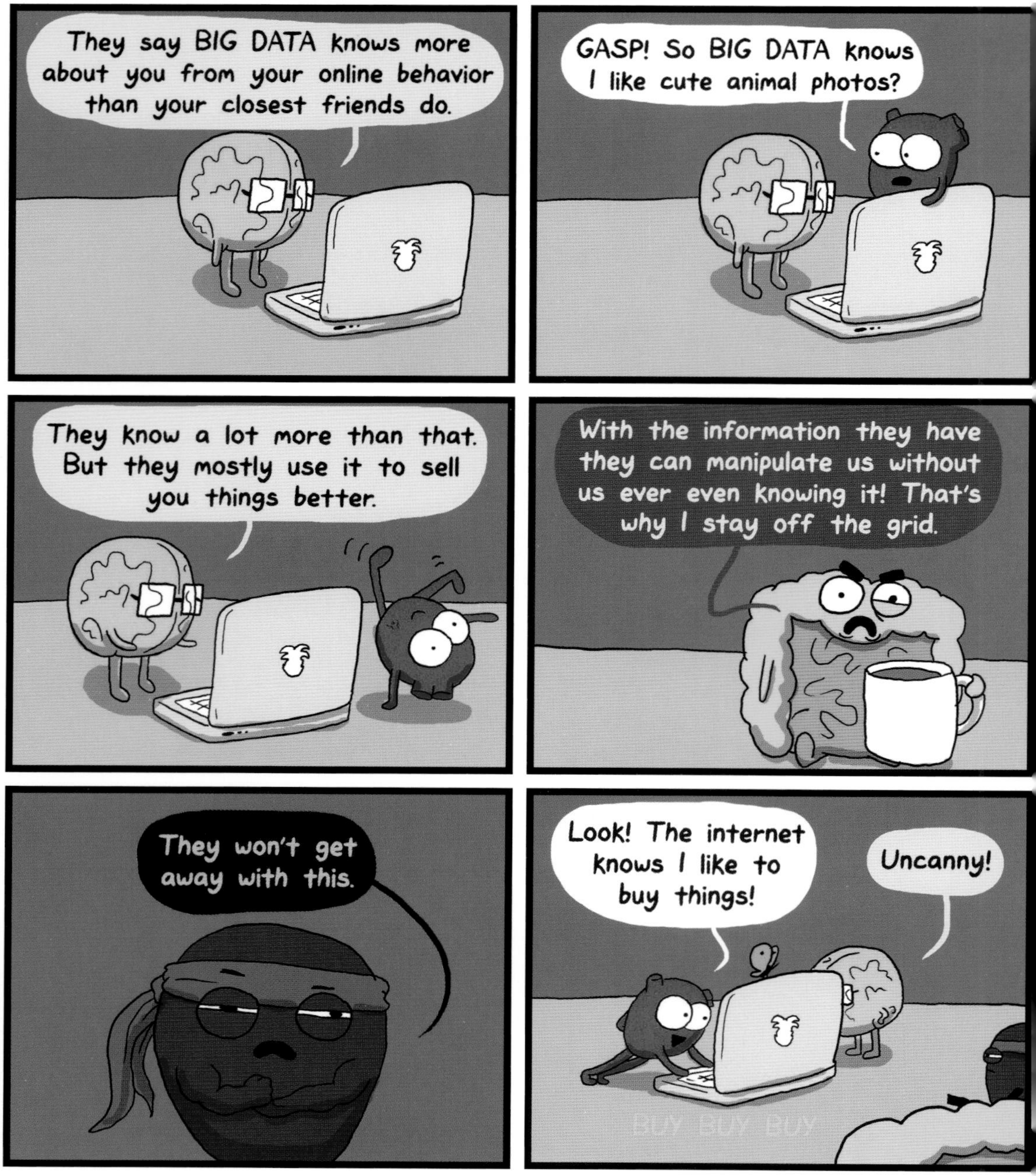
They say BIG DATA knows more about you from your online behavior than your closest friends do.
GASP! So BIG DATA knows I like cute animal photos?
They know a lot more than that. But they mostly use it to sell you things better.
With the information they have they can manipulate us without us ever even knowing it! That's why I stay off the grid.
They won't get away with this.
Look! The internet knows I like to buy things!
Uncanny!
BUY BUY BUY

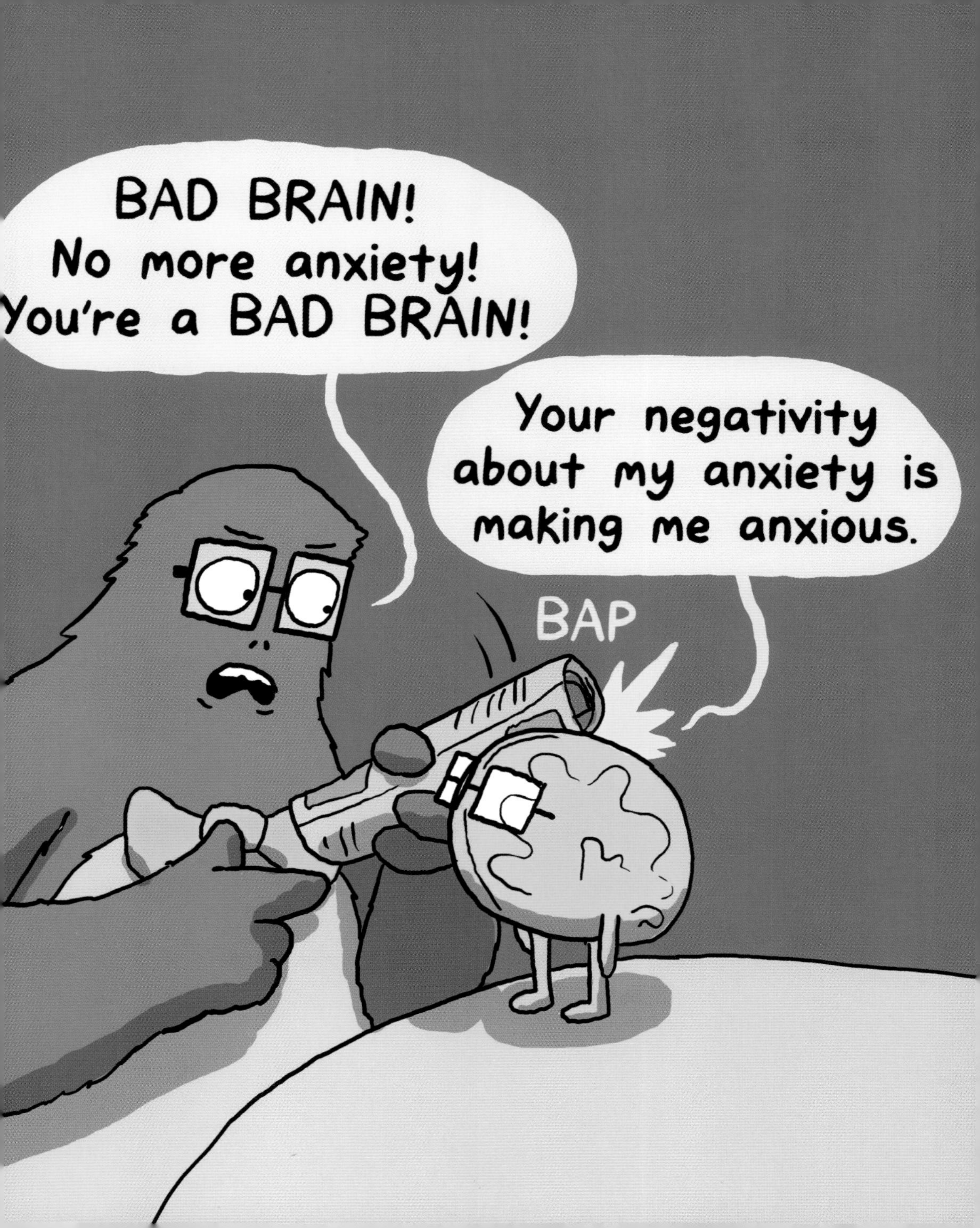
BAD BRAIN! No more anxiety! You're a BAD BRAIN!
Your negativity about my anxiety is making me anxious.
BAP

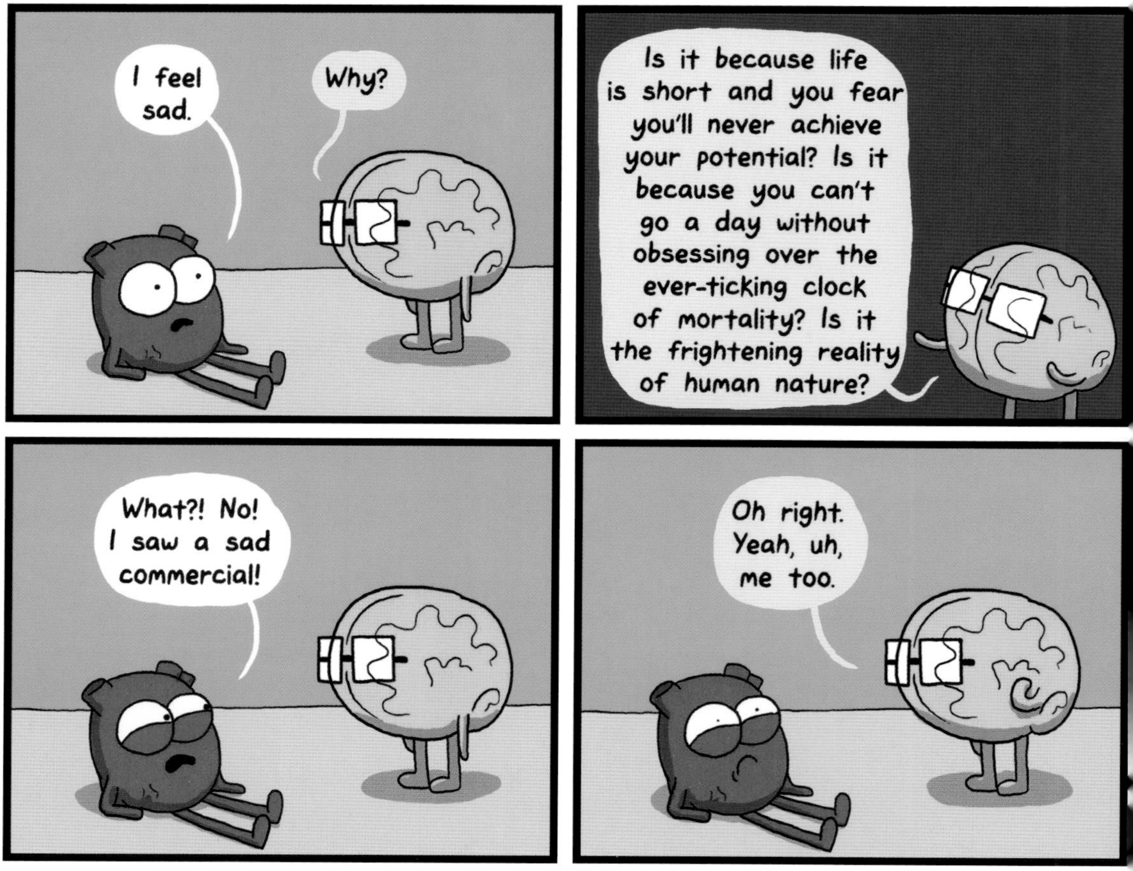
I feel sad.
Why?
Is it because life is short and you fear you'll never achieve your potential? Is it because you can't go a day without obsessing over the ever-ticking clock of mortality? Is it the frightening reality of human nature?
What?! No! I saw a sad commercial!
Oh right. Yeah, uh, me too.

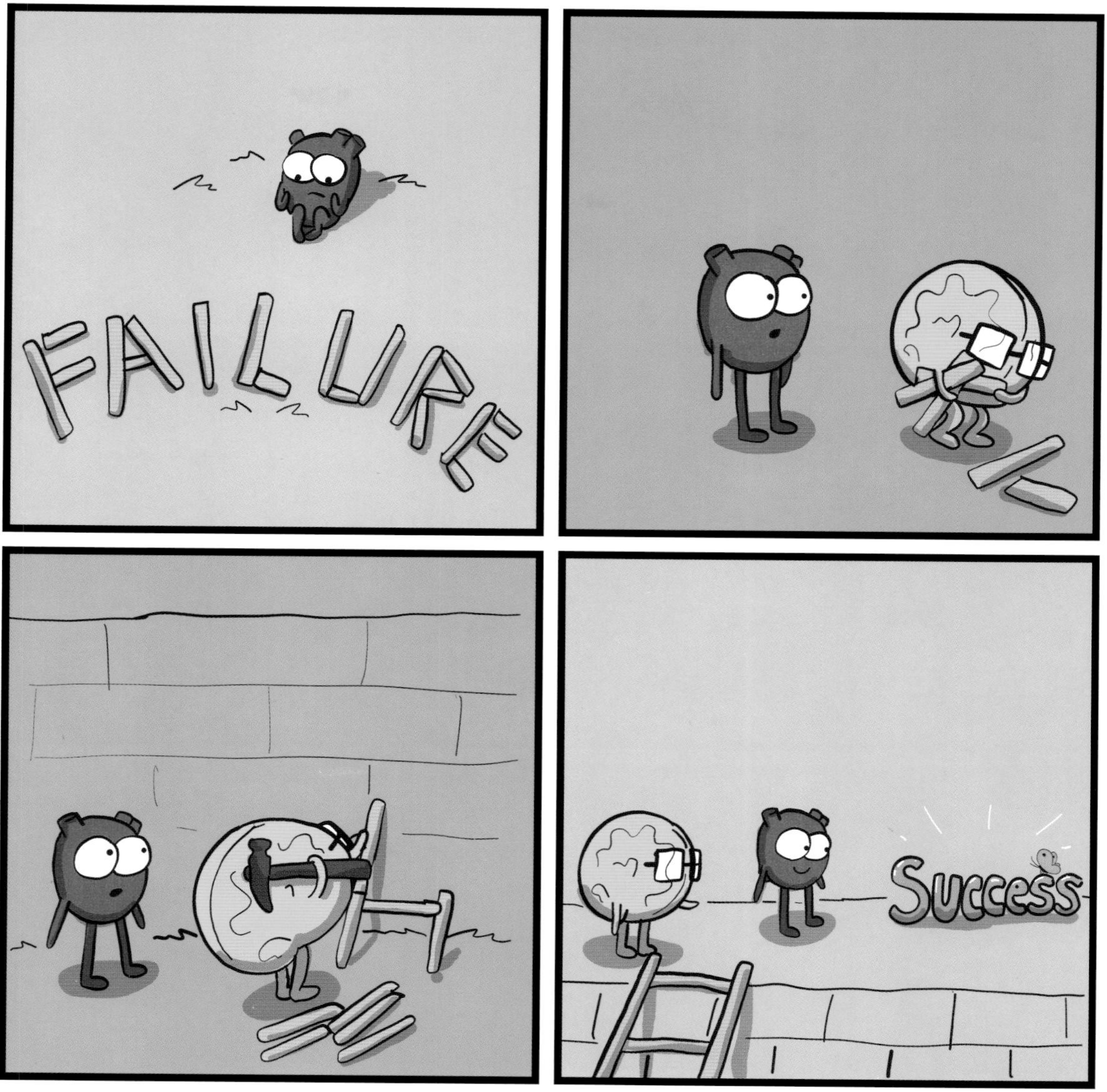
FAILURE
SUCCESS

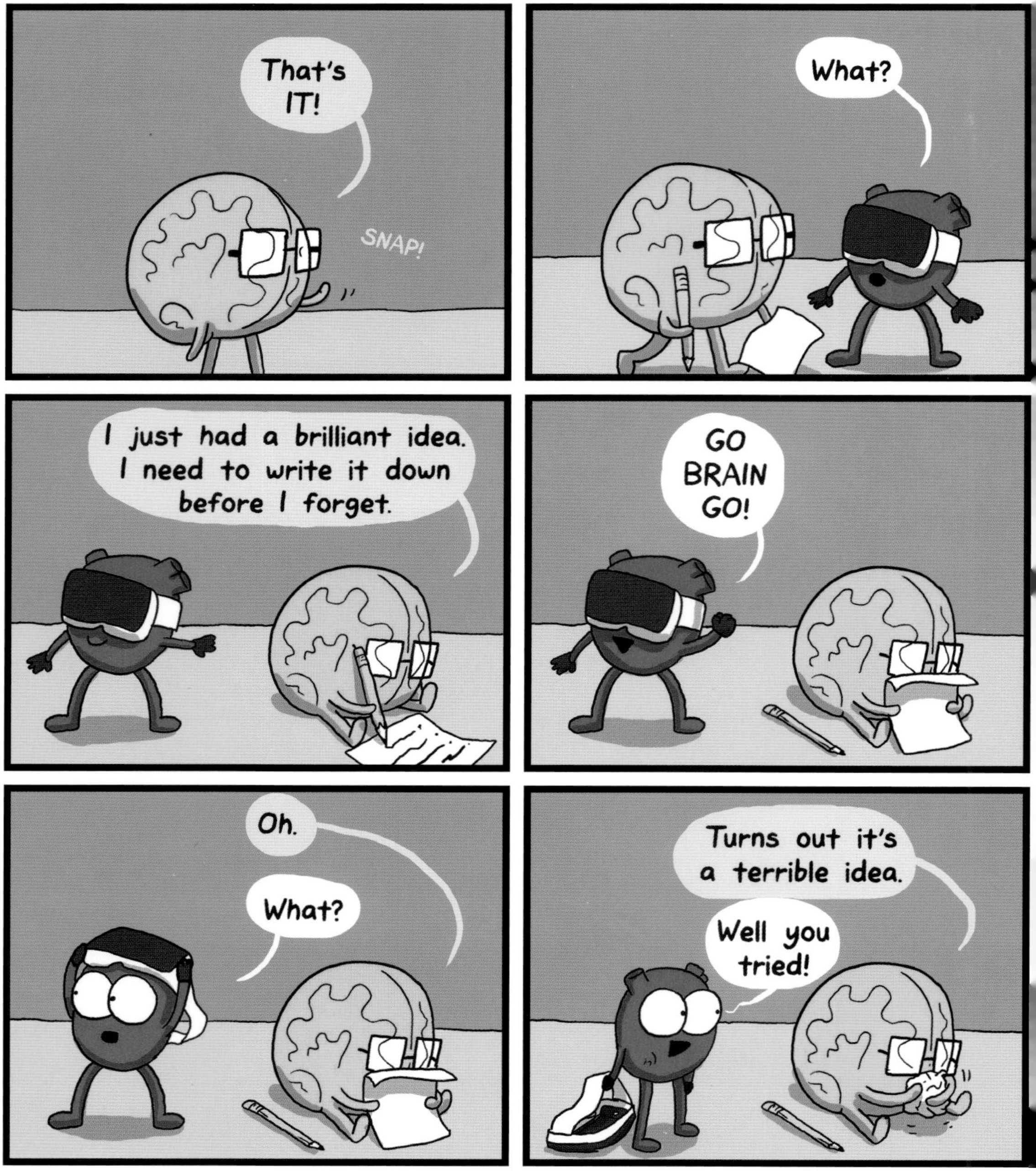
That's IT!
SNAP!
What?
I just had a brilliant idea. I need to write it down before I forget.
GO BRAIN GO!
Oh.
What?
Turns out it's a terrible idea.
Well you tried!

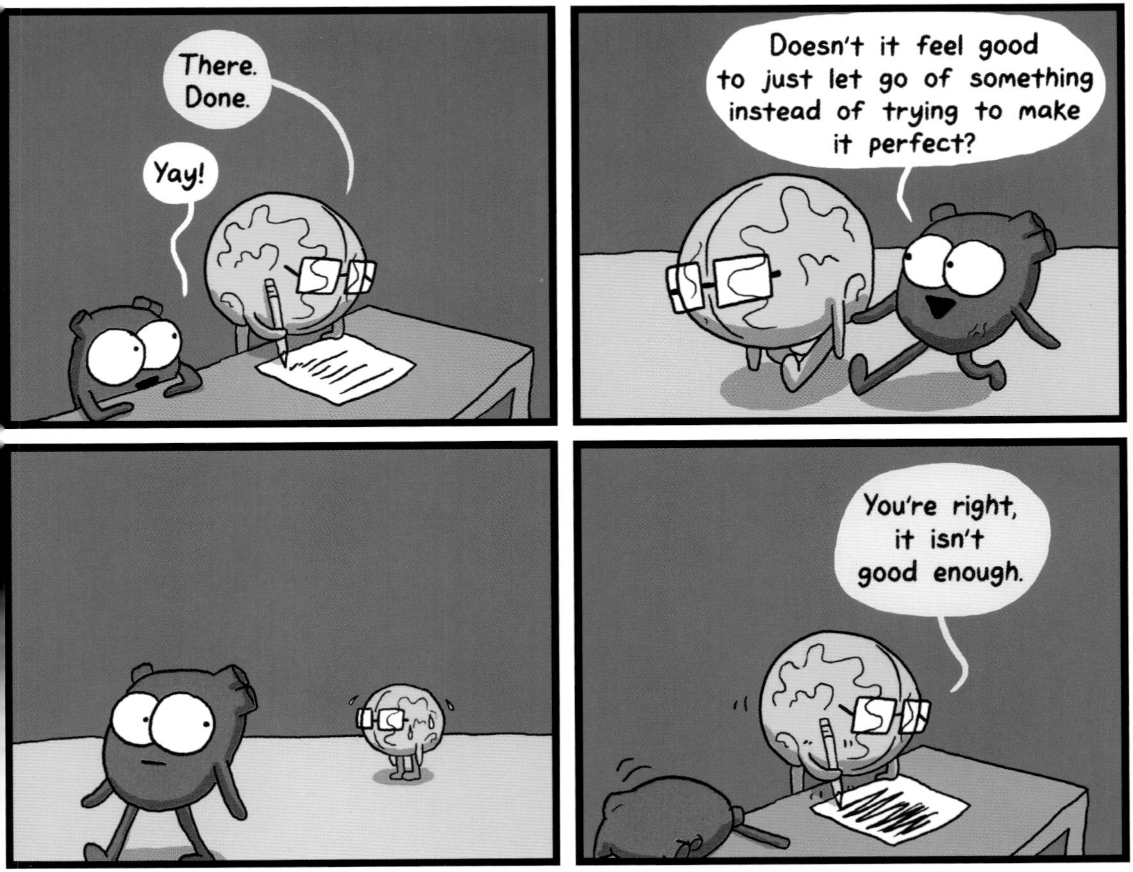
There. Done.
Yay!
Doesn't it feel good to just let go of something instead of trying to make it perfect?
You're right, it isn't good enough.

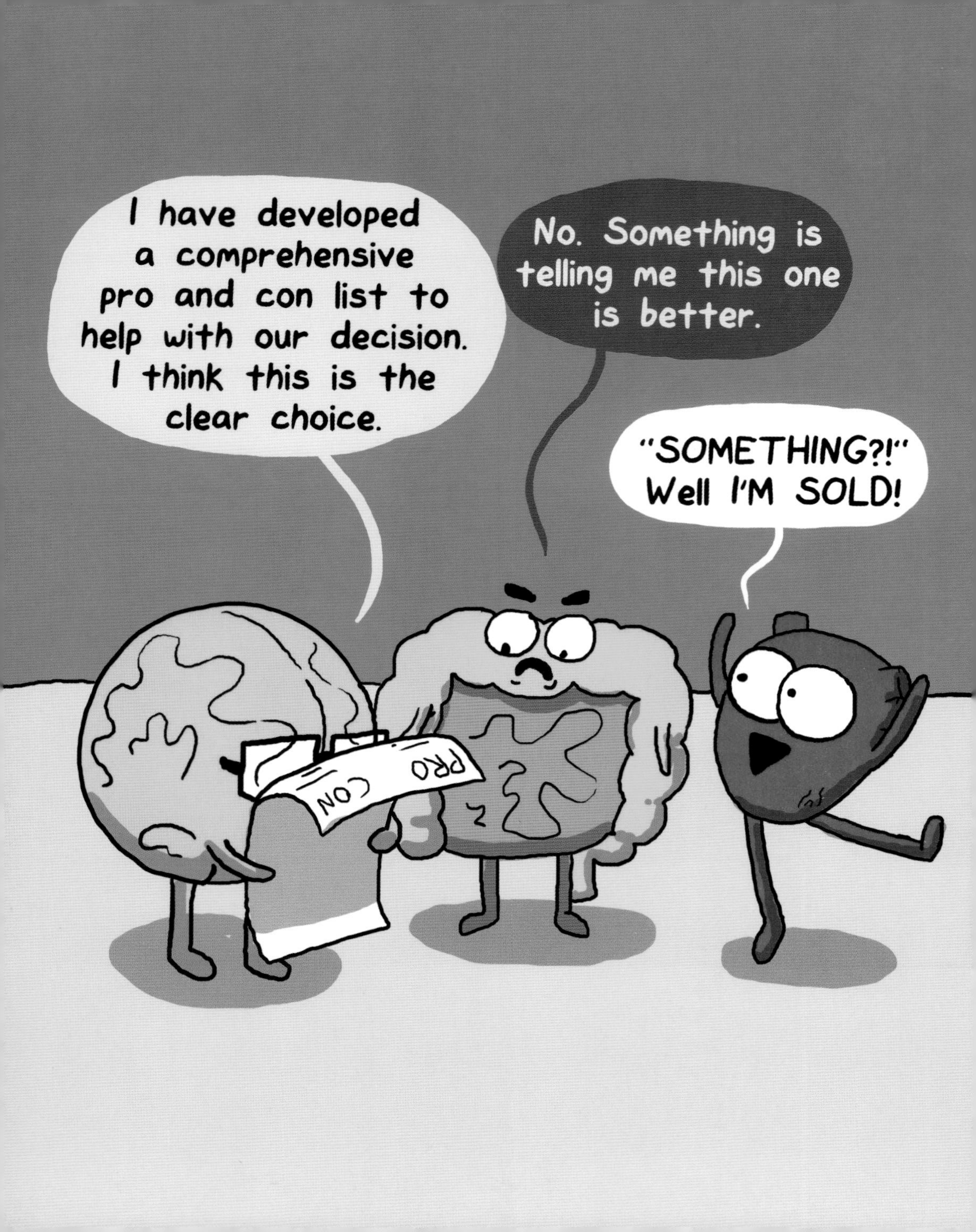
I have developed a comprehensive pro and con list to help with our decision. I think this is the clear choice.
No. Something is telling me this one is better.
"SOMETHING?!" Well I'M SOLD!
PRO
CON

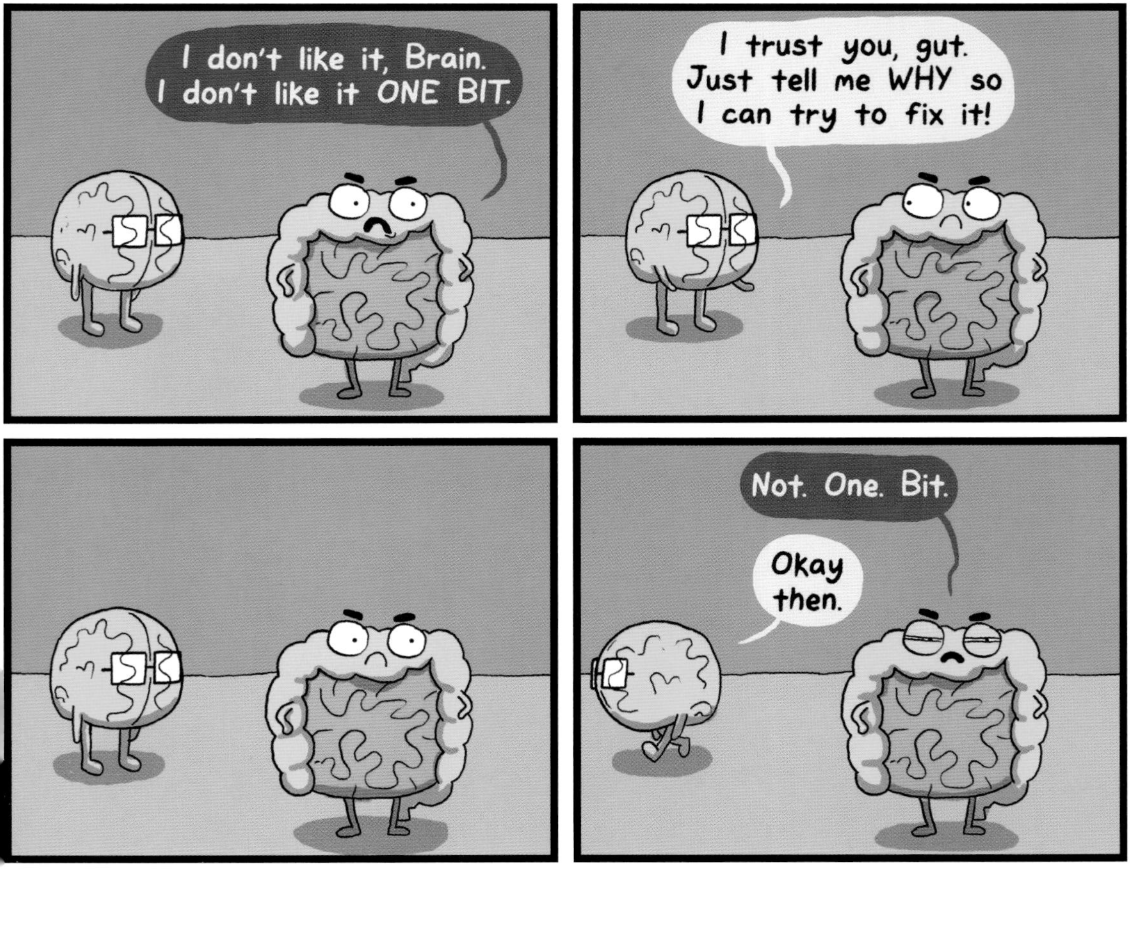
I don't like it, Brain. I don't like it ONE BIT.
I trust you, gut. Just tell me WHY so I can try to fix it!
Not. One. Bit.
Okay then.

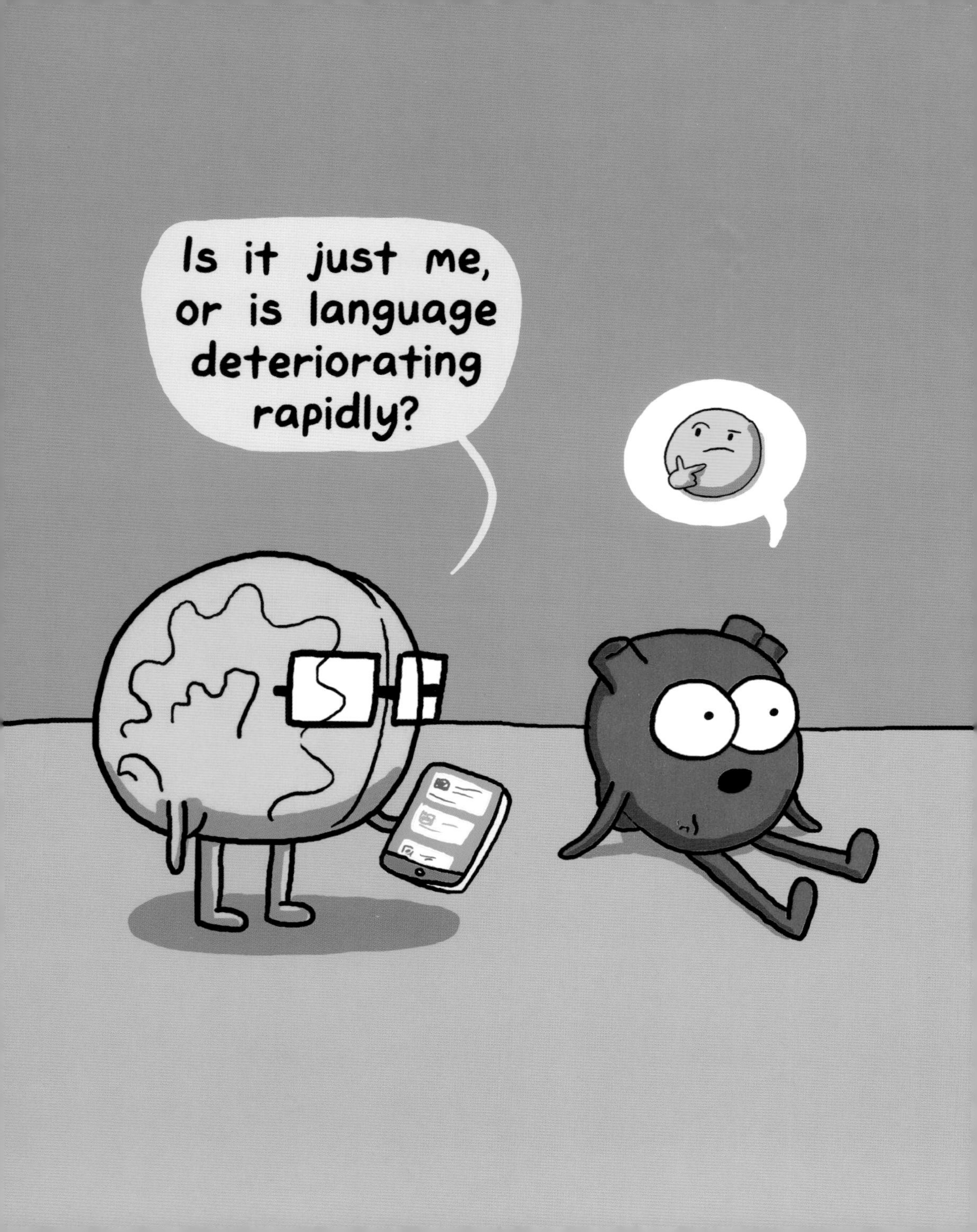
Is it just me, or is language deteriorating rapidly?

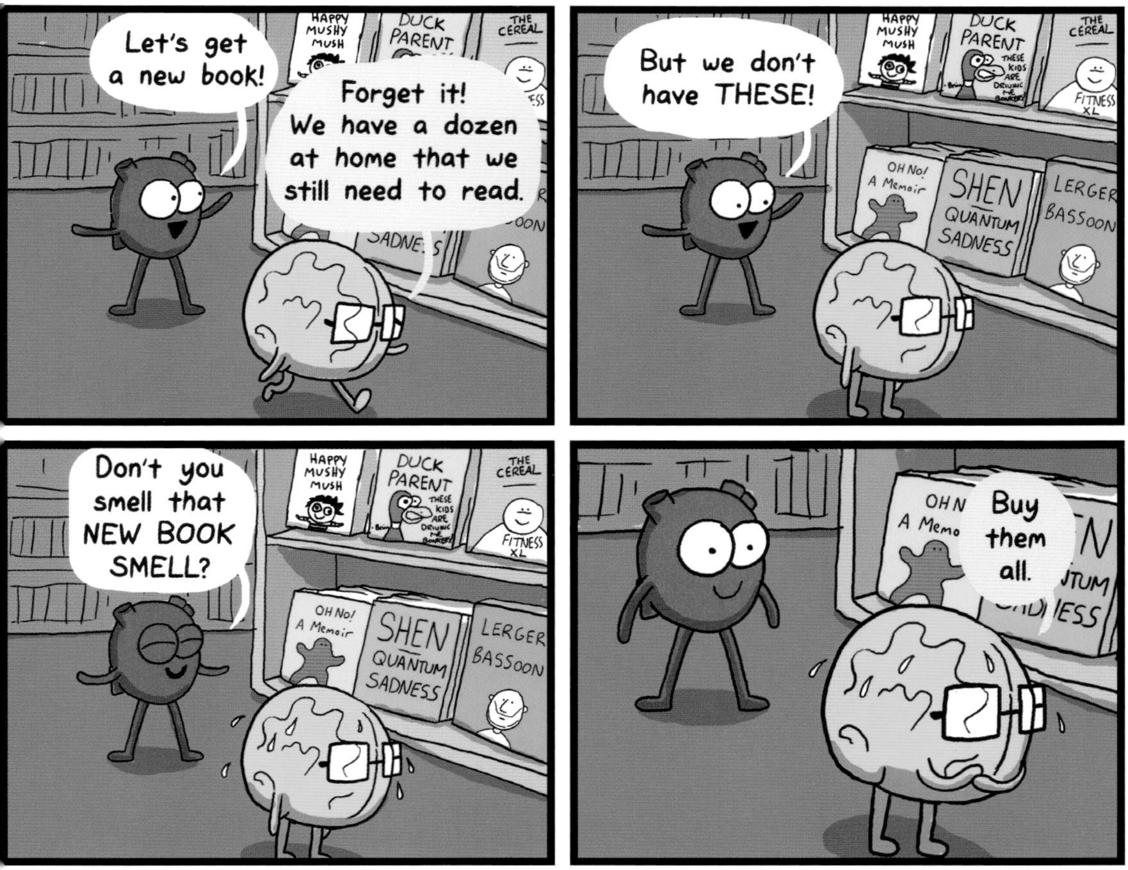

Let's get a new book!
Forget it! We have a dozen at home that we still need to read.
HAPPY MUSHY MUSH
DUCK PARENT
THE CEREAL
But we don't have THESE!
THESE KIDS ARE DRIVING ME BONKERS!
FITNESS XL
OH No! A Memoir
SHEN QUANTUM SADNESS
LERGER BASSOON
Don't you smell that NEW BOOK SMELL?
Buy them all.

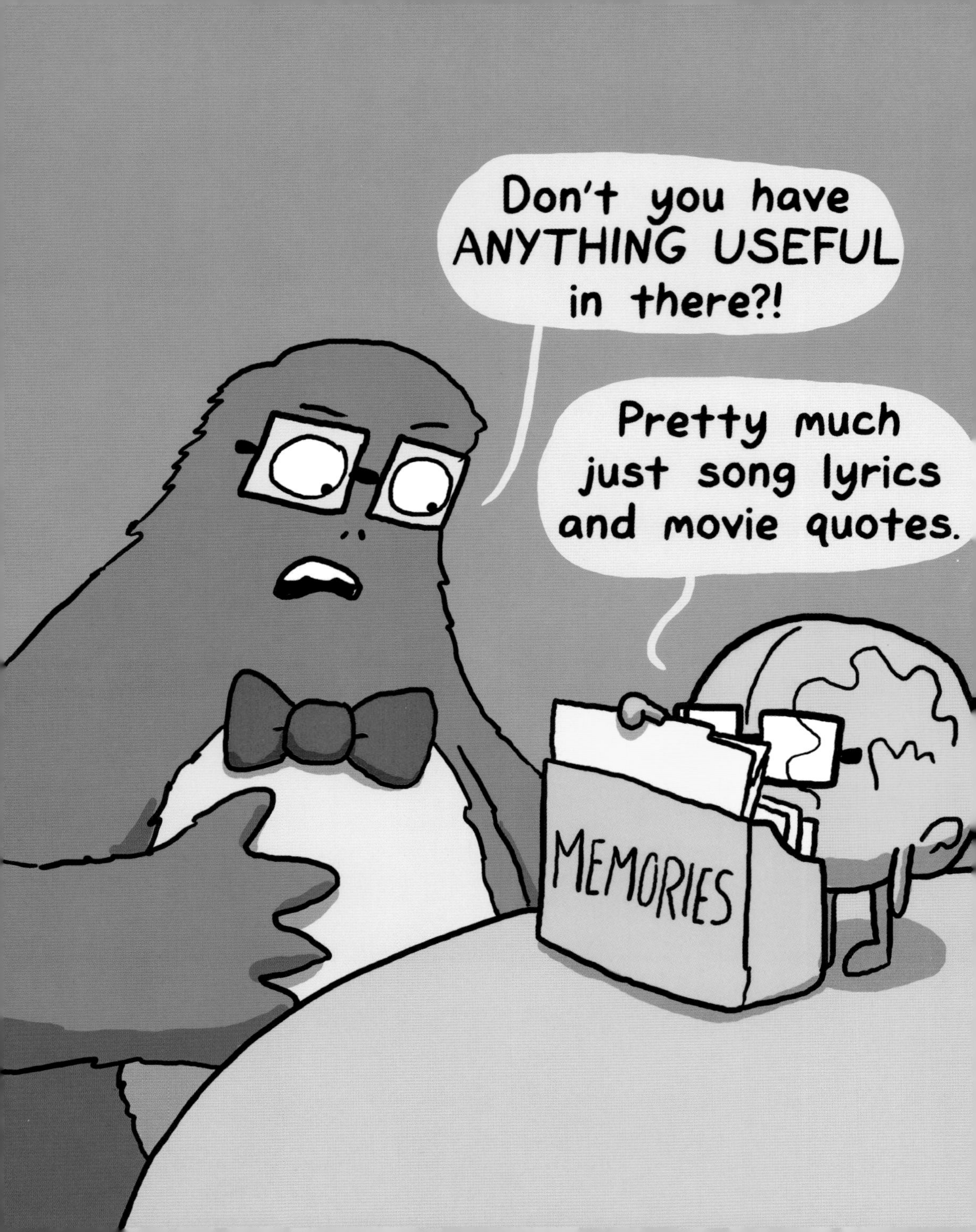
Don't you have ANYTHING USEFUL in there?!
Pretty much just song lyrics and movie quotes.
MEMORIES

New Experiences
NEW IDEAS

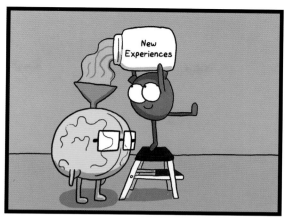

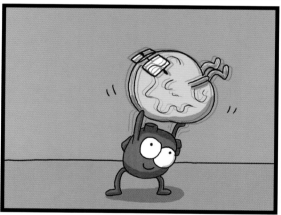

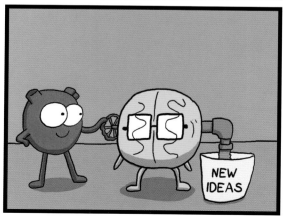

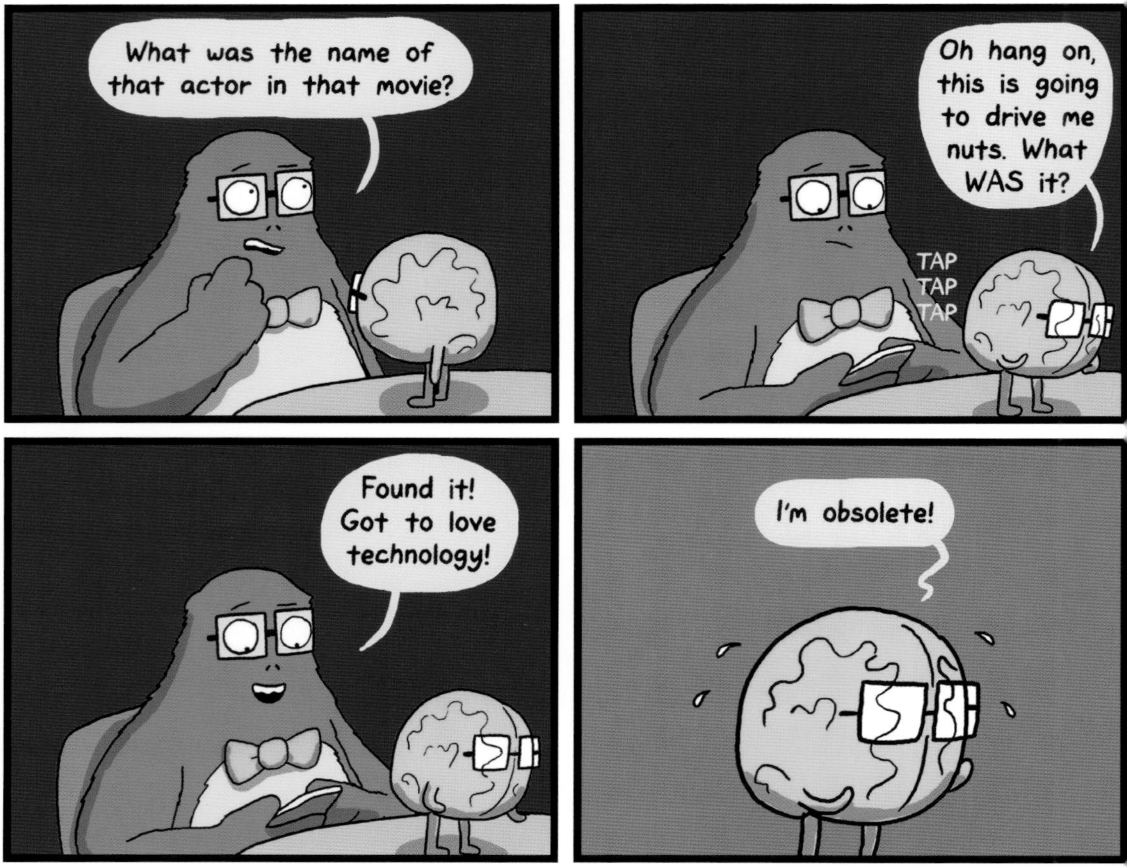
What was the name of that actor in that movie?
Oh hang on, this is going to drive me nuts. What WAS it?
TAP TAP TAP
Found it! Got to love technology!
I'm obsolete!

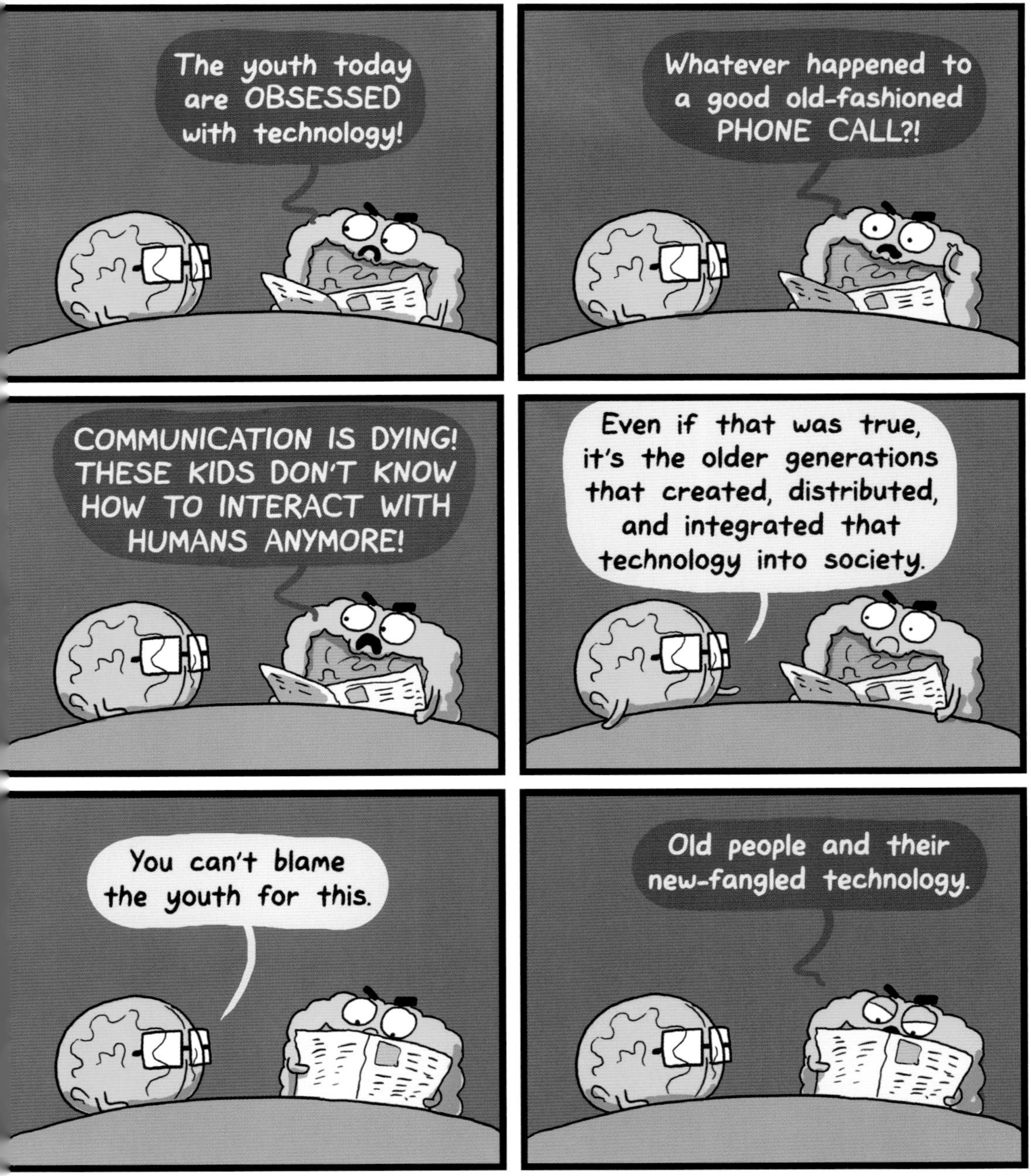
The youth today are OBSESSED with technology!
Whatever happened to a good old-fashioned PHONE CALL?!
COMMUNICATION IS DYING! THESE KIDS DON'T KNOW HOW TO INTERACT WITH HUMANS ANYMORE!
Even if that was true, it's the older generations that created, distributed, and integrated that technology into society.
You can't blame the youth for this.
Old people and their new-fangled technology.

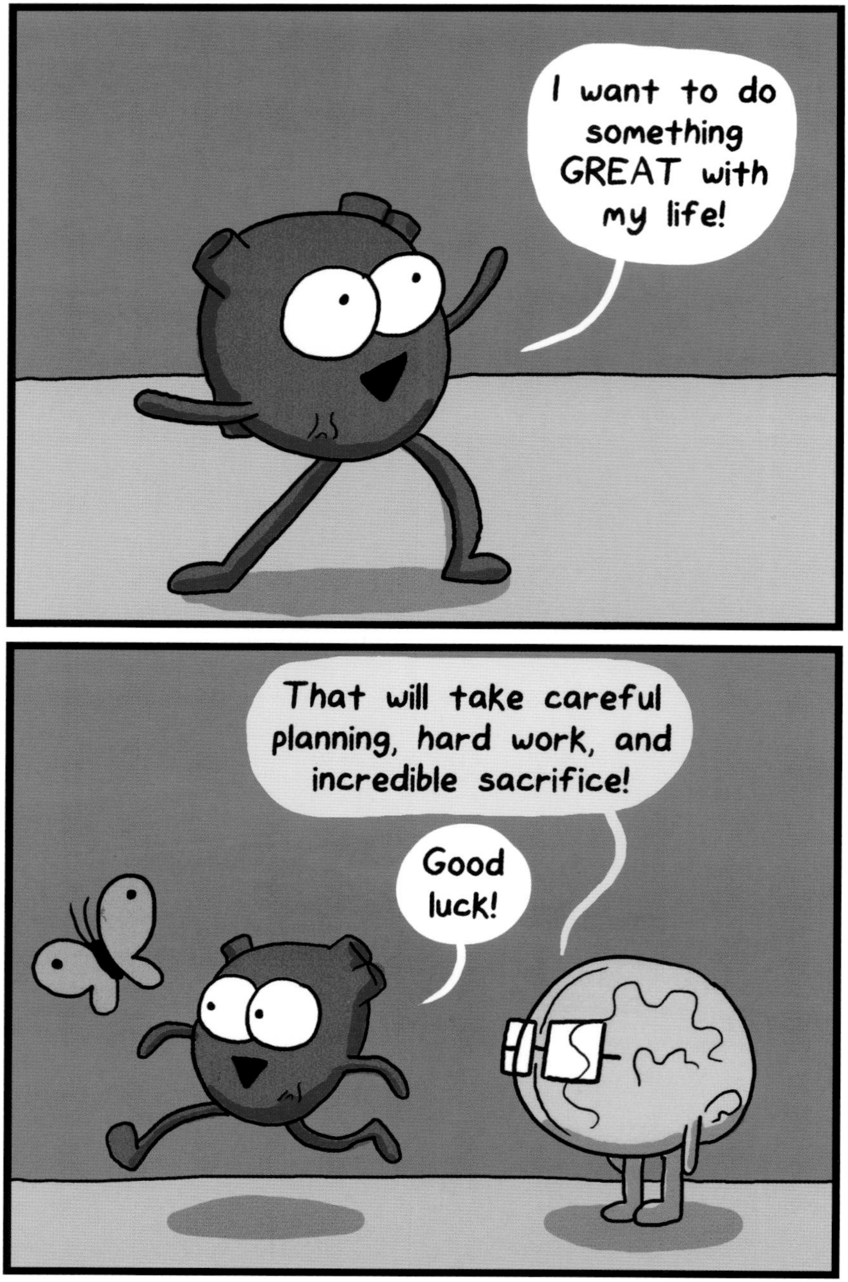
I want to do something GREAT with my life!
That will take careful planning, hard work, and incredible sacrifice!
Good luck!

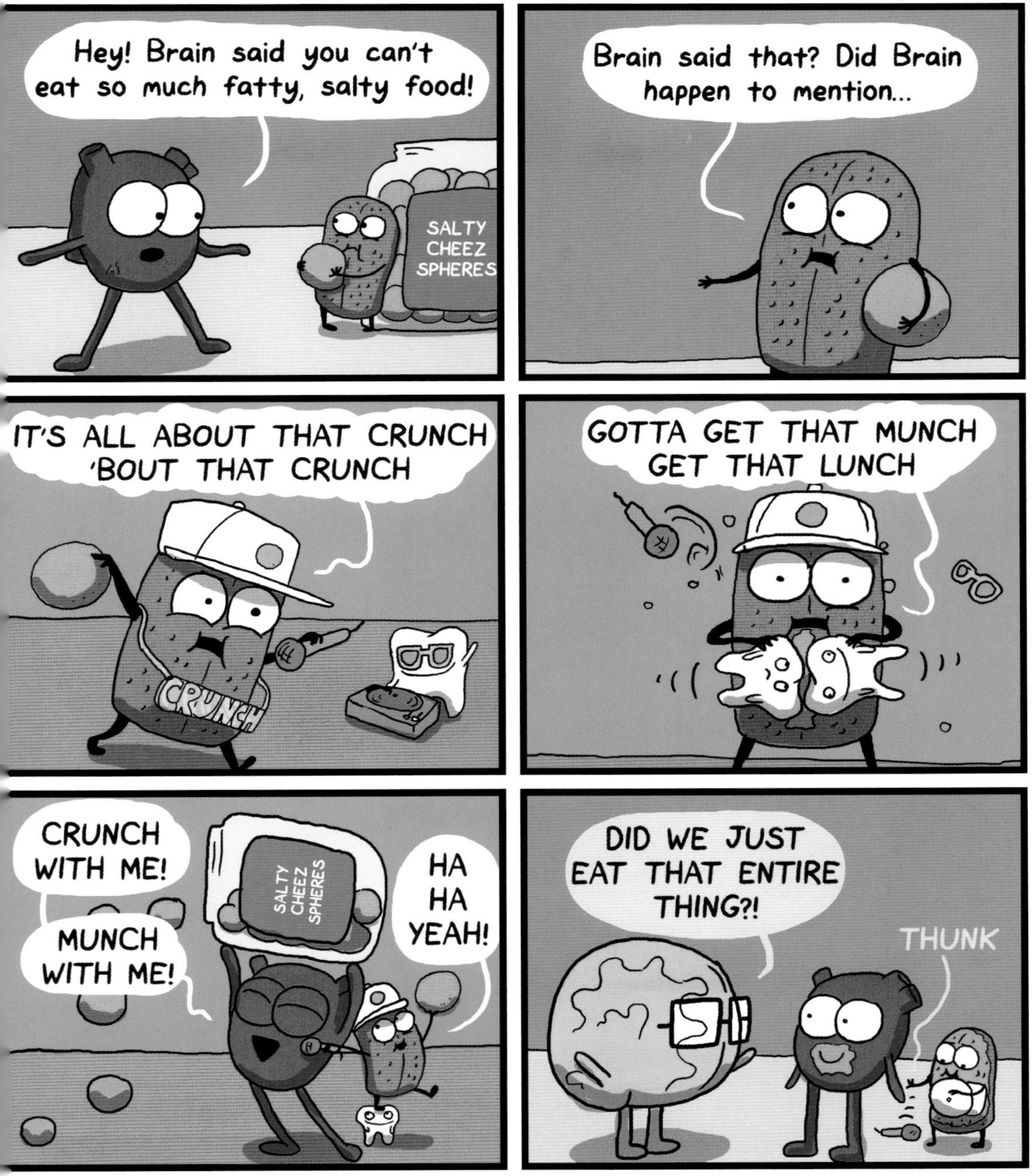
Hey! Brain said you can't eat so much fatty, salty food!
SALTY CHEEZ SPHERES
Brain said that? Did Brain happen to mention...
IT'S ALL ABOUT THAT CRUNCH 'BOUT THAT CRUNCH
CRUNCH
GOTTA GET THAT MUNCH GET THAT LUNCH
CRUNCH WITH ME!
MUNCH WITH ME!
SALTY CHEEZ SPHERES
HA HA YEAH!
DID WE JUST EAT THAT ENTIRE THING?!
THUNK

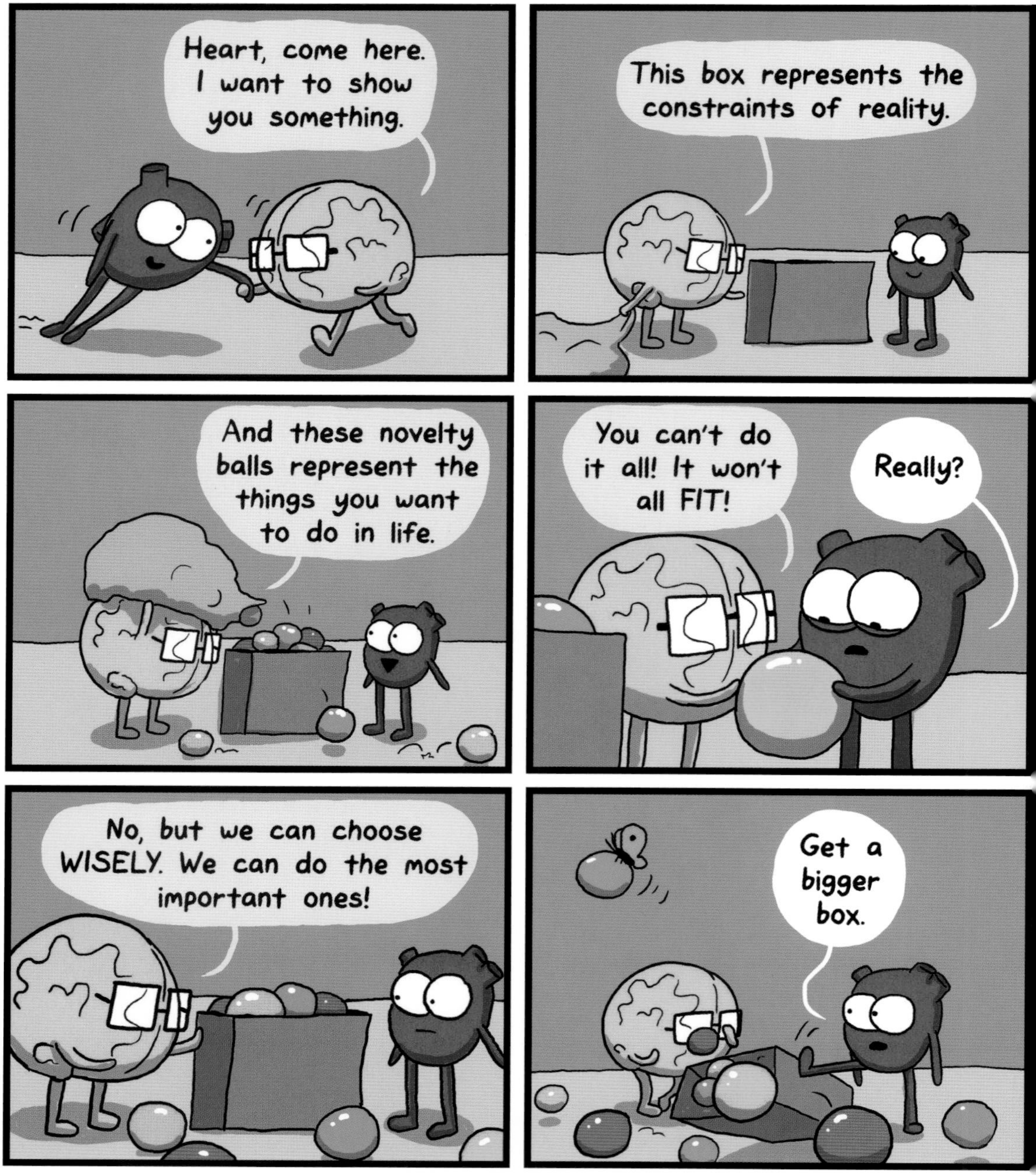

Heart, come here. I want to show you something.
This box represents the constraints of reality.
And these novelty balls represent the things you want to do in life.
You can't do it all! It won't all FIT!
Really?
No, but we can choose WISELY. We can do the most important ones!
Get a bigger box.

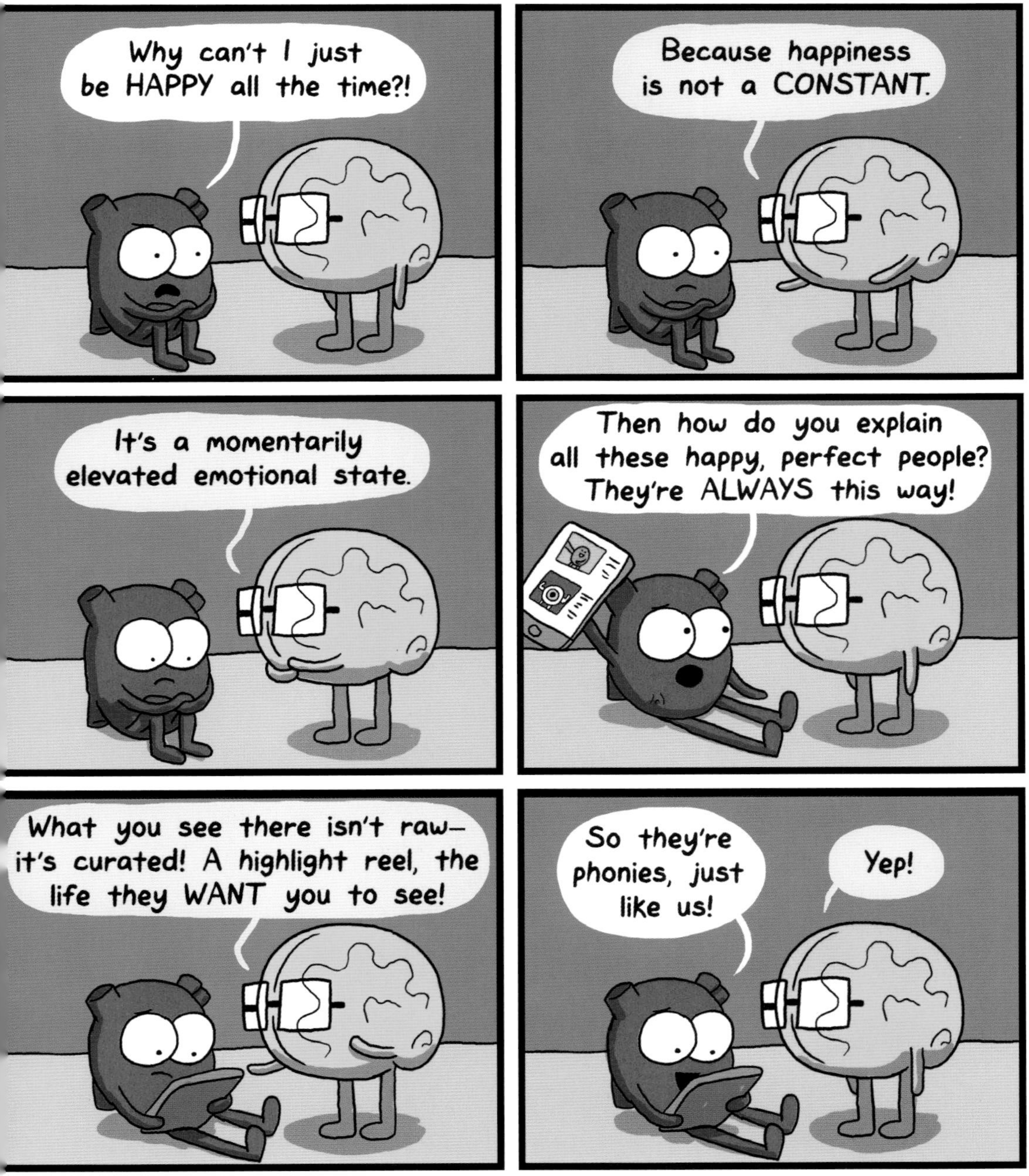
Why can't I just be HAPPY all the time?!
Because happiness is not a CONSTANT.
It's a momentarily elevated emotional state.
Then how do you explain all these happy, perfect people? They're ALWAYS this way!
What you see there isn't raw— it's curated! A highlight reel, the life they WANT you to see!
So they're phonies, just like us!
Yep!

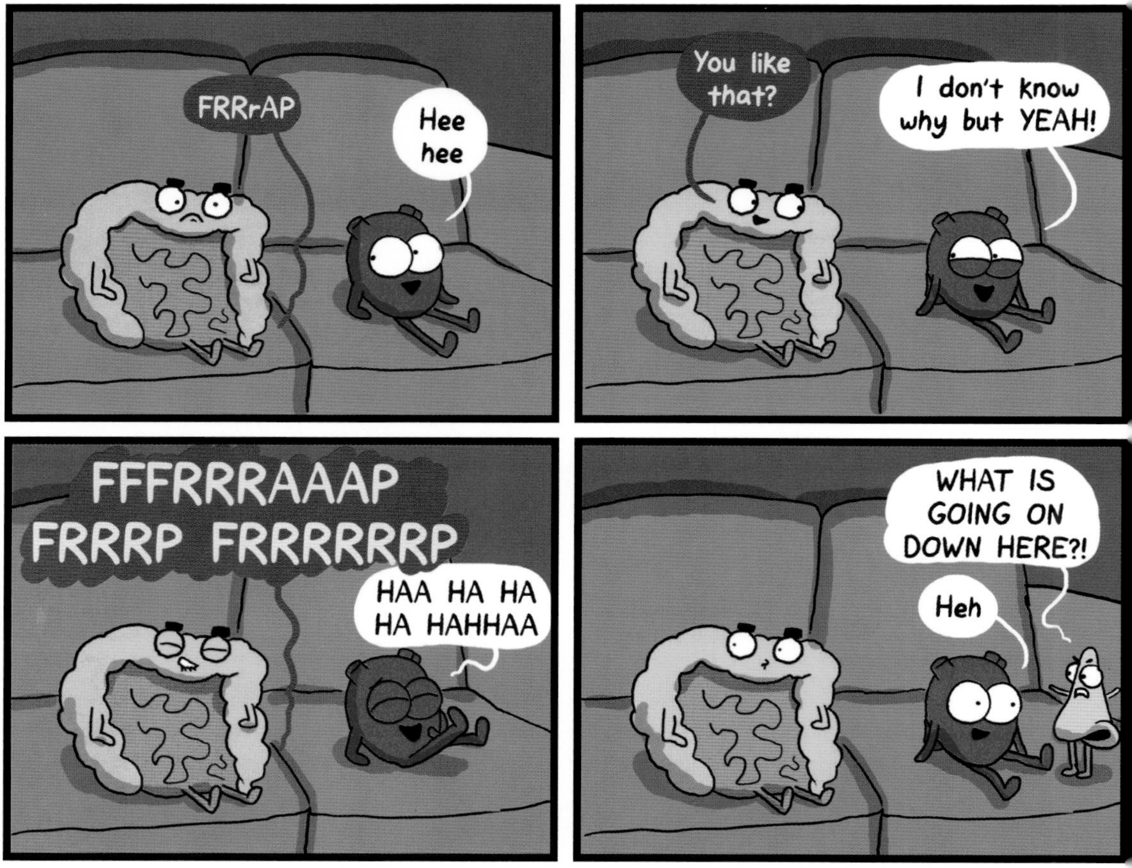
FRRrAP
Hee hee
You like that?
I don't know why but YEAH!
FFFRRRAAAP FRRRP FRRRRRRP
HAA HA HA HA HAHHAA
WHAT IS GOING ON DOWN HERE?!
Heh

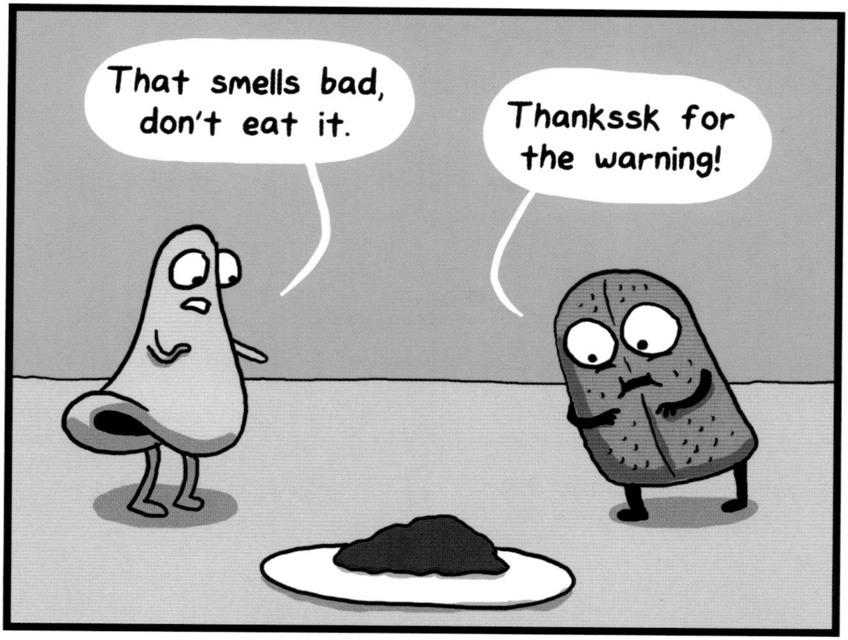
That smells bad, don't eat it.
Thankssk for the warning!

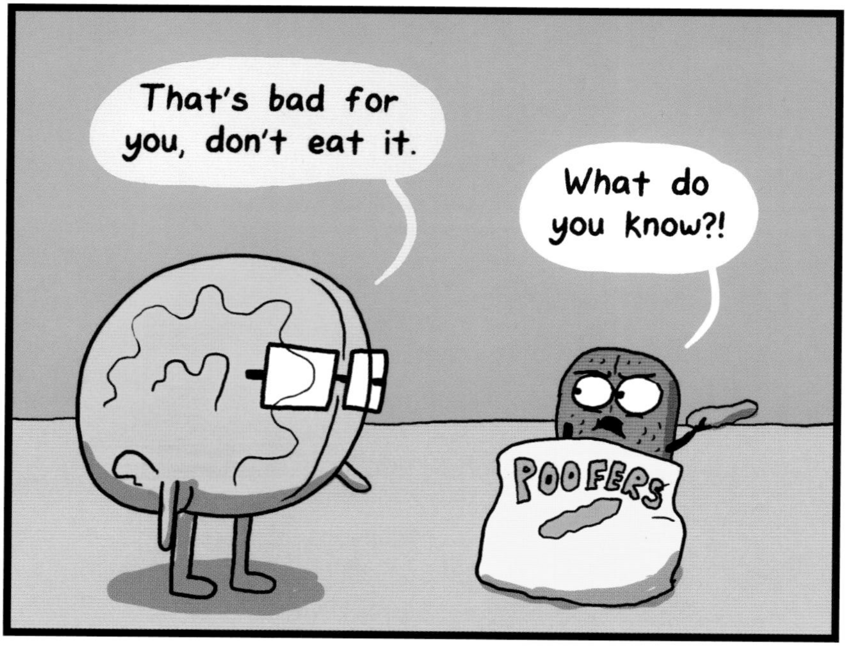
That's bad for you, don't eat it.
What do you know?!
POOFERS

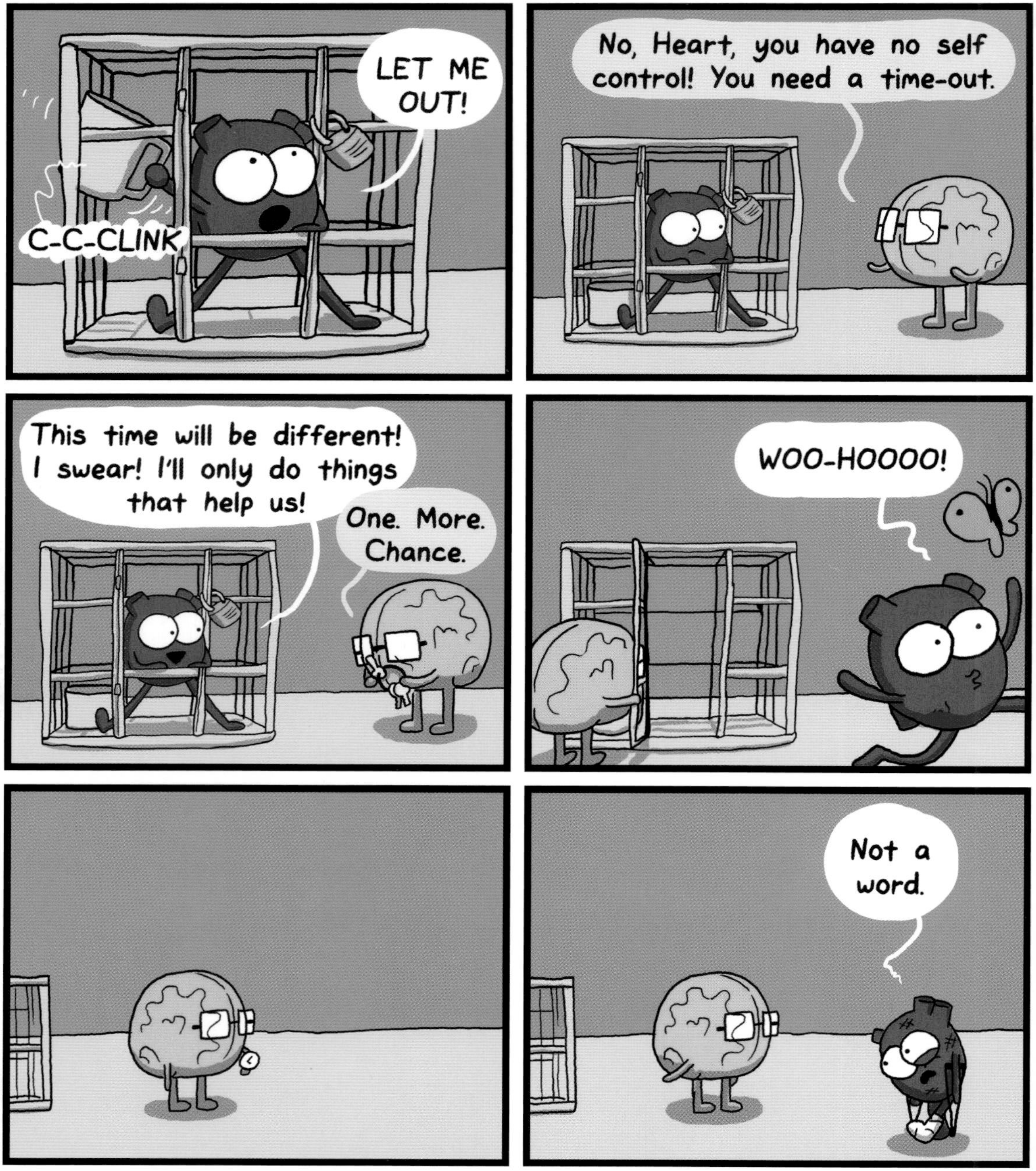
LET ME OUT!
C-C-CLINK
No, Heart, you have no self control! You need a time-out.
This time will be different! I swear! I'll only do things that help us!
One. More. Chance.
WOO-HOOOO!
Not a word.

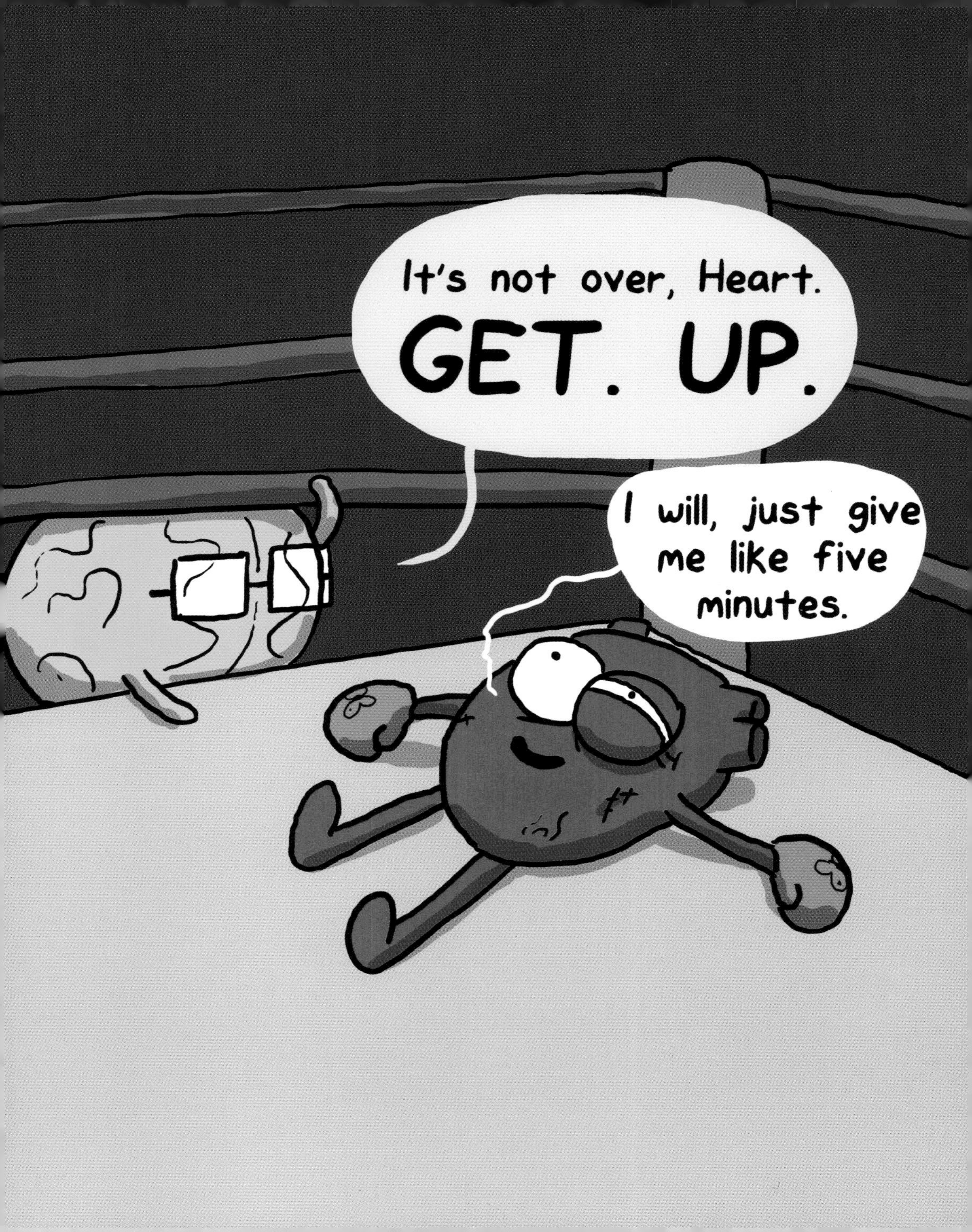
It's not over, Heart.
GET. UP.
I will, just give me like five minutes.

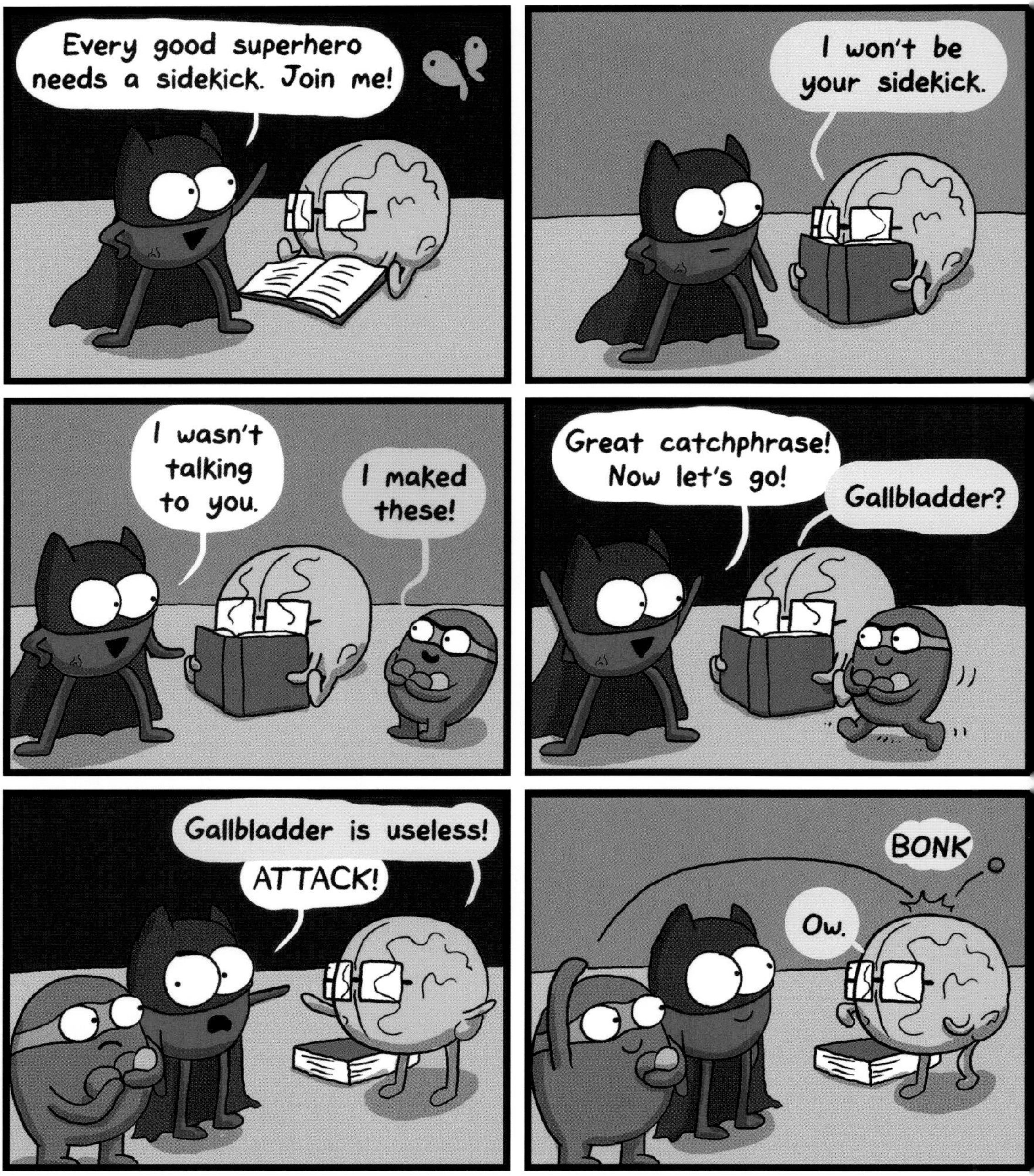
Every good superhero needs a sidekick. Join me!
I won't be your sidekick.
I wasn't talking to you.
I maked these!
Great catchphrase! Now let's go!
Gallbladder?
Gallbladder is useless!
ATTACK!
BONK
Ow.

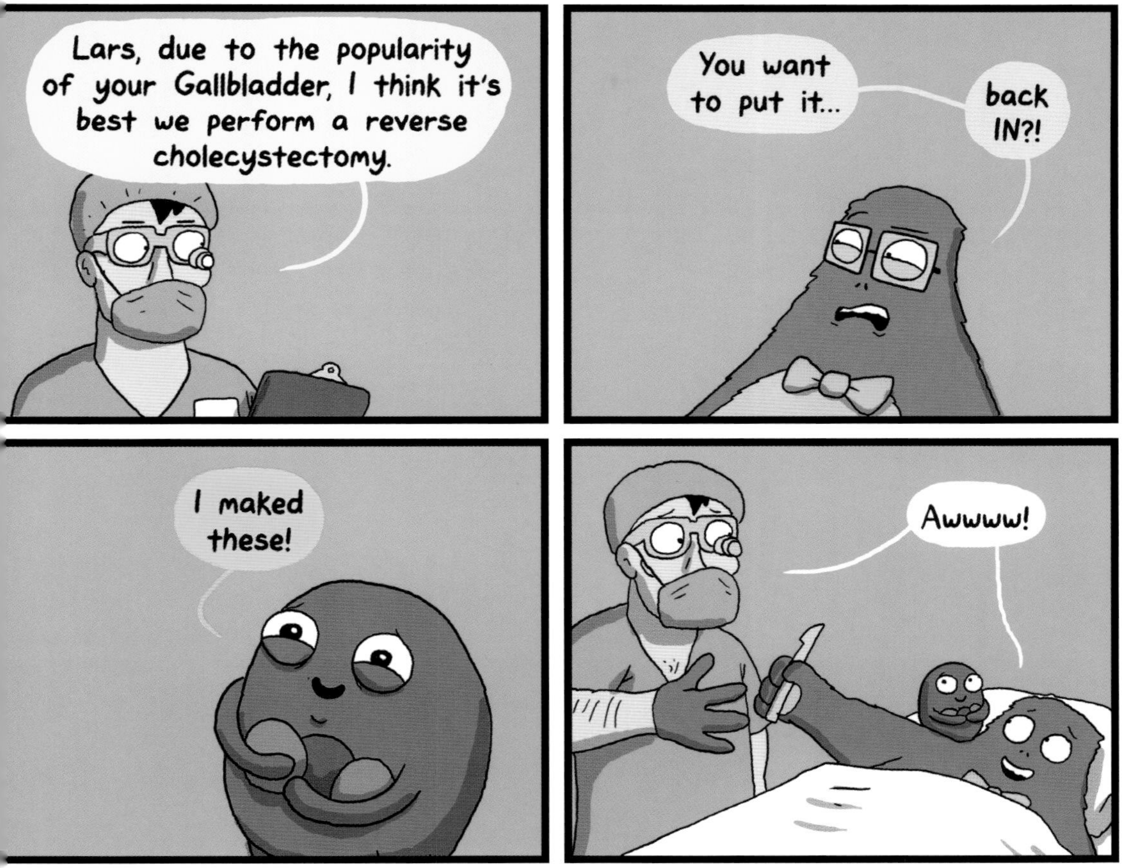
Lars, due to the popularity of your Gallbladder, I think it's best we perform a reverse cholecystectomy.
You want to put it...
back IN?!
I maked these!
Awwww!

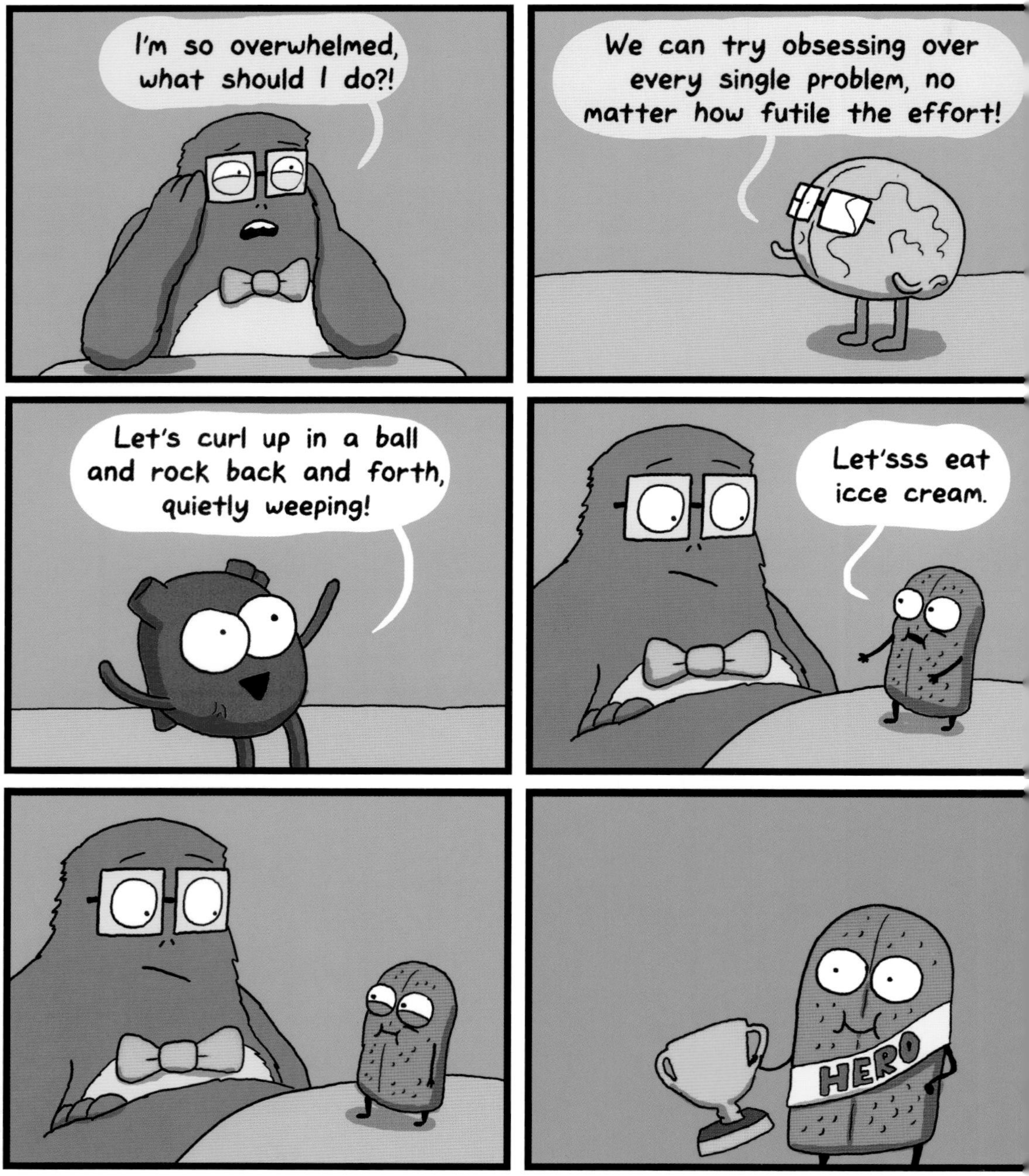
I'm so overwhelmed, what should I do?!
We can try obsessing over every single problem, no matter how futile the effort!
Let's curl up in a ball and rock back and forth, quietly weeping!
Let'sss eat icce cream.
HERO

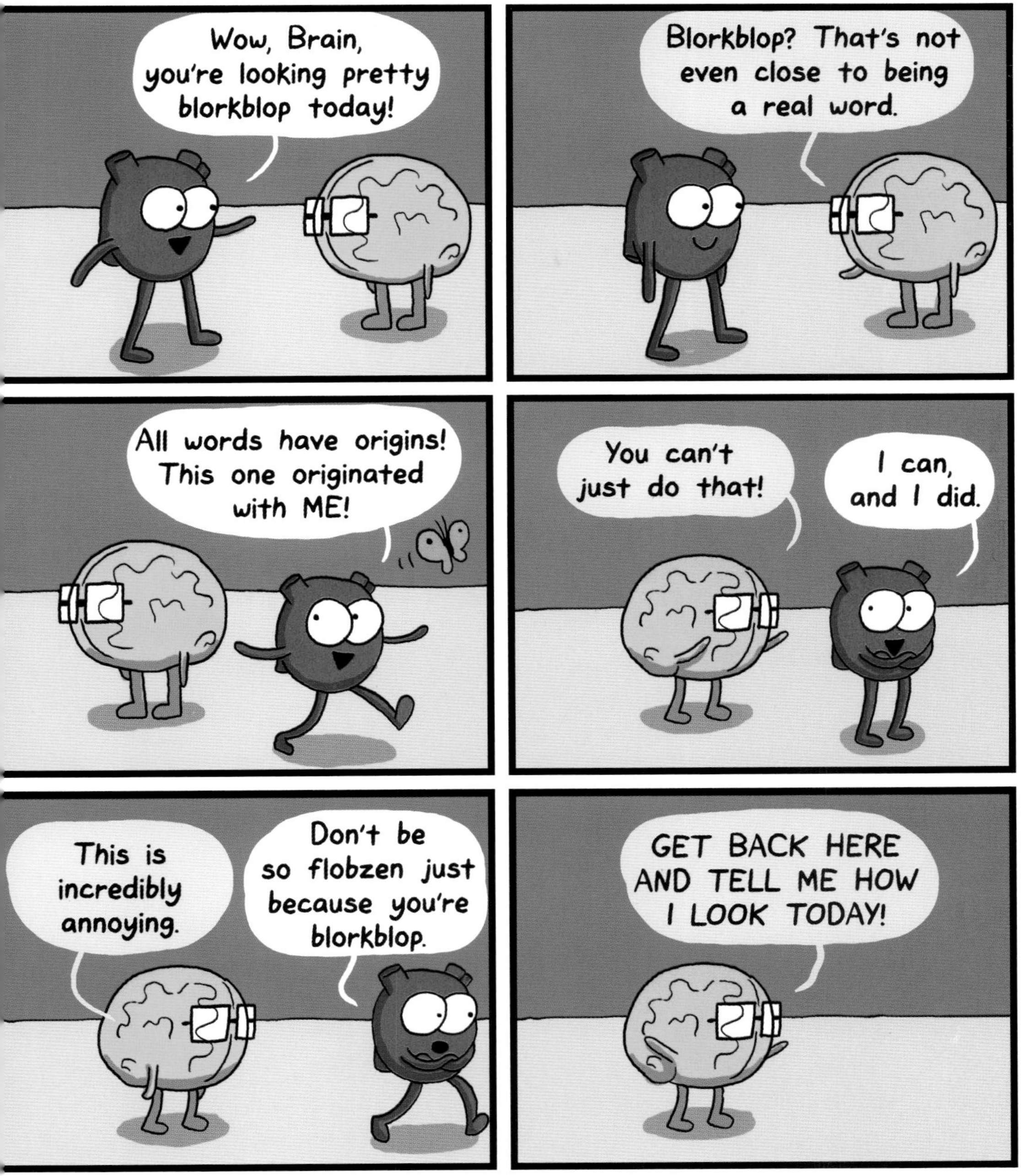
Wow, Brain, you're looking pretty blorkblop today!
Blorkblop? That's not even close to being a real word.
All words have origins! This one originated with ME!
You can't just do that!
I can, and I did.
This is incredibly annoying.
Don't be so flobzen just because you're blorkblop.
GET BACK HERE AND TELL ME HOW I LOOK TODAY!

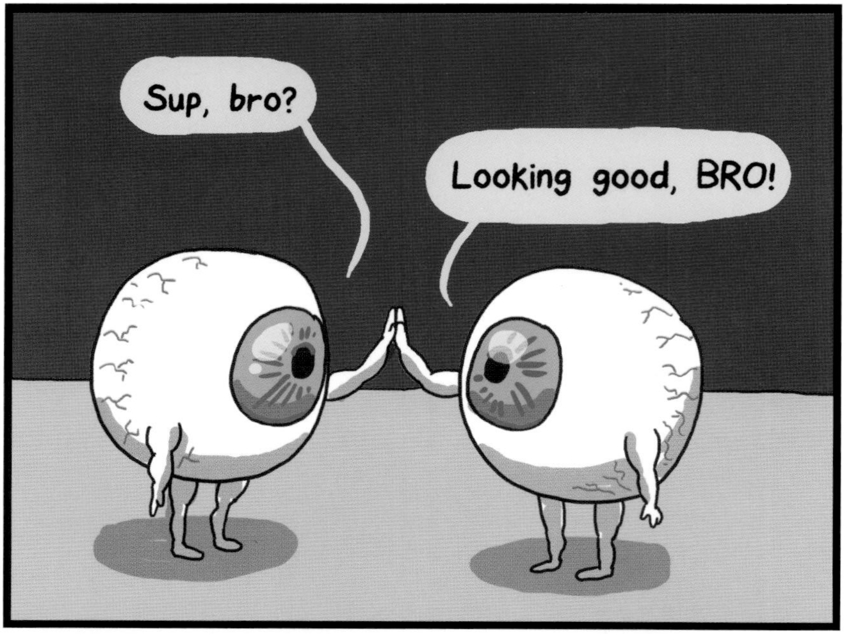
Sup, bro?
Looking good, BRO!

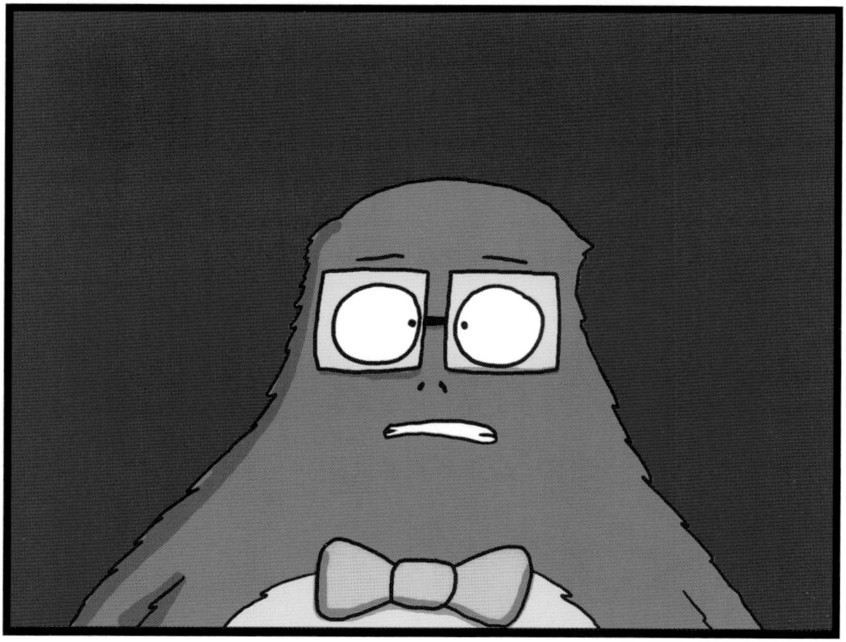

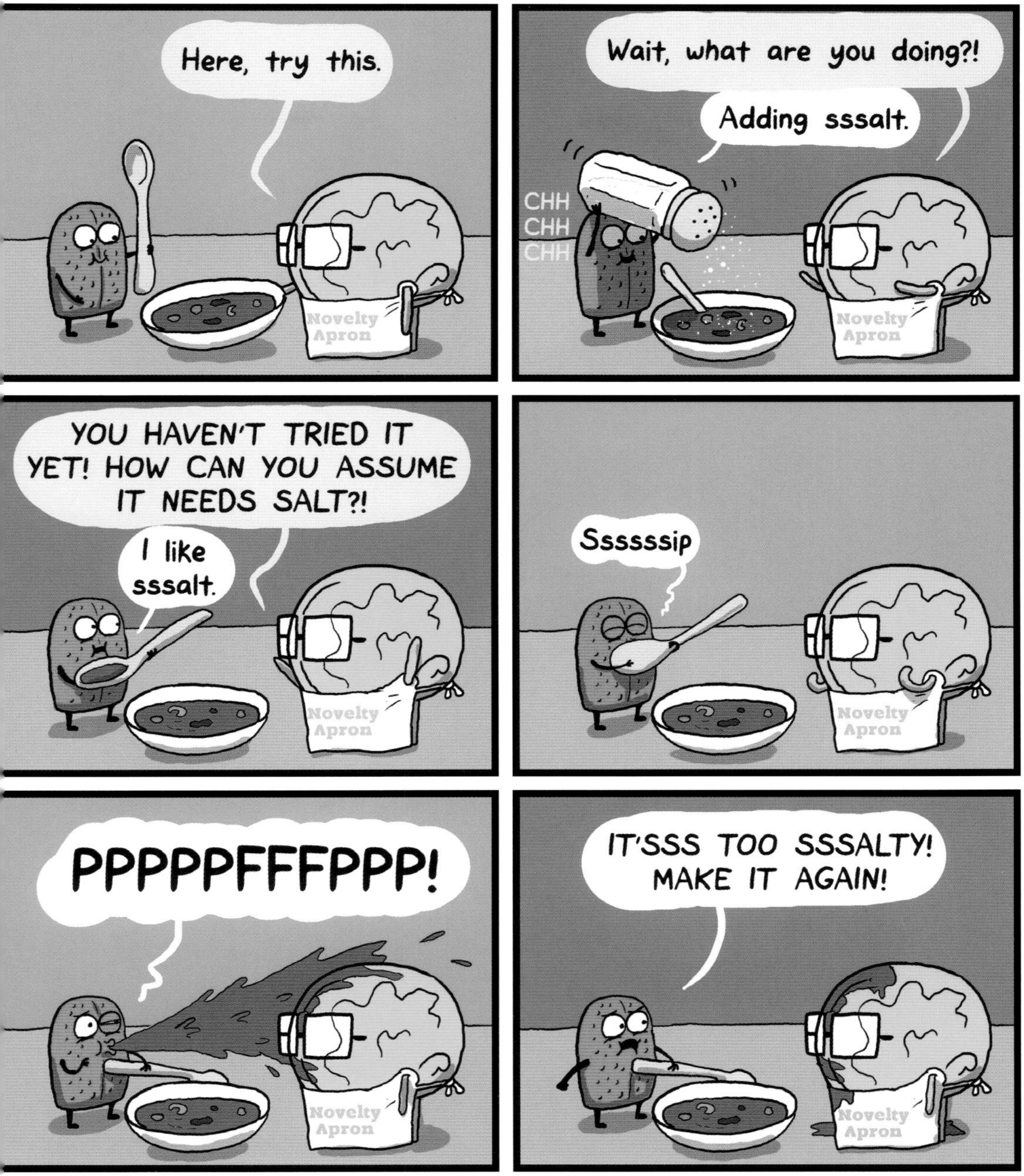
Here, try this.
Wait, what are you doing?!
Adding sssalt.
CHH
CHH
CHH
Novelty Apron
YOU HAVEN'T TRIED IT YET! HOW CAN YOU ASSUME IT NEEDS SALT?!
I like sssalt.
Sssssssip
PPPPPFFFPPP!
IT'SSS TOO SSSALTY! MAKE IT AGAIN!

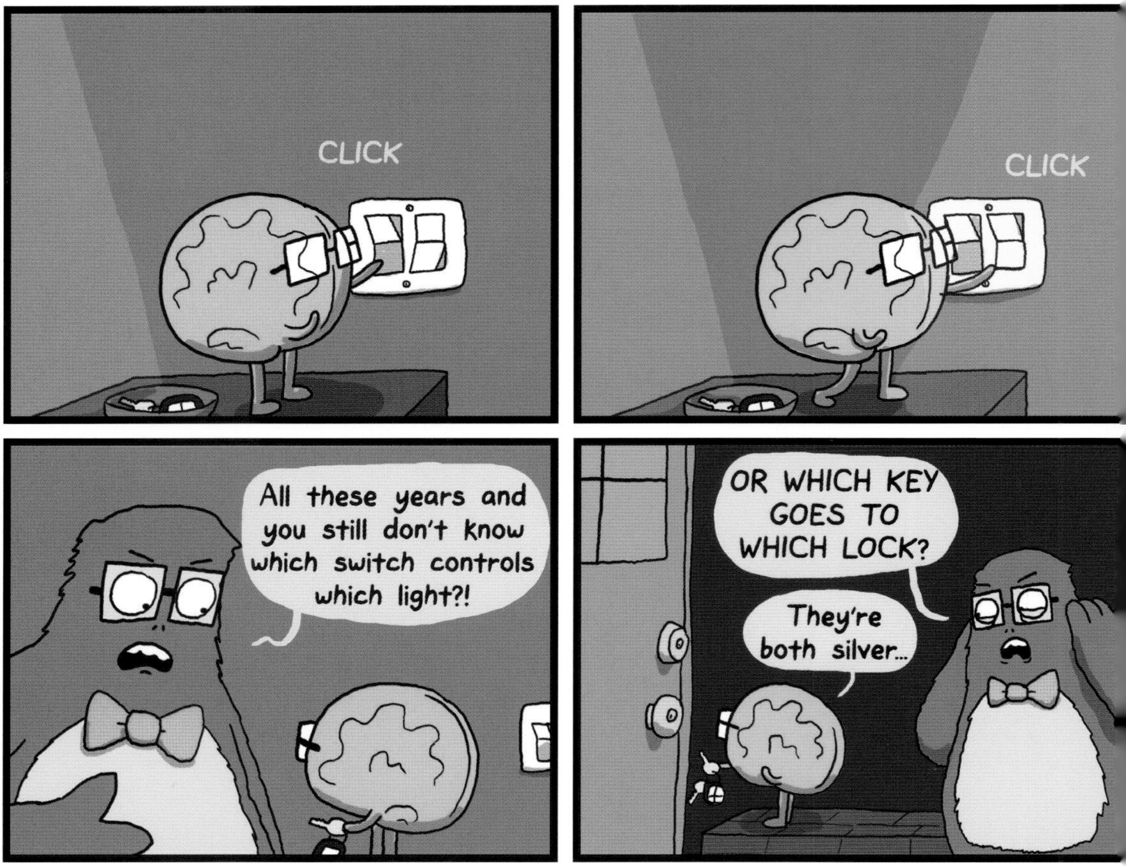
CLICK
CLICK
All these years and you still don't know which switch controls which light?!
OR WHICH KEY GOES TO WHICH LOCK?
They're both silver...

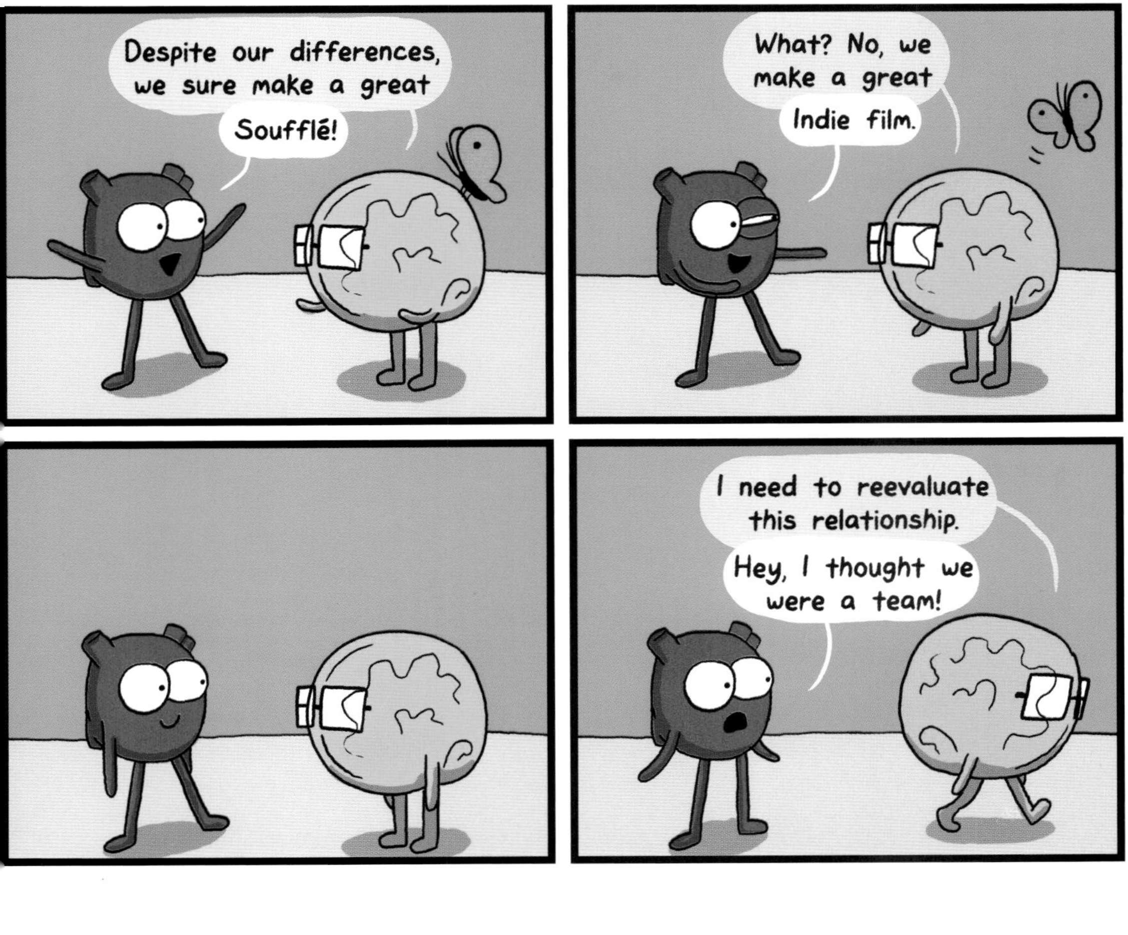
Despite our differences, we sure make a great
Soufflé!
What? No, we make a great
Indie film.
I need to reevaluate this relationship.
Hey, I thought we were a team!

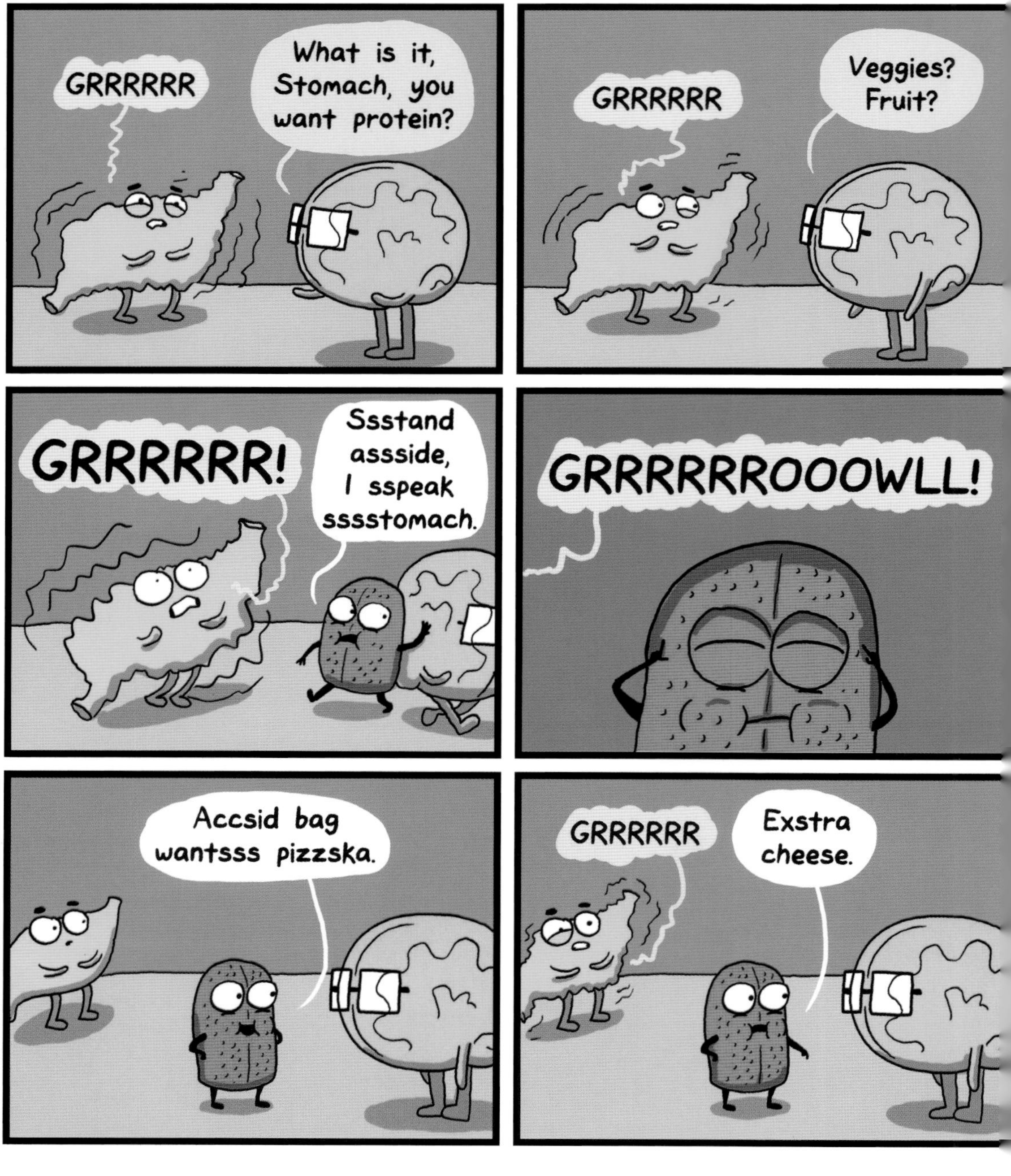
GRRRRRR
What is it, Stomach, you want protein?
GRRRRRR
Veggies? Fruit?
GRRRRRR!
Ssstand assside, I sspeak sssstomach.
GRRRRRROOOWLL!
Accsid bag wantsss pizzska.
GRRRRRR
Exstra cheese.

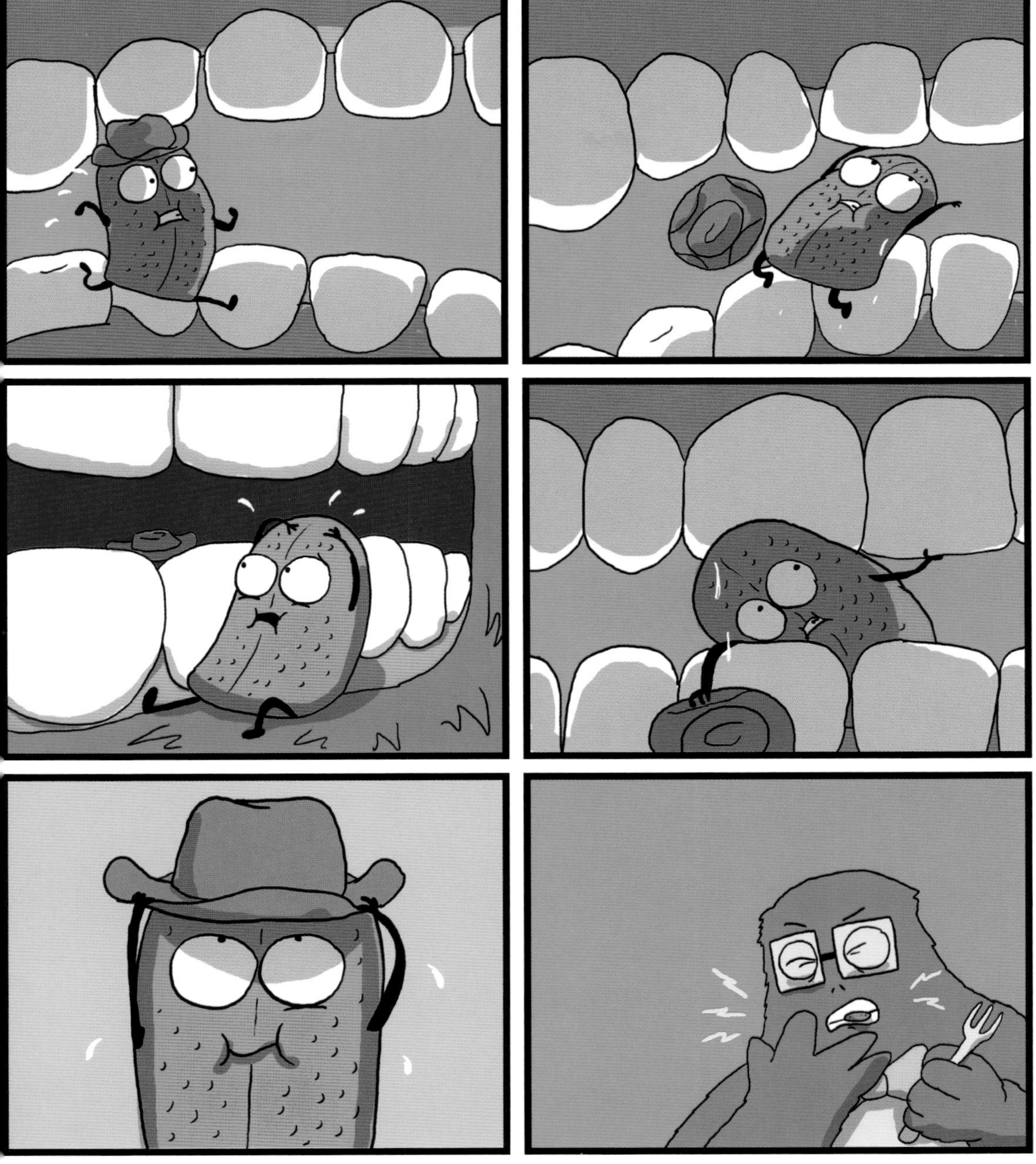

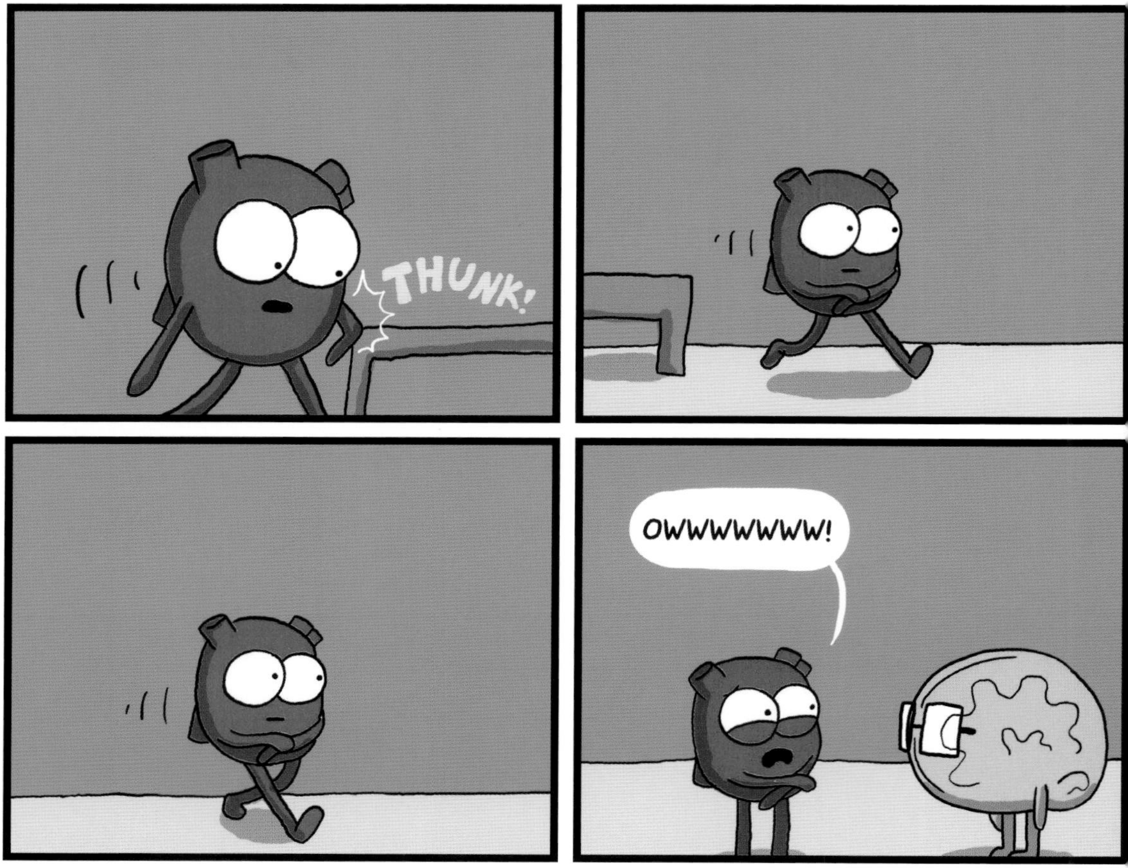
THUNK!
OWWWWWWW!

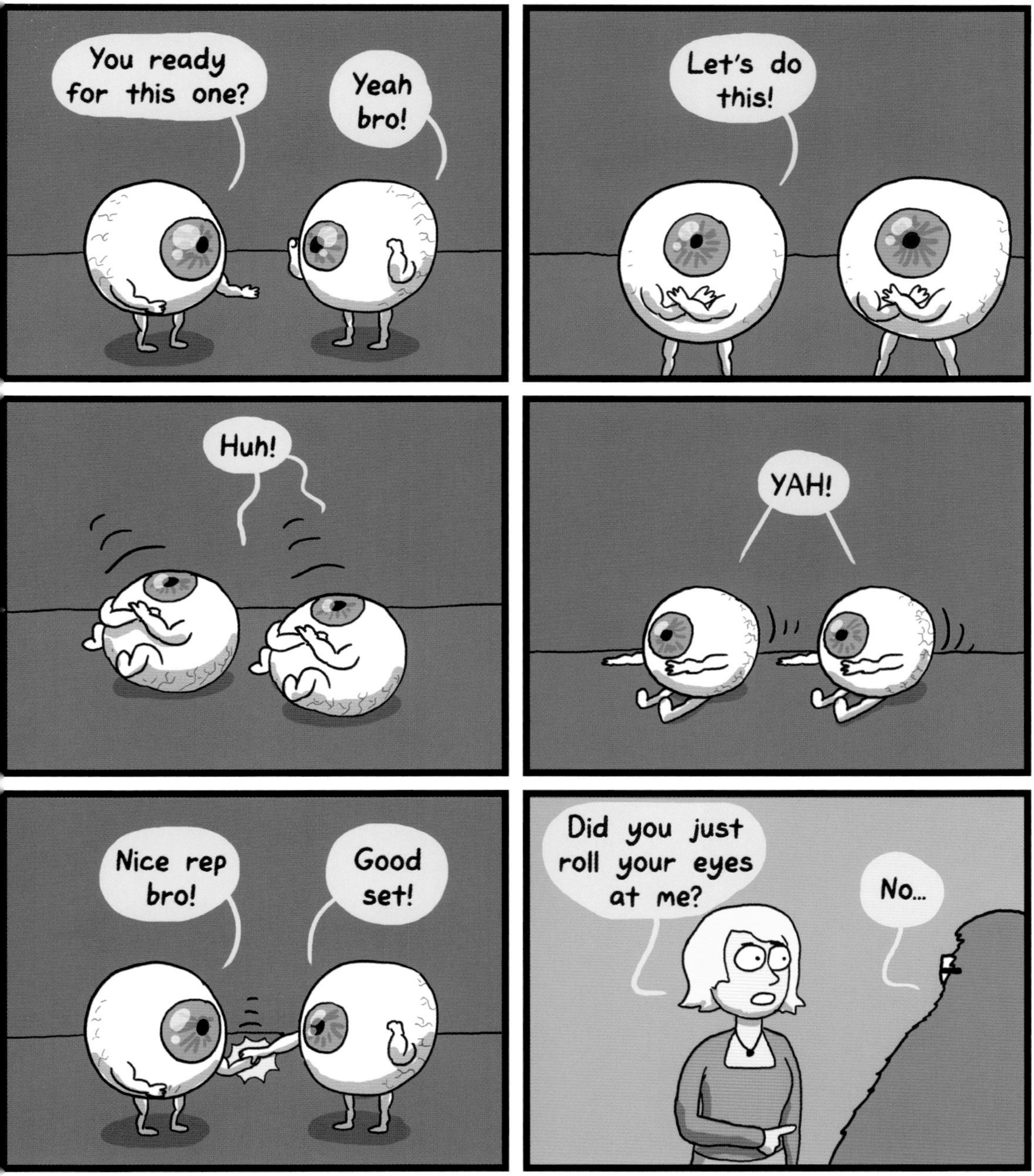
You ready for this one?
Yeah bro!
Let's do this!
Huh!
YAH!
Nice rep bro!
Good set!
Did you just roll your eyes at me?
No...

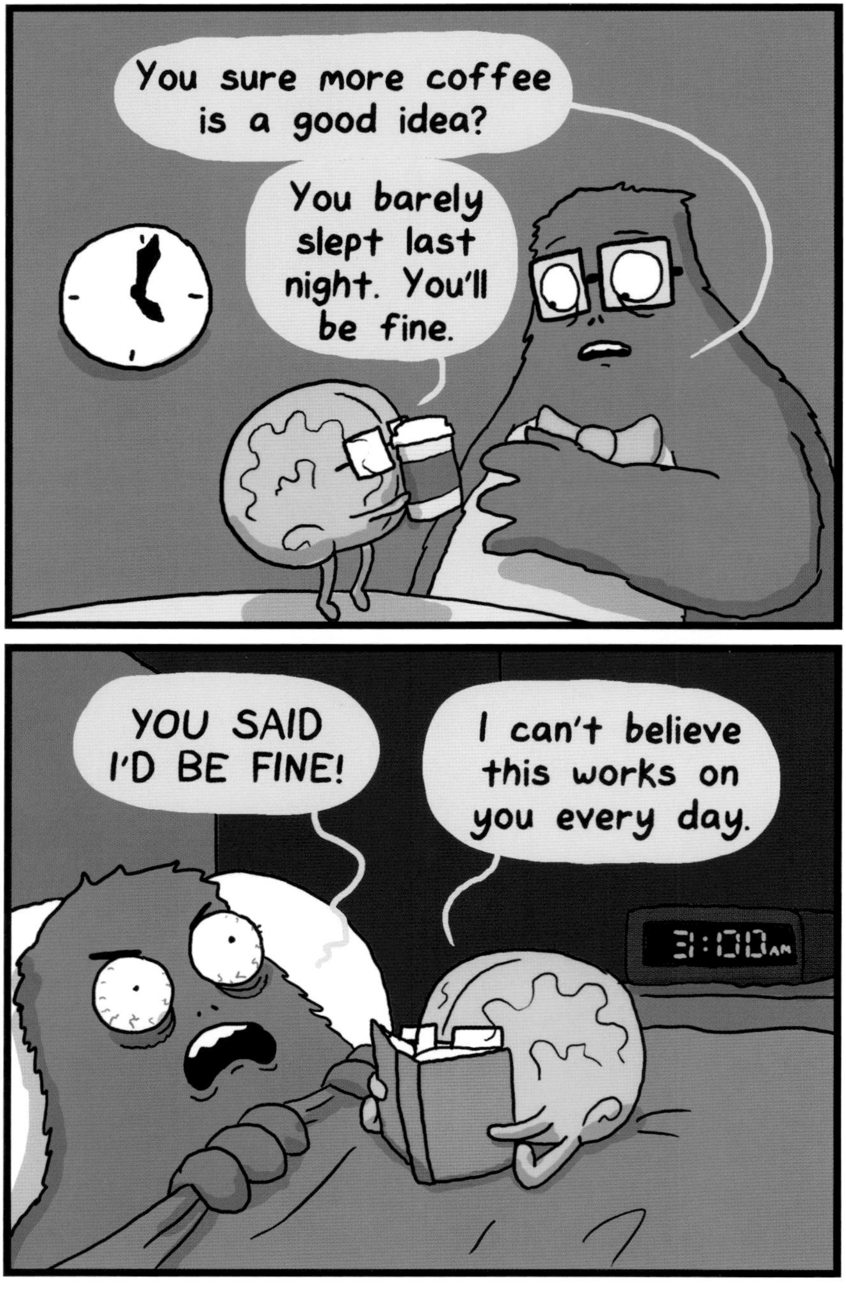

You sure more coffee is a good idea?
You barely slept last night. You'll be fine.
YOU SAID I'D BE FINE!
I can't believe this works on you every day.
3:00 AM

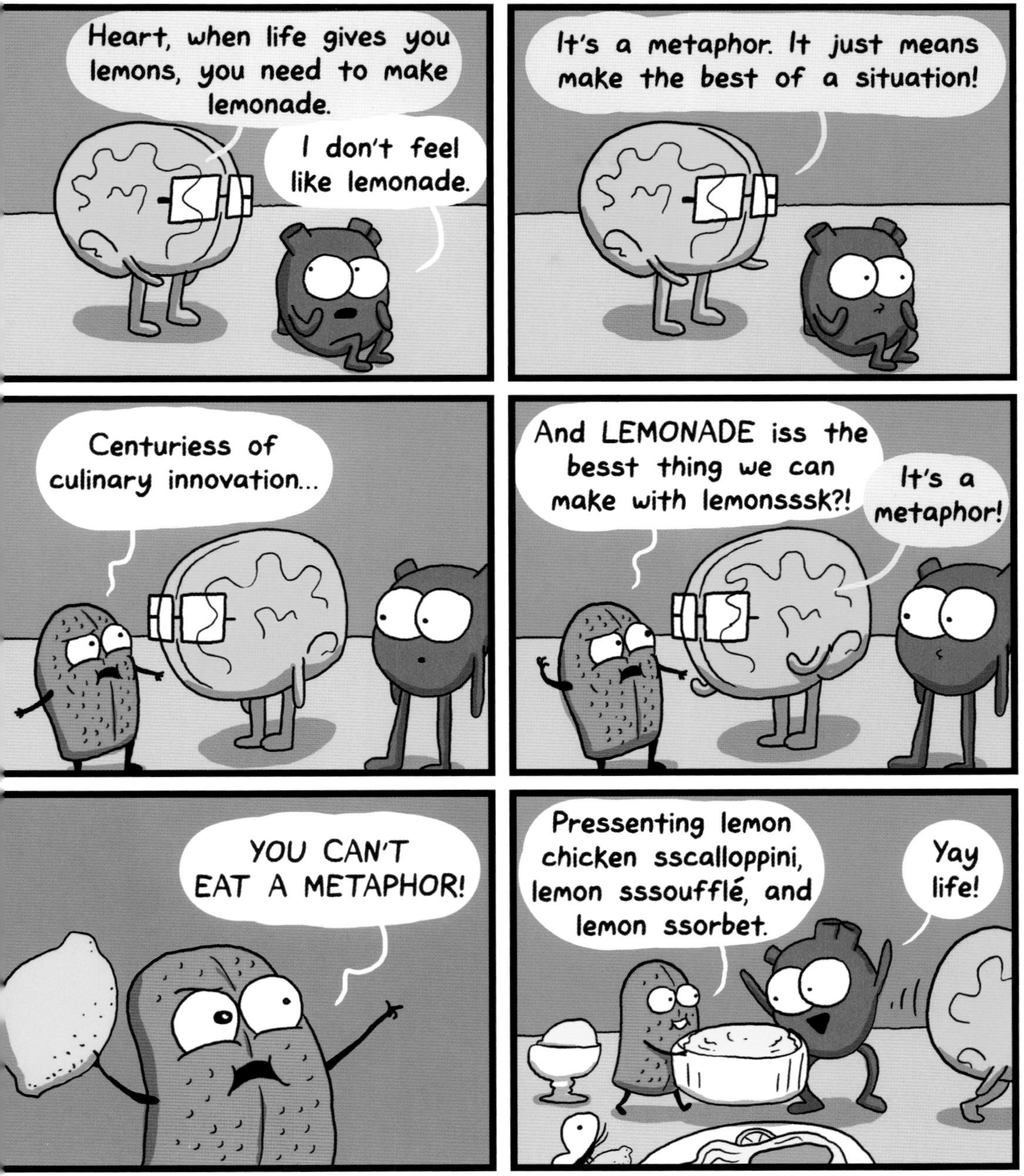
Heart, when life gives you lemons, you need to make lemonade.
I don't feel like lemonade.
It's a metaphor. It just means make the best of a situation!
Centuriess of culinary innovation...
And LEMONADE iss the besst thing we can make with lemonsssk?!
It's a metaphor!
YOU CAN'T EAT A METAPHOR!
Pressenting lemon chicken sscalloppini, lemon sssoufflé, and lemon ssorbet.
Yay life!

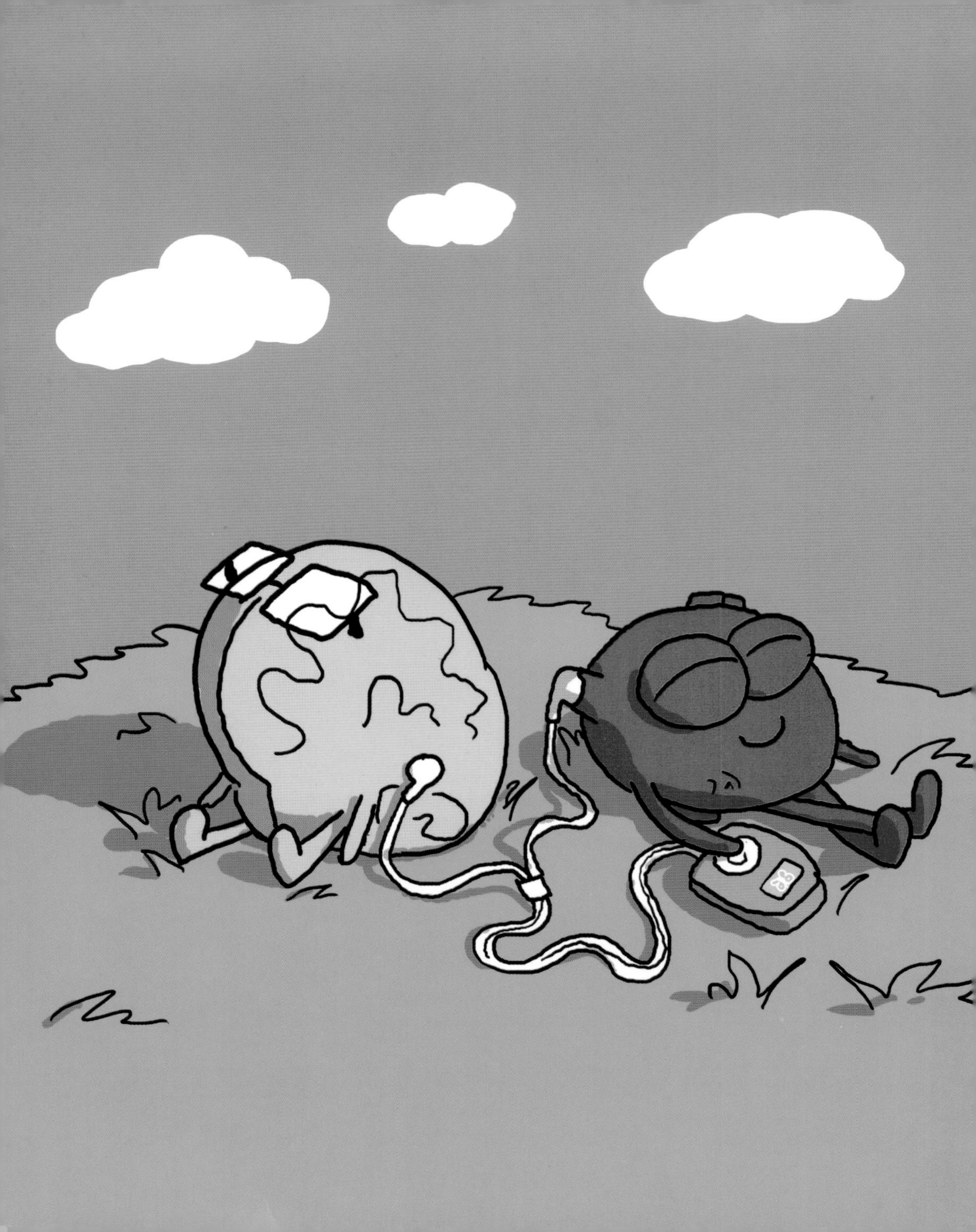

"Simultaneously deeply insightful and delightfully lighthearted, *Body Language* is a wonderful read that will make you laugh at life's many nuances."

—Sarah Andersen, author of *Adulthood Is a Myth* and *Big Mushy Happy Lump*

From the *New York Times* bestselling creator of the hugely popular Awkward Yeti comics comes the third collection in his *Heart and Brain* series.

Heart and Brain: Body Language continues the adventures of the loveably conflicted sentimental Heart and rational Brain, as well as other bodily inhabitants like Gallbladder, Muscle, and Tongue.

Warmhearted and laugh-out-loud funny, these comics bring our inner struggles to vibrant, humorous life.

It's book three and I'm still not on the cover. I'm beginning to suspect that it's on purpose...

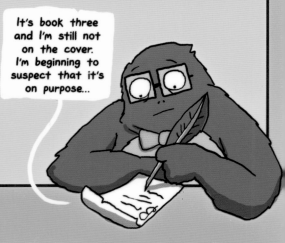

About the Author

Nick Seluk decided to pursue his lifelong dream of being a professional cartoonist after serving nine years in the corporate world as a graphic designer. In his childhood, he drew inspiration from classics such as *Calvin and Hobbes*, *The Far Side*, *Garfield*, and *The Simpsons*.

Nick lives with his wife, three young kids, and a lovable, ornery old dog in the suburbs of Detroit.

Heart and Brain and a growing cast of organs can be found at theAwkwardYeti.com and on most social media sites.

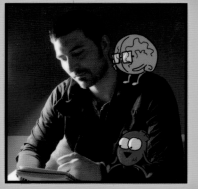

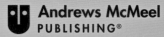

Andrews McMeel
PUBLISHING®

www.andrewsmcmeel.com

theawkwardyeti.com

Printed in China

$14.99 U.S.A. (*$19.99 Canada*)

ISBN: 978-1-4494-8712-6

51499

9 781449 487126